disaster and memory,

disaster and memory

CELEBRITY CULTURE AND THE
CRISIS OF HOLLYWOOD CINEMA

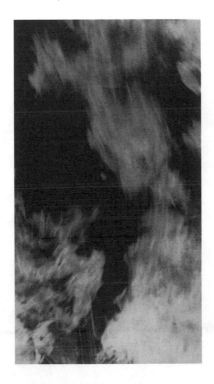

Wheeler Winston Dixon

COLUMBIA UNIVERSITY PRESS

NEW YORK

Columbia University Press

Publishers Since 1893

New York   Chichester, West Sussex

Copyright © 1999 by Columbia University Press

Library of Congress Cataloging-in-Publication Data

Dixon, Wheeler W.

Disaster and memory   :   celebrity culture and the crisis of
Hollywood cinema   /   Wheeler Winston Dixon.

p.   cm.

Includes bibliographical references and index.

ISBN 0–231–11316–1 (cloth   :   alk. paper).

ISBN 0–231–11317–X (pbk.   :   alk. paper)

1. Motion pictures—Miscellanea.   I. Title.

PN1994.D54   1999

791.43—dc21   98–27256

Casebound editions of Columbia University Press books are printed
on permanent and durable acid-free paper.

Printed in the United States of America

c 10 9 8 7 6 5 4 3 2 1

p 10 9 8 7 6 5 4 3 2 1

For Gwendolyn

CONTENTS

While the death of Diana Spencer, Princess of Wales, certainly triggered my work in *Disaster and Memory*, the topics considered in this book have long fascinated me. As the reader will soon discover, my discussion of the media's reception and coverage of Diana's death serves as the jumping off point for a series of extended meditations on the cult of celebrity, the nature of public surveillance, the role of the print and television media in shaping the words and images that form the fabric of our shared communal consciousness, and the role of the public as a coproducer of the wave of emotion surrounding Diana's death. The roots of the public's fascination with the life and death of Diana Spencer, I would argue, are grounded in a cult of personality which has gradually overtaken the world as a congruent whole, brought together yet separated by global cable, broadcast and satellite networks, and international print publications which can service many different markets around the world simultaneously.

In this text I trace much of this phenomenon from the midcentury point, the 1950s, when television first became a pervasive influence in our lives. To do so, I discuss at length the careers of two somewhat marginalized fifties icons who sought to re-create their public image by taking control of the director's chair—Ida Lupino and Richard Carlson. In the 1950s, both actors were well-known personalities at the height of their respective careers, yet both sought to fashion an entirely new vision of their public selves. Lupino re-created herself as a tough, no-nonsense "noir" director who refused to submit to societal norms that denied her the opportunity to direct her own films and to deal with topics that mattered to her. Carlson channeled his film career in a new direction by doing away with the stock leading man characterizations that were forced upon him in the early fifties (at the rate of up to five feature films per year), substituting instead the the figure of existentialist "hero" as suicide and social outcast in his films as an actor-director.

Throughout this book I examine the role of the televisual media (cable, videocassettes, instant print magazines and newspapers, pictures stored in digital memory and then recalled with the push of a button)

to explore the ways in which the story of Diana Spencer, Princess of
Wales, caught the enduring attention of the general public. Although
there are certainly other mitigating factors in the enshrinement of
Princess Diana as a posthumous pop media icon, the public's overwhelming response to and embrace of the visual immediacy and hypersurveillance that only television affords transformed a senseless and
violent accidental death in a Parisian car crash into an occasion for international mourning. It is this phenomenon, and the concomitant acceptance of both Hollywood stars and European royalty as objects of ado-
ration and veneration, that I wish to discuss. Diana's death was only
one of many in 1997. Why did it have such an enormous worldwide
impact? And why did the media seize the spectacle of Diana's sixteen
years of public life with such intensity and scrutiny? These are just a few
of the topics I wish to examine here, along with related areas of critical
and theoretical concern.

The author wishes to thank Jan Jarvis for her superb and painstaking
research on this project, as well as Janet Moat, Mandy Rowson, and Ian
O'Sullivan of the British Film Institute; Dana Miller for her skill and dili-
gence in typing my often hard-to-read handwritten manuscript; and the
members of the Department of English, the University of Nebraska, Lincoln, for their encouragement and support of my work. I would especially like to thank my chair, Dr. Linda Pratt, for her support of my work
over the past several years. Brief sections of this manuscript appeared previously in *Popular Culture Review* (my comments on *Riders to the Stars*); *Lit-
erature/Film Quarterly* (the material on Godard's *For Ever Mozart*); *Films in
Review* (the discussion of the figure of the child in contemporary horror
films); and *Classic Images* (my work on the films of Ida Lupino, and on the
British teleseries of producer Ralph Smart). My thanks to all the editors
of these publications for allowing me to reprint this material here. Full
acknowledgment is as follows: "The Auteur as Elegist: Richard Carlson's
Riders to the Stars," *Popular Culture Review* 9, no. 2 (August 1998), Felicia
Campbell, Editor; "For Ever Godard: Notes on Godard's *For Ever
Mozart*," *Literature/Film Quarterly* 26, no. 2 (1998), James Welsh, Editor;
"Ida Lupino: In the Director's Chair," *Classic Images* 248 (February 1996):
14–16, 18, 20, 22; "*The Invisible Man, Secret Agent*, and *The Prisoner*: Three
British Teleseries of the 1950s and '60s," forthcoming, *Classic Images*,
Robert King, Editor; and "The Child as Demon in Films Since 1961," *Films
in Review* 37, no. 2 (February 1986): 78–83, Roy Frumkes, Editor. All of
these materials have been extensively revised and updated for their inclu-

sion here. Finally, I want to thank those colleagues who have been particularly supportive of my work, especially Tom Conley, Mark Reid, Marcia Landy, James Welsh, Felicia Campbell, Lloyd Michaels, Frank Tomasulo, David Desser, Steven Shaviro, Suzanne Regan, Tony Williams, and Jean-Pierre Geuens.

PREFACE

disaster and memory

THE MOVING IMAGE IN CRISIS

diſaſter and memory

First of all, we must understand that we are living in the final years of the twentieth century. The numerous technological, social, political, and epidemiological changes during the past one hundred years—even from the midcentury mark—are both striking and curiously cyclical. The Internet and the web, both in their infancy, roughly parallel the development of the cinematograph almost exactly a century ago. AIDS and HIV infections, once the stuff of science fiction, have become routine markers of mortality. "Information" is tightly controlled, channeled, and manipulated by a few giant conglomerates; what we receive at the end of the "news filter" is a precensored, predigested diet of titillation and gossip, lacking both the style and substance of empirical factual reportage.

Yet certain alternative voices creep through the dominant superstructure of the news media. Sometimes these stories are buried in national newspapers, far from the front page, and occasionally they appear in antiestablishment journals. Chat rooms on the Internet offer a variety of wild speculation and gossip, all of it infected with a tossed-off flavor of instantaneous composition and dissemination. But as we crest on the wave of the twentieth century, slouching uneasily toward the millennium (whether it starts in the year 2000 or 2001 is itself a matter of contentious debate), the public discourse of our century's conclusion is framed by a series of disturbing polarities: the embrace of spectatorial violence versus the search for political and social peace; the desire for escapist entertainment, coupled with a near-prurient absorption in the most private details of the lives of total strangers; the denial of the body in what is undoubtedly the opening decades of an unforeseeably protracted battle against a series of worldwide epidemics, as augured by HIV and AIDS; and a desire to sacrifice personal freedom for an antiseptic fantasyland of manufactured domestic tranquillity, as typified by the move toward "gated" communities, or compounds like the Disney Corporation's "instant town," Celebration, U.S.A.

At the same time, televisual media mini-conglomerates have sprung up in the late 1990s which aggressively and shamelessly cross-plug each other, not surprisingly since they are often owned by the same parent organization: NBC's *Dateline* plugs *People* magazine as part of its ostensible news programming, to better publicize both corporate entities; MSNBC cannibalizes the stock news footage from NBC's library into an ultra-cheap retrospective show entitled *Now and Then*; Ted Turner's various networks (CNN, Headline News, TNT, the Cartoon Network, and Turner Classic Movies) relentlessly promote each other's interests in crossover advertisements. But it goes much further than this. Turner was acquired in the late 1990s by Time Warner, which owns the cable networks HBO, Cinemax, and other cable providers (it also has a share in Court TV, Comedy Central, and Black Entertainment Television). This, of course, is in addition to its publishing and motion picture production interests, in which it competes with Disney/ABC and Viacom/MTV, two other giants in the cable industry. The Viacom/MTV bloc owns Nickelodeon, VH1, MTV, Showtime, The Movie Channel (TMC), TV Land, and M2, in addition to a 50 percent stake in the USA and Sci-Fi Channel networks. Disney/ABC controls not only the ABC network and its various on-line progeny (all the individual cable and broadcast networks mentioned above maintain a significant web presence) but also the Disney Channel, 80 percent of ESPN1 and ESPN2, 50 percent of Lifetime, and 37.5 percent of A&E and the History Channel (*see* Dempsey, 1). This in itself explains why these particular cable networks dominate the current programming fare offered by most cable operators (such as Falcon Cable and Cablevision); they're all various "narrowcasting" elements of the same organization.

But even this is only a fragment of the overall televisual and theatrical motion picture landscape. While CBS/Westinghouse scrambles to get its own cable network off the ground, paying a reported $1.55 billion in stock for ownership of the Nashville Network and Country Music Television (CMT) (Dempsey, 1), cable suppliers such as TCI also own an interest in the various channels they provide to the public, including a stake in all the previously mentioned Time Warner services, plus "The Discovery Channel, The Learning Channel, The Family Channel, E! Entertainment Television, Court TV, Encore and Starz" (Dempsey, 84). Thus distribution and production of programming are vertically integrated in the style of late nineties' production, distribution, and exhibition all owned by a few major players who control the overwhelming majority of home televisual programming, whether disseminated by a cable operator or supplier, or through a direct satellite broadcast (dish) system. No matter which system the viewer chooses, the "choices" are the same: slices of the same monolithic visual block, each channel relentlessly counterpromoting the other.

Packages of new channels are thus spun off from existing channels by the major conglomerates and parceled out with previously existing cable channels in a presold set of offerings that are often forced upon cable suppliers in a "take it or leave it" manner, thus mimicking the nearly century-old theatrical distribution practices of *block booking* and/or *blind bidding*, in which theater owners were forced to take a series of inferior films from a major studio in order to obtain rights to one or two blockbuster releases (block booking), often without even seeing the product they were being sold (blind bidding). When Ted Turner purchased Metro-Goldyn-Mayer, he quickly sold the physical assets of the company (real estate, buildings, and the like), but retained control of MGM's most important asset: a motion picture library of more than five hundred feature films, plus numerous shorts, cartoons, one-reelers, and promotional films, all of which he programmed first on his TNT network (with commercials) and later on TCM (Turner Classic Movies) without sponsor interruptions.

This explains why American Movie Classics (AMC), which is primarily (75 percent) owned by the cable supplier Cablevision, but which currently owns none of the films it programs, is looking at the back inventory of both Columbia and Universal as potential acquisitions, in return for a percentage of AMC (Dempsey, 84). The most important property for these cable channels is product programming—which they can cycle and recycle in various packages, specials, documentaries, and clip compilations to their subscribers. The former MGM building is a repository only of memories; the real property of MGM (as well as of Universal, Paramount, Twentieth Century Fox, Columbia, Warner Brothers, and the other Hollywood studios) is their back library of theatrical motion pictures, which Turner now owns.

Similarly, in theatrical motion pictures, we are witnessing the same cross-plugging and conglomerate practices which now dominate our viewing at home. It makes sense; motion picture production is now a ruinously costly affair, with films like James Cameron's *Titanic* approaching the $200 million mark by many estimates, simply for its negative cost, before any exhibition, distribution, or promotion expenses are added in. *Titanic* (1997) is essentially a remake of Roy Ward Baker's *A Night to Remember* (1958). Unlike Baker's film (and the ones that preceded it, including Werner Klingler and Herbert Selpin's 1943 Nazi version, and Jean Negulesco's 1953 Hollywood film, both also simply called *Titanic*), Cameron's *Titanic* offers spectacle in the place of substance and cynically attempts to capture the audience's attention through the use of an archetypal Romeo and Juliet "star cross'd lovers" conceit. Contemporary teen idol Leonardo

DiCaprio appears in the film as the fictive Jack Dawson, an American sketch artist who wins two tickets to the *Titanic*'s maiden voyage in a last-minute poker game, while Kate Winslet portrays rich heiress Rose DeWitt Bukater, another passenger on the ill-fated ship, who falls into Dawson's arms to escape an arranged marriage with one Cal Hockley (Billy Zane). The entire story is told in flashback, narrated by a very elderly Rose (Gloria Stuart), who survives the disaster through a series of fortuitous circumstances; Jack Dawson perishes in a suitably heroic manner.

Titanic strives to live up to its title, and indeed, in budget, length (195 minutes), and sheer aural/visual spectacle, it certainly does so, but Cameron simultaneously reduces the human element of the tragedy to a series of schematic caricatures. Jack is entirely true and brave; Rose is a misunderstood rich girl who adores Picasso and Monet; Cal is a ruthless, sneering villain, straight out of a Victorian melodrama. The music cues relentlessly attempt to manipulate our emotions (now you should cry; now you're scared), the dialogue is astonishingly wooden (when the *Titanic* first hits the iceberg, Jack declares solemnly, "This is bad"), and every other character in the film (with the possible exception of Kathy Bates as Molly Brown) is marginalized in a foredoomed attempt to focus our attentions solely on the young lovers, to the expense of all the other passengers.

In contrast, *A Night to Remember* views the *Titanic* disaster as a series of interlocking human tragedies, in which each character is given an equal amount of screen time, and no one story overwhelms the others. Further, Baker's film, while quite convincingly brutal in its final sequences of the disaster, never allows the spectacle to overpower the human aspect of the drama. Thus, *A Night to Remember* emerges as a profoundly moving and emotional tragedy on all levels, rather than a mammoth disaster spectacle masquerading as a heterotopic teenage love story, aimed primarily at PG-13 audiences. In addition, the budget for *A Night to Remember* was also much smaller than that of the 1997 *Titanic*—slightly over $1,000,000.

Indeed, at the midcentury point a major studio release could be whipped up for as little as $210,000 (Eugene Lourie's *The Beast from 20,000 Fathoms*, 1953), utilizing a series of back-projection plates, a papier-mâché dinosaur left over from *Bringing Up Baby*, and Ray Harryhausen's then state-of-the-art stop-motion special effects. Lourie shot the film in a mere twelve days; the film was then sold outright to Warner Brothers for $450,000, launched with a media campaign costing less than $100,000, and released to a gross of $5 million (Lourie, 234–41). The $210,000 figure included, incidentally, the rights to Ray Bradbury's short story, "The Fog Horn," which served as the basic narrative backdrop for the piece. Similarly, in 1956 Ray Harryhausen provided a series of spectacular special effects depicting the destruction of Washington, D.C., by a fleet of alien spacecraft in Fred F. Sears's *Earth vs. the Flying Saucers*, completed in less than two weeks for slightly less than $200,000, which also opened to respectable box office figures and later served as the template for Roland Emmerich's mega-budgeted remake *Independence Day* (1996), a film costing nearly $100 million to create and promote. As of this writing, the average budget of a theatrical motion picture for the negative cost alone is approximately $50 million—plus the expenses for prints, advertising, and promotion; nearly fifty years ago American International could produce such films as Roger Corman's *The Pit and the Pendulum* (1961) in Panavision and Pathécolor for a mere $300,000, a figure that seems risible today. Numerous other disaster films of the fifties, sixties, and seventies brought about the destruction of cities, countries, and even entire civilizations in a compellingly low-budget manner. Maurice Yacowar cites a series of basic "types" of conventional generic disaster films in his excellent essay "The Bug in the Rug: Notes on the Disaster Genre," detailing a group of "Natural Attack," "Ship of Fools," "The City Fails," Monster, Survival, War, Historical and Comic Disaster films, in which women and men face disaster and usually escape without serious consequences, except in the more ambitious examples of the genre. Thus John Guillermin and Irwin Allen's *The Towering Inferno* (1974) becomes roughly equivalent to Fritz Lang's *Metropolis* (1926); in each film, the hub of a gigantic city collapses (in Guillermin and Allen's film an enormous skyscraper, in Lang's an underground worker's city) while frantic efforts are made by various figures of authority to reestablish order. In all these films, as Yacowar notes, a series of conventions or archetypes are at work, including the use of various cast members to dramatize racial and/or social inequities, and the fact that the genre disaster film isolates its characters in order to place them in a position of peril, in which "all systems fail" inexorably, one after the other (see Yacowar, 261–79). All these films were created for comparatively little money; almost without exception, their special effects (the "disaster" sequences, specifically, or their very reason for existing as cinema entertainments) have become dated and unconvincing with the passage of time, and the increasing reliance on digital special effects. But though technology continues to evolve, the disaster film continues to thrive in ever-more-rarified territory, the cost of production driven up into the $50–90 million range through the demands of increased star salaries, lavish sequences of destruction, and international ad campaigns which routinely launch a film in thousands of theaters simultaneously.

As costs have risen, so have the concomitant risks of production, resulting in a spate of big-budgeted sequels (hardly a new practice, of course: consider the *Bowery Boys/East Side Kids/Dead End Kids* films of the thirties through the fifties, or the *Sherlock Holmes, Blondie, Henry Aldrich, Andy Hardy, Hopalong Cassidy, Charlie Chan*, or the *Whistler* series from the same approximate era). But where the modest genre films of an earlier era were content to support an A feature of greater artistic and aesthetic ambition on the bottom half of a double bill, today's genre films have become the main attraction, the dominant force in motion picture production and exploitation, because (as with all genre films and/or sequels), they are to a large extent a presold, pretested quantity whose qualities and limitations are known to the audience before they enter the theater, or see a trailer, or view a promo clip on television during an interview with one of the film's star commodities.

An excellent example of this is Les Mayfield's 1997 remake of Robert Stevenson's *The Absent-Minded Professor* (1961), this time around simply titled *Flubber*, after the gooey, endlessly elastic substance accidentally created by a befuddled, lovable college professor working at home in his basement laboratory. The original film, modestly budgeted, shot in black and white with Fred MacMurray as the star, has been transmogrified in the 1997 version into a multimillion-dollar digital special effects festival, starring Robin Williams as the absent-minded Professor Philip Brainard, and featuring a host of technical tricks which become the sole focus of the film's narrative thrust and/or aesthetic ambition. Both films, the original and the remake, are primitive genre entertainment, but the new version lacks the virtue of any originality (it is merely a carbon copy of the first film, with increased technical wizardry and a robot sidekick, Weebo, to hype up the action), and, unlike the original film, exists in a cinematic landscape where nearly every other major studio release is a genre film as well (Rogers 1997a). In addition, Disney is shrewdly banking on baby boomers' memories of the first film to bring parents to the sequel with their offspring, in a psychic construct which thus ensures a return to the past for the adult viewer, and a presold customer in the child viewer, who is thus primed for the numerous sequels which usually follow a major studio genre release, sequels which now bypass the theatrical marketplace altogether and are released, in mass quantities, as straight-to-tape home videos. After Disney successfully released *Aladdin* in theaters in

1992, *Honey, I Shrunk the Kids* in 1989, and *Beauty and the Beast* in 1991, subsequent sequels were simply released to home video, having been sufficiently presold to both parents and their children by virtue of the initial theatrical outing.

Indeed, it is the sameness of these films that assures audiences that they will not be challenged, confused, or surprised in anything other than the most elementary manner. The classical Hollywood cinema model has been exhausted through overuse of narrative closure, reliance on excess of spectacle, hypertechnic sound tracks, and the like, to the point that the contemporary cinema has become simply a memory of itself, a replaying of old roles and outmoded plotlines, all fueled by the inexorability of a "star" system that manufactures and then discards the protagonists of this phantom automatism. Thus Masayuki Sao's 1997 film *Shall We Dance?*—a Japanese production clearly targeted directly at Western audiences—exudes a sense of forced Orientalism with each succeedingly calculated frame, or Nick Cassavetes' 1997 *She's So Lovely* emulates the work of his late father without adding any element of true risk or experimentation to the proceedings. Anthony Minghella recycles the spectacle of David Lean's ultracolonialist *Lawrence of Arabia* (1962), a 222-minute blockbuster from the era of *The Sound of Music* (1965) and *Mary Poppins* (1964) in his 1996 film *The English Patient*, a conflation, as Jonathan Miller suggested to me, of Barbara Cartland's novels and the character of "Biggles," the 1940s aviator-hero featured as the central protagonist in a series of books that captured the imagination of British schoolboys in post–World War II Britain (Dixon interview). The commercial and mainstream critical success of this Best Picture Oscar-winner should thus come as no surprise because the film itself was designed and marketed precisely for the purpose of providing the public with a simplistic romantic adventure, complete with a "sympathetic" Nazi as the film's ostensible hero, and bodice-ripping scenes straight from the back cover jacket blurb of a Harlequin romance novel. Similarly, Steven Spielberg's *Schindler's List* (1993), clocking in at a mammoth 195 minutes, uses black-and-white cinematography merely for effect in its disturbingly sanitized retelling of the Holocaust, commercially but not aesthetically eclipsing either Alain Resnais's *Night and Fog* (*Nuit et Brouillard*, 1955), a short film that nevertheless brings the carnal brutality of the Nazi regime into sharper and more clinical focus than Spielberg's work, or Claude Lanzmann's *Shoah* (1985), a 570-minute film that relentlessly documents the testimony of both victims and perpetrators of the Holocaust with a carefully considered, meditational camera eye.

For *The Scarlet Letter* (1996), Roland Joffe reworked Hawthorne's novel so that it now incorporates a generically acceptable narrative closure; Richard Attenborough's *Gandhi* (1982) reduces a curiously complex character to the one-dimensionality of a cardboard religious icon; Alan Parker's *Mississippi Burning* (1988) reframes the civil rights conflict through the eyes of two white FBI agents, Gene Hackman and Willem Dafoe; Sydney Pollack's *Out of Africa* (1985) romanticizes the early days of Kenyan colonialist domination by the British empire; Randal Kleiser's *It's My Party* (1996) turns a fatal AIDS infection into an excuse for a series of maudlin farewells and a two-day, Capraesque party in which the protagonist is reconciled with his estranged lover and extended family before committing suicide with an overdose of barbiturates; Jonathan Demme's *Philadelphia* (1993) similarly manages to snare audience sympathy through a series of clichés and stereotypes in its tale of a gay attorney, Andrew Beckett (Tom Hanks), fired from his job at a high-powered law firm because he has contracted the AIDS virus.

Beckett's eventual courtroom victory and martyr's death are eerily mirrored by Irwin Winkler's artificially upbeat conclusion to *Guilty by Suspicion* (1991), Winkler's revisionist take on the Hollywood blacklist of the late 1940s and early 1950s. When Robert De Niro defies the House Committee on Un-American Activities (HUAC) against the advice and counsel of his associates in the final scene of the film (just as Woody Allen did in Martin Ritt's 1976 film *The Front*), we are participating in a cathartic yet completely unrealistic fantasy of the supposedly inevitable triumph of good over the machinations of criminal governments or the intractable exigencies of disease. Bob Fosse's 1974 *Lenny* sanitizes the brilliant scatology of the late comic; Tim Burton's 1994 *Ed Wood* creates a happy ending in which Wood's film *Plan Nine from Outer Space* (1959) is released to an enthusiastic public reception; in fact, the film received a few desultory theatrical bookings before being dumped unceremoniously into television syndication in the early 1960s—even failure becomes a resounding success in the Hollywood genre machine.

Compare these films to Alfred Hitchcock's *Psycho* (1960) or *Vertigo* (1958), Blake Edwards's *Breakfast at Tiffany's* (1961), Robert Aldrich's *Kiss Me Deadly* (1955), Billy Wilder's *Some Like It Hot* (1959), Richard Brooks's *Cat On a Hot Tin Roof* (1958), Mike Nichols's *Who's Afraid of Virginia Woolf?* (1966), Howard Hawks's *Scarface* (1932), Leo McCarey's *Duck Soup* (1933), Frank Capra's *It Happened One Night* (1934), Fritz Lang's *Fury* (1936), William Wellman's *Public Enemy* (1931), Tod Browning's *Freaks* (1932), W. S. Van Dyke's *The Thin Man* (1934), or any other of several thousand possible examples from the first seventy-five years of the Dominant Holly-wood cinema, and the vacuousness of the current product becomes instantly and painfully apparent.

With the current pervasive utilization of computer-generated image technology, which arguably reaches its contemporary zenith in the digi-tal creature effects of Phil Tippett in Paul Verhoeven's *Starship Troopers* (1997), the theatrical motion picture has become the repository of spec-tacle above all other considerations. But even the brilliantly digitized arachnid warriors of Verhoeven's film can't disguise its essential empti-ness; although Verhoeven acknowledges the film's various stylistic and thematic debts to Capra's *Why We Fight* series and Leni Riefenstahl's Nazi propaganda films, he has basically created a film in which the updated nightmare insects (reminiscent of Gordon Douglas's *Them!*, 1954) meet the cast of the teleseries *Baywatch*. Casper Van Dien, Dina Meyer, and Denise Richards are perfect icons for a new cinema age: plas-tic, perfect, endlessly interchangeable action figures without depth and/or emotion.

Nor is Verhoeven shy in annotating his various cinematic homages in the film. In an interview he noted directly that "the first shot [in the film] is taken from [Riefenstahl's] *Triumph of the Will* (1935) . . . when the sol-diers look at the camera and say, 'I'm doing my part!' That's from Riefen-stahl. We copied it" (Svetkey, 8). As to the profusion of Nazi-styled uni-forms, insignias, giant eagles, and other paraphernalia sprinkled through-out the film's visual design, *Starship Troopers'* screenwriter, Edward Neumeier, explained that "the reason for all the German uniforms and everything is because the Germans made the best-looking stuff. Art direc-tors love it" (Svetkey, 8). Verhoeven avows that his underlying purpose in making the film was to "use subversive imagery to make a point about society. I tried to seduce the audience to join [the futuristic] society, but then ask, 'What are you really joining up for?' " (Svetkey, 9). Yet the protofascist imagery, and the equally lockstep ideology propounded by both the film and Robert Heinlein's 1959 source novel of the same name is so enthusiastically triumphant that one can see why the film generated more than $22 million on its opening weekend; once again, it makes fas-cism chic.

This desire for control, community, and a commonality of shared experience has been exemplified on a global scale by the media frenzy over the violent death of Diana Spencer in the aftermath of an automo-bile accident in Paris on Sunday, August 31, 1997. Salman Rushdie was perhaps the first writer to draw the comparison between the death of

Diana and the public's fascination with spectacles of violent vehicular carnage as presented in David Cronenberg's film *Crash* (1996). But as Rushdie himself admitted, the connection is an obvious one. Noted Rushdie: "It is one of the darker ironies of a dark event that the themes and ideas explored by [J. G.] Ballard [British author of the novel *Crash*, on which the film was based] and Cronenberg, themes and ideas that many in Britain have called pornographic, should have been lethally acted out in the car accident that killed Diana, Princess of Wales, Dodi Fayed, and their drunken driver" (Rushdie, 68).

Rushdie goes on to argue that the public's desire to possess Diana through the lens of the camera, to possess the simulacrum of her silver gelatin image printed on the page, in conjunction with the relentless pursuit of what are now being termed the "Stalkerazzi," together conspired to bring about the circumstances leading up to Diana's death. "In Diana's fatal crash, the camera (both as reporter and lover) is joined to the automobile and the star, and the cocktail of death and desire becomes even more powerful than the one in Ballard's book" (38). Rushdie then goes on to suggest that, in view of the Windsors' treatment of Diana during her marriage to Prince Charles, "the Royal Family itself . . . may just possibly be on the way out" (69), dethroned by an outraged public who at long last have had enough with the inequitable rule of a capricious monarchy, one that grows increasingly unpopular (or so it would seem) with the British public day by day.

Other commentators, most notably Christopher Hitchens, are far less sympathetic to Diana's posthumous celebrity and far more suspicious of her motives. Even the otherwise laudatory Rushdie admits that Diana had learned how to use the media to create a suitable image of herself for public consumption:

> Diana, Princess of Wales, became skillful at constructing the images of herself that she wanted people to see. I recall a British newspaper editor's telling me how Diana composed the famous shot in which she sat, alone and lovelorn, in front of the world's greatest monument to love, the Taj Mahal. She knew, he said, exactly how the public would 'read' this photograph. It would bring her great sympathy, and make people think (even) less well of the Prince of Wales than before. Diana was not given to using words like 'semiotics,' but she was a capable semiotician of herself. With increasing confidence, she gave us the signs by which we might know her as she wished to be known. (Rushdie, 68)

Picking up on this, Hitchens argues that Diana's ultimate triumph of construction was not only her image as a "lovelorn" mother of two, cast aside by the unfeeling members of the Royal Family. Comparing Diana with Agnes Bojaxhiu, or Mother Teresa, Hitchens commented that "both had spent their careers in the service and the pursuit of the rich and powerful. Both had used poor and sick people as 'accessories' in their campaigns. And both had succeeded in pulling off the number-one triumph offered by the celebrity culture—the achievement of a status where actions are judged by reputation and not the other way around" (Hitchens, 7). Indeed, Diana's carefully managed photo ops in service of the poor and the afflicted are reminiscent of the staged newsreels in John Schlesinger's *Darling* (1965), in which Diana Scott (Julie Christie) becomes "Princess Diana" when she marries an Italian prince. Princess Diana Spencer's own later public appearances were themselves mini-masterpieces of press manipulation. Staged for the mutual benefit of a press corps (and its public) that couldn't get enough of her visage (she was on the cover of *People* magazine an astounding forty-three times), and for Diana's personal benefit as a young divorcée fighting to hang on to the trappings of power and wealth with feverish intensity, they served everyone's purposes admirably. Hitchens notes that "by her embrace of the Fayed family, [Diana made it clear] what sort of company and society she considered desirable. Nonetheless, it seemed that every person in Britain believed she cared for them individually and would be at her happiest when dining in a homeless shelter" (7). In the event itself, the mass media coverage in the aftermath of the death of Diana Spencer was remarkable not only for its quantity but also for the overwhelming uncritical sentimentality that characterized its appearance in newspapers, television, and on various web sites and Internet chat groups around the world.

As Jacqueline Sharkey noted in her essay, "The Diana Aftermath," news coverage for the week of August 31 to September 6, 1997, could aptly be summarized with the phrase "All Diana, All the Time." In that week CBS, NBC, and ABC devoted a total of 197 minutes on their main evening broadcasts alone to Diana's violent death and a seemingly endless recapitulation of her life, complete with video clips of her marriage to Prince Charles, footage of the Princess and her sons on vacation, images of scandal and ceremony commingled into a continuous stream of almost unceasing media coverage. E! Entertainment Television broadcast the funeral of Diana live, as did CNN, CNBC, MSNBC, and numerous other cable services around the world. MSNBC and several other cable and/or broadcast networks replayed a video of the wedding of

Diana and Prince Charles intact (except for commercial interruptions) the day after her death, for added horrific contrast.

In the days following the fatal accident, Diana became the ultimate medieval consumerist icon, the sign that far from abandoning the idea of the British Royal Family, the world audience, to say nothing of the British public, demanded not only a monarchy but its continuation, as Diana's two young sons now stand directly in line for accession to the throne. Even the tabloid press rushed to consecrate Diana in death. While the *National Enquirer*'s headline the week before her death had shrieked "Di Goes Sex-Mad—'I Can't Get Enough!' " (Sharkey, 21), in the ensuing weeks the *Enquirer* and other supermarket tabloids would serve up a newly minted Diana for public consumption, a thirty-six-year-old humanitarian cut down in the prime of her life by the unwanted attentions of an irresponsible press corps that refused to leave her alone. The more respectable journals profited as well: *Time* sold 850,000 issues on the nation's newsstands the week of Diana's death, about "650,000 [issues] more than normal" (20).

A week later, a commemorative issue of *Time* magazine devoted exclusively to Diana sold an astounding 1.2 million copies, "the two largest sellers in the history of the magazine, according to Managing Editor Walter Isaacson" (Sharkey, 20). Fifteen million people watched a special edition of *60 Minutes* covering Diana's life and death on August 31, 1997, an hour-long show hastily assembled on the very day of her death (Sharkey, 20). Nor did the media viewing frenzy abate within a few days, or even a week; "the week of September 15—two weeks after Diana died—broadcast networks devoted more time to the Princess and the British Monarchy than any other story" (Sharkey, 20). Compare these figures to the sixteen minutes of nightly network news time Mother Teresa received when she died on Friday, September 5, less than a week after the accident that claimed Diana's life; in that same week, Diana dominated the nightly network news airtime by nearly a ten-to-one ratio.

Diana's companion in death, Emad Mohamed "Dodi" al-Fayed, received almost no coverage at all; his father, the Egyptian tycoon Mohamed al-Fayed, owner of the department store institution Harrods and an unsuccessful suitor for British citizenship, arranged for an immediate burial, which was discreetly carried out away from the glare of news cameras and their attendant publicity. Clearly, the death of Diana Spencer dominated the public consciousness during the first weeks of September 1997 as no other story had previously been able to do. What was it about Princess Diana's troubled life and violent death that so riv-

eted the readers and viewers of the world, some essence th[a]
posedly newsworthy spectacles lacked? Why was Diana's
keenly felt, more adroitly exploited, more avidly consum
deaths of John or Robert Kennedy, Martin Luther King, the
Challenger disaster, Pearl Harbor, or, to be concise, any
celebrity death and/or international catastrophe of the er
century?

In part, the answer lies in the sheer profusion of the news media a
able to disseminate Diana's image-in-death. One of the last images we
have of Diana, perhaps the absolute last, is her ghostly presence as she
exits from the Ritz Hotel through a revolving door, captured for one last
time on a hotel surveillance camera. Diana's image has been cropped,
scanned, digitized and reconstructed in literally hundreds of thousands of
photographs, miles of film and videotape, and then sluiced out to a waiting, eager public through magazines, newspapers, web sites, cable networks, broadcast networks, local television stations, academic journals,
CD-ROMs, DVDs, home video cassettes, not to mention (particularly
after her death) postage stamps, coffee mugs, place mats, dish towels,
commemorative dinner plates, porcelain dolls, memorial "coins" cus-
tom-stamped by various private mints, and various and sundry other
items.

No wonder that on December 1, 1997, a group of attorneys filed a peti-
tion in London on behalf of the Diana, Princess of Wales Memorial Fund
to have Diana's face certified as a trademark with Britain's patent office,
in the hope of controlling the flood of exploitational materials created to
merchandise her image. Indeed, as late as mid-December 1997, a site
existed on the World Wide Web offering two "nude" photographs of
Diana for public consumption, free for anyone to download without cost
of any kind. A Princess Di look-alike still offers her services on the web
for "TV, film and photo opportunities, corporate and commercial advertising, corporate and commercial entertaining ('meet and greet'), promotional and charity work, personal appearances, [and] modeling,"
although the person whose image she resembles has passed from the
realm of the living into the shared sarcophagus of collective visual memory. And a transcript of the parodic "Top Ten Surprises in the Princess
Diana Interview" from *The Late Show with David Letterman* for November
21, 1995, is still archived on the web, including the fictitious claims that
"[it] turns out she's Mexican" and "[she] works nights at Euro-Hooters."

But can we blame the social parodists? In life, Diana was the subject of
at least four TV movies, including Peter Levin's *The Royal Romance of*

Charles and Diana (1982), starring Christopher Baines as Prince Charles and Catherine Oxenberg as Diana; James Goldstone's *Charles and Diana: A Royal Love Story* (1982), with David Robb and Caroline Bliss as Charles and Diana; John Powers's *Charles and Diana: Unhappily Ever After* (1992), with Roger Rees as Charles and Catherine Oxenberg reprising her role from *The Royal Romance of Charles and Diana*; and Kevin Connor's *Diana: Her True Story* (1993), featuring Serena Scott Thomas and David Threlfall in the key roles. Across the decade of these fictional representations of Diana's life, we can trace not only the "romance novel" narratives imperative of the two 1982 films but also the final images of Hollywood royalty busily engaged in bringing the fictive Diana's story to flickering life. Olivia de Havilland (as the Queen Mother), Dana Wynter (Queen Elizabeth), Stewart Granger (Prince Philip), and Ray Milland all appeared in *Royal Romance*; Christopher Lee (Prince Philip), Rod Taylor (Edward Adeane), and Charles Gray (Earl Spencer) graced *A Royal Love Story*. Interestingly, in the 1982 *Royal Love Story*, both Andrew Parker-Bowles (former "Chad and Jeremy" rock star Jeremy Clyde) and Camilla Parker-Bowles (Jo Ross) are presented as friends of the couple, wishing them all the best; by 1992's *Unhappily Ever After*, Jane How's Camilla is seen as an implacable adversary bent on wrenching the Royal marriage asunder.

By the time of 1993's *Diana: Her True Story*, Camilla's role (now played by Elizabeth Garvie) has been so enlarged as to render her third in a cast of more than twenty-five principal players, and the public revision of Diana's life in the Royal Family has come full circle. Based on Andrew Morton's book of the same title, *Diana: Her True Story* presents Diana as a victim of cruelty and careless indifference, in stark contrast to the happy newlyweds of the 1982 film. But which version are we to regard as authoritative? None of them. All are fictions, disguised as docudramas, created with an intended audience uppermost in the producer's mind. The first two films promised romance, pageantry, and medieval splendor; the second pair of films promised scandal, decadence, and insider information. In all four cases, the films are merely constructs, designed to merchandise and exploit Diana Spencer's image without her direct participation in the project.

You can have Diana's image without actually having Diana's image in these films, which offer at length the Baudrillardian conceit of a copy without an original, based as they are on a public persona manufactured by Diana and her advisers with skill, marketing sense, and an omnipresent eye for the public's appetite for spectacle. During the sixteen years of Diana's relationship with the House of Windsor, Diana mastered the art of presenting to the public exactly the image she wished them to have of her, precisely the impression that she sought to leave with the press and public who were her real courtiers in the world of the public's view.

And yet, Diana's entire childhood and early schooling seemed to prepare her for such a destiny. Born on July 1, 1961, at Park House near Sandringham, in Norfolk, into a family of considerable means, Diana's early life was one of pleasure and power, commingled with the usual domestic entanglements that shape one's interior landscape. Her mother, the Viscountess Althorp, was only twenty-five when Diana was born; her father, Viscount Althorp, was thirty-seven. She had two older sisters, Jane and Sarah, and Diana's birth was followed by that of her younger brother, Charles. The family lived in a palatial house on the Queen's Estate at Sandringham, and at Althorp House, the family estate, in the English Midlands. Diana never felt particularly at home in the vast, museumlike precincts of Althorp House, and much preferred Park House, which was both more intimate and more modern. Nevertheless, Diana's life was one of privilege and power, in close proximity to members of the Royal Family, with Princes Andrew and Edward as occasional afternoon guests, and invitations to "the Queen's winter home" (Morton, 14). But tensions between Diana's mother and father, exacerbated by a series of medical tests Lady Althorp was forced into by her husband after the birth of the couple's son John in 1959, who was born badly deformed, and "survived for only ten hours" (Morton, 10). In 1967 the couple separated, throwing the entire family ménage into psychic chaos. A bitter divorce followed, scattering the children into a variety of boarding schools and temporary living arrangements. Diana's father won custody of the children, and Lady Althorp subsequently married Peter Shand Kydd, a wealthy young entrepreneur (Morton, 16–18). Diana would immerse herself in the romantic novels of Barbara Cartland, her step-grandmother, while a succession of wildly variable "nannies" did little to compensate for the loss of her mother as a result of the divorce (Morton, 19).

Diana was an avid TV viewer, preferring shows like the pop music review *Top of the Pops* and *Coronation Street*, one of the longest-running soap operas in British television history. Indeed, Diana's fascination with soap operas did not diminish with the passage of time. As she entered the Royal Family, she still kept abreast of the plotlines of the most popular British soaps, so that she could discuss them with her constituents as an immediate shared common interest (Morton, 28). She also took ballet lessons, and attended the Riddlesworth Hall preparatory school in Norfolk, moving on to the West Heath School in Kent in 1974. Her formal education was completed at a finishing school in Rougemont, Switzerland. In 1977, Diana first met Prince Charles during a day of outdoor shooting "in the middle of a ploughed field near Nobottle Wood on the Althorp estate" (Morton, 35). Diana was hardly the center of the prince's attention on this occasion, for Prince Charles was at the time involved in a brief flirtation with Diana's sister, Sarah.

But as the relationship between Charles and Sarah diminished, Charles's interest in Diana grew, and she was invited to the prince's thirtieth birthday party at Buckingham Palace in November 1978 (Morton, 37). By the winter of 1979, Diana was moving closer to a relationship with Charles. Charles himself was already deeply involved in a friendship with Camilla Parker-Bowles, who was happy to accompany the prince on his various outdoor sporting trips, while the British public as a whole wanted Prince Charles to settle down and produce an heir to the throne (Morton, 48). In July 1980, Diana and Charles were thrown together during a weekend barbecue at the house of Commander Robert de Pass and exchanged confidences surrounding the Earl of Mountbatten's death and the ensuing funeral procession in Westminster Abbey. Diana expressed great sympathy for Charles's sadness on that occasion, and from that moment on Charles began to aggressively court Diana Spencer (Morton, 49).

By September, Charles asked Diana to join him at Balmoral Castle, for the weekend of the Braeman games (Morton, 51). That weekend she got her first taste of what her hypersurveillant future as a member of the Royal Family would be like when two photographers and a newspaper reporter spotted her fishing with Prince Charles in the Dee River (Morton, 51). Within days Diana was stalked outside her apartment by a bevy of paparazzi, who forced her to pose for photographs at a moment's notice and followed her to the Young England Kindergarten School, where she was working as a teacher. From the moment her connection with Prince Charles was discovered, her private identity and any claim she may have once had to anonymity were finished. On Friday, February 6, 1981, Prince Charles formally proposed to Diana Spencer (Morton, 56). The engagement was announced on February 24, 1981, and Princess Diana left her own flat for the last time. By now, she had an armed bodyguard from Scotland Yard who accompanied her everywhere. As she left her apartment, the bodyguard told Diana, "I just want you to know that this is the last night of freedom in your life, so make the most of it" (Morton, 58). After that, Diana belonged more to the public, and to the press, than to herself.

Diana Spencer thus passed from a somewhat unstable and calamitous, if privileged, upbringing into the glaring spotlight of unceasing international celebrity within a matter of a few years. From the moment she entered the prince's orbit, her life was no longer her own. In rapid succession she gave birth to two sons, Princes William (born July 21, 1982) and Harry (born September 15, 1984). Private and public life commingled into a continual dialogue with the public, which often overshadowed her increasingly formal relationship with her husband. In 1982, in a somewhat bizarre quirk of fate, Diana traveled to Monaco to represent the queen at the funeral of Princess Grace, who had died in an automobile accident on September 14. The two women had met before Diana's marriage to Prince Charles at a social event at London's Goldsmith Hall on March 9, 1981, and were photographed chatting amiably amidst their star-studded surroundings.

As many other observers have noted, Grace and Diana's lives had, sadly, a great deal of commonality. Diana died after her Mercedes slammed into a wall in a tunnel under the Place de l'Alma trying to escape a pursuing flock of paparazzi; although she remained conscious for several hours following the accident, her wounds were so severe that she could not possibly have survived. Princess Grace died when her car went off the road on a steep thoroughfare outside of Monaco, hurtled down a precipice, and landed in a culvert. Both Diana and Grace were "commoners" who had married royalty; neither was particularly happy in her marriage. As Diana attended Grace's funeral, she could not possibly have imagined that as a consequence of her own fame, she, too, would die in a violent automobile accident fifteen years later. As an observer noted, "Both princesses felt betrayed in their marriages. But Diana, at least, looked as though she was starting a new life. For Grace, it was already too late" (August, 5A).

In 1983, Diana and Charles toured New Zealand and Australia on a formal visit, and soon official visits (with her two sons in tow) to Brazil, South Korea, Nigeria, Canada, Portugal, Cameroon, Japan, Spain, and other countries followed. By this time, too, Diana was already deeply involved in the charity work that would consume much of the rest of her life, particularly on behalf of persons with HIV/AIDS, and the international abolition of land mines. After her separation from Charles in December of 1992, and their subsequent divorce in August 1996, this work increased, as Diana took on an increasingly demanding schedule of lectures, fund-raising events, and public appearances.

On September 12, 1996, Diana attended the thirtieth anniversary meeting of the International Leprosy Association in London; also in September she attended various charity events for breast cancer. In early January 1997, Diana visited the Diana Red Cross Handicap Hospital in Angola and shortly thereafter turned her attentions to Bosnia, where her campaign against the use of antipersonnel land mines continued in earnest. While in Angola, she also visited various hospitals in Luanda, the capital city, and on January 17, 1997, she attended a meeting of the Red Cross in Washington, again to discuss the issue of land mines as a negative force in maintaining international territorial domains. Diana auctioned off many of her dresses collected over the years at a gala event at Christie's; she comforted Elton John after fashion designer Gianni Versace was senselessly shot to death in front of his house in July 1997. By this time, Diana had evolved into a highly accomplished public speaker and could easily hold the podium, as she did in a series of cancer research fund-raising events in June 1997 in Chicago, Washington, D.C., and London. And as all this charitable work progressed, as Diana was firmly involved in establishing both a new public and private persona for herself, she met Dodi al-Fayed, much to the general disapproval of the press and public, who regarded Mohamed al-Fayed and his son as interlopers in British society, who attempted to buy their respective ways into public favor.

Yet Mohamed Fayed had known Diana "since childhood" (Spoto, 149), before her involvement with the Royal Family, and so Diana's vacation with the Fayed family could easily be seen as an extension of her financially comfortable yet emotionally tempestuous childhood. Gradually, Diana and the younger Fayed became more deeply involved, although Diana remained uncertain about the true nature of her relationship with Dodi. As she told one confidant in the last month of her life, "I haven't taken such a long time to get out of one poor marriage in order to get into another one" (Spoto, 165). Dodi Fayed indeed had something of a reputation as an international playboy and had produced or served as coproducer on such films as Hugh Hudson's *Chariots of Fire* (1981), George Roy Hill's *The World According to Garp* (1982), and Steven Spielberg's *Hook* (1991). Fayed, a billionaire's son, was thus no stranger to power and celebrity. At the time of his involvement with Diana, the forty-two-year-old sometime film producer, who partied in a series of lavish rented mansions in Beverly Hills at a reported cost of $20,000 to $35,000 a month, was already noted for his high-living, extravagant lifestye. Dodi Fayed was an inveterate partygiver, whose guests included Ryan O'Neal, Robert Downey, Jr., Brooke Shields, Tony Curtis, and other Hollywood celebrities. A graduate of Sandhurst Military Academy and a junior officer in London for the United Arab Emirates, Fayed would drift from house to house, party to party, often traveling in the company of his father on their multimillion-dollar yacht. Dodi Fayed's life, then, was also a life of power and wealth, and many social observers saw in Diana's relationship with Dodi Fayed a parallel between Jackie Kennedy's romance and subsequent marriage to multimillionaire shipping entrepreneur Aristotle Onassis.

Diana herself professed to be uneasy with the lavish presents that Dodi pressed upon her: "I don't want to be bought. I have everything I want. I just want someone to be there for me, to make me feel safe and secure," she told a friend (Spoto, 165). But within days, all these concerns would be swept aside by the simple yet unalterable fact that Diana herself had ceased to exist altogether. When she left the Ritz Hotel at 12:15 A.M. on the night of August 31, 1997, and was seen drifting ethereally through the revolving doors of the hotel for one final public moment before her departure from this world, how could she have known that, within a matter of minutes, the black 1994 Mercedes S-280 she and her companions were traveling in would be reduced to a hunk of scrap metal? "The front end [of the car was] telescoped into the engine, which was forced almost through the driver's seat. Inside the pile of rubble, Henri Paul and Dodi al-Fayed were dead, their bodies hideously mangled. [The driver] Trevor Rees-Jones was seriously injured [and] Diana, Princess of Wales was near death. It was 12:24 [A.M.]" (Spoto, 176). Extricated from the wreck, Diana and Rees-Jones were rushed to the Hôpital de la Pitié-Salpêtrière, but due to the difficulty in retrieving them from the wrecked automobile, they were not admitted until two in the morning. Despite intensive labors by a medical team that worked feverishly to bring Diana back to life, Diana went into cardiac arrest and died at 4 A.M. on August 31, 1997 (Spoto, 177).

And thus, it was all over, except for the memorial tributes that would soon follow her death and, in a peculiar manner, eclipse and perhaps even transcend the public reception she had been afforded in life. Which brings us back to David Cronenberg's film *Crash* (1996). Reviled upon its initial release, but praised almost immediately by cognoscenti as a nearly "religious masterpiece" (in Bernardo Bertolucci's words), *Crash* is a meditation of the exigencies of fame, the certainty of posthumous sainthood for celebrities dying young, the links between public consumerism of images of violent death and scandal and the needs of the imagistic/material entertainment marketplace, and the desire, above all, of the public to *possess*, through multiple exposures and serial repetition, the essence of the person whom they admired and/or emulated in life, and consequently enshrined in death. In Cronenberg's film, James Ballard (an obvious homage to the author upon whose novel the film is based) is employed as a director of crash-test films in which automobiles are slammed into a variety of walls, concrete pillars, and other objects, while being photographed by Ballard and his crew in tortuous slow motion. Actor James Spader, bland, detached, curiously removed from the cataclysmic spectacles he designs and executes on a daily basis, is an ideal choice for the character of Ballard.

Ballard's home life is equally bizarre. While he is ostensibly married to Catherine (Deborah Kara Unger), both Ballard and Catherine aggressively sleep with other people, preferring liaisons with strangers in public and potentially embarrassing situations to conventional heterotopic coupling. When we first meet Catherine, she is engaged in adulterous sex in an otherwise deserted airplane hangar; moments later, we meet Ballard, frenziedly fucking his camera assistant in a darkroom between camera setups. That evening, at home, both compare their sexual experiences, which seem transparently designed to spice up their own relationship. Shortly thereafter, as Ballard is driving in his car, he is involved in an automobile accident with Helen Remington (Holly Hunter), in which the body of Remington's male companion is thrown by the force of the impact through Ballard's windshield and on to the front seat of his car.

As Remington and Ballard stare transfixedly at each other in the aftermath of the collision, a curious bond of mutual understanding seems to forge between them. Transferred to the same hospital for treatment, Ballard meets Vaughan (Elias Koteas), who masquerades as a medical technician at the facility, while Remington recuperates nearby. In reality, Vaughan is a car crash fetishist, the leader of a subculture dedicated to recreating the final moments of various celebrities who have died in violent car crashes, correct down to the smallest detail. After his release from the hospital, Ballard finds that he is unable to return to his job with full energy, and discovers himself being increasingly drawn in by Vaughan and the members of his cult, including stunt driver Colin Seagrave (Peter MacNeil) and Gabrielle (Rosanna Arquette), whose mangled legs are kept in place by a series of metal braces which extend from her feet to her chest.

At an invitation from Vaughan, Ballard and Remington attend an elaborately staged reenactment of the car crash that killed James Dean on September 30, 1955. As Vaughan addresses a hushed crowd assembled in a set of hastily erected bleachers, he assures the members of his rapt audi-nce that everything in the re-creation they are about to witness is absolutely authentic, down to the detailing on Dean's silver Porsche Spyder, a car that was Dean's favorite mode of transportation. Only one week after the completion of filming on George Steven's *Giant* (1956), Dean was killed at 5:59 P.M. in an accident "at the intersection of Routes 41 and 466 near Paso Robles, California" (Parish, 13). Dean was traveling at 86 mph at the time of the impact. Dean's passenger, one Rolf Weutherich, received a broken leg and head injuries as a result of the impact, while the driver of the other car, Donald Turnupseed, suffered only minor injuries.

Vaughan lovingly details the circumstances leading up to the accident and notes that Weutherich, although he escaped death in this crash, would die in a similar road accident some twenty-six years later in Germany. With Seagrave playing the role of James Dean in a perfect replica of Dean's beloved Porsche Spyder, and cult follower Brett Trask (John Stoneham, Jr.) reenacting Turnupseed's role in the accident, Vaughan himself steps into the passenger seat of the Porsche in the role of Weutherich. The Porsche, complete to the detailing of James Dean's nickname for the car, "Little Bastard," emblazoned across the trunk, backs up for a quarter of a mile, while the car driven by Brett Trask does the same. And then, at a signal from Vaughan, the two cars charge forward in the night, without, as Vaughan notes, "any safety padding, helmets, roll cages or seat belts of any kind," and finally collide in a brutal crash in front of the enthralled spectators, who break into frenzied applause as the reenactment concludes.

What they have been reconstructing, Vaughan tells the crowd, is "*one moment,* but it was a moment that would create a Hollywood legend." Transfixed by the spectacle he has just witnessed, Ballard rises to his feet in the stands in a mixture of anticipation and excitement. Are the stunt drivers all right? Trask emerges from the Turnupseed car, shaken but intact, and the audience rewards his efforts with a rousing round of applause. But Cronenberg's relentlessly tracking camera is more circumspect in its approval and examination of the scene. As Howard Shore's appropriately mesmerizing music score swells in the background, Cronenberg's camera drifts in a meditational trance past the wreck of the Turnupseed car, inhaling every detail of the damage, and then comes to rest on Dean's Porsche. Both Vaughan and Seagrave remain immobile inside the car. "Is this part of the act, or are they really hurt?" Ballard asks Remington. "You never know with Vaughan," she replies. "It's his show."

Slowly, painfully, Vaughan slides out of the wreck. Microphone in hand, he continues his narration of the crash and its aftermath, noting that Rolf Weutherich spent a year in the hospital recovering from his injuries, while Donald Turnupseed "was found wandering about in a daze, but basically unhurt. James Dean died of a broken neck, and became *immortal*." At this, the crowd once again breaks into furious applause, which is interrupted only by the sudden appearance of the police, who have been monitoring the activities of the group. The crowd scatters into the woods, but it is clear that there will be other meetings and other reenactments, in the future. After all, who does not desire immortality, to be frozen forever in the public gaze in the perfect iconic image of youth, health, and desire? As Ballard drifts deeper into the sub-culture of Vaughan's group, he confronts and becomes increasingly engaged in a performance art enterprise that conflates ritualistic sex with car crashes. The cult members replay crash-test videos (the very films, in some instances, that Ballard directs) to analyze the key moments of impact, and plan to restage Jayne Mansfield's fatal crash, complete with her four Chihuahua dogs. Soon Vaughan, Catherine, and Ballard find themselves engaging in a series of chance, violent encounters on the road, in which minor collisions, bumping at high speeds, and near-accidents replace sex as an emotional and intellectual stimulant. Vaughan and Ballard pick up a prostitute (Yolande Julian) at the airport and engage in sex in a car on the highway. Catherine and Vaughan fuck in the back seat of Ballard's car, as he drives through a car wash. Ballard and Vaughan fuck in the back seat of Vaughan's beat-up car by the side of an industrial viaduct. In perhaps the film's most notorious sequence, Ballard, fixating on Gabrielle's leg braces and the various scars that traverse her body, fucks one of the wounds in her leg, in the back of yet another anonymous vehicle, carried away by a passionate conflation of love, death, and desire. Throughout all this, members of the cult sporadically meet in a series of derelict buildings to smoke marijuana, watch more crash tapes, and swap scrapbooks of photos of particularly brutal car crashes. During one meeting, Ballard is surprised to discover that Vaughan has a scrapbook of photographs documenting Ballard's crash with Helen Remington's car. The scrapbook includes photos of Ballard's battered body right after the accident, taken by Vaughan while Ballard was in the hospital. Despite this invasion of privacy, Ballard finds himself increasingly drawn into the cult. During a late-night conversation with Vaughan, Ballard describes his entire experience with the group as "very satisfying."

"That's the future, Ballard, and you're already a part of it," Vaughan esponds. "You're beginning to see that there's a benevolent psy-hopathology that beckons towards us. For example, the car crash is a fer-ilizing rather than a destructive event. A liberation of sexual energy, mediating the sexuality of those who have died, with an intensity that's impossible in any other form to experience. To live that, that's my pro-ect." Just how seriously Vaughan takes this quest is made eerily manifest when Vaughan, Ballard, and Catherine accidentally come across a spec-acular multicar crash on the highway. As Vaughan slows the car to a crawl to inspect the wreckage, he realizes that the spectacle he is wit-nessing is the Jayne Mansfield car crash fatally reenacted from a painfully detailed series of news photos by Colin Seagrave, which has been staged without Vaughan's participation. "You couldn't wait," Vaughan mur-nurs, addressing Seagrave's corpse, more in disbelief than anything else. As Catherine sits down next to a dazed but otherwise unhurt victim of the carnage, carelessly smoking a cigarette, Ballard looks on in a mixture of amazement and wonder bordering on admiration. Vaughan moves smoothly among the wreckage of the tangled automobiles, photograph-ing everything, attempting to capture the essence of the entire event on film. Police and ambulance workers go about their tasks, prying car doors open with crowbars and other rescue tools. No one stops or questions Vaughan as he carefully, and lovingly, documents Colin Seagrave's final performance piece.

At length, Vaughan himself is killed in a car crash, a destiny he pur-sued with the intensity of a religious zealot. Only Catherine and Ballard are left to play the game. In the final scene of the film, Ballard purpose-fully runs Catherine off the road. Though stunned and shaken, Catherine has escaped serious injury. Lovingly caressing her bruised body, Ballard whispers, "Maybe next time. Maybe next time." For the characters who inhabit the world of *Crash*, sex = death – immortality as long as the object of one's desire perishes in an automobile accident. Only through violence can one achieve immortality, pop iconic sainthood. The mem-bers of Vaughan's group have themselves tattooed with scars they find particularly arousing. Cronenberg in *Crash* is offering nothing less than a meditation on our spectatorial fascination with violence, death, and destruction, the reasons behind the public's continued fascination with spectacles of death and brutality. As Cronenberg himself commented on his reasons for making the film,

I had to make the movie to *find out* why I had to make the movie. It was not something that was obvious to me. . . . As human beings, our sense of what's beautiful or repulsive is only skin deep, even when it comes to our own bodies. I'm always interested in taking something which seems repulsive at the beginning of the film and making it appear beautiful and inevitable by the end. . . . [The viewer is] hopefully entering into the psychology of the characters. I'd like people to be thinking, "even though I would have thought that these feelings were completely distant and impossible for me, I do have a kinship with these characters." As soon as you've made one connection like that, you can start to make others. . . . [The characters in *Crash*] seek life, even if they're seeking it through death or danger. And I think that's very human. (Pizzello, 43–47)

The *Faces of Death* series of videotapes, in which animals and humans (with tape culled from a variety of medical, news, and documentary sources) are ritualistically slaughtered to satiate the gaze of the camera, have become justly notorious for their infamous content. But what of Christopher Lewis's *The Ripper* (1985), Clive Barker's *Nightbreed* (1990), Wes Craven's *Scream 2* (1997), Jim Gillespie's *I Know What You Did Last Summer* (1997), Bill Rebane's *Blood Harvest* (1987), Joe Giannone's *Madman* (1981), William Lustig's *Maniac* (1980), and numerous other slasher films which have flooded theatrical and home video screens since the early 1970s? In *Nightbreed*, in fact, it is Cronenberg himself who plays the central role in the film, as a psychiatrist/serial killer who relentlessly roams the film's bleak landscape, searching for new victims (among them an aging John Agar) to dispatch. *Nightbreed* was directed by Clive Barker, most famous as a writer of splatter horror stories and novels, in which graphic violence as text is taken to a new degree of specificity, and as the director and author of *Hellraiser* (1987), a particularly brutal and vicious horror film that was followed by two sequels, *Hellbound: Hell Raiser II* (1988) and *Hellraiser III: Hell on Earth* (1992), neither of which Barker himself directed. The point here is not to excoriate these films, which are nothing more than synthetic concoctions of a latex, prosthetic makeup and stage blood (with increasing quantities of computer-generated imagery to distort the human body into even more improbable contortions for our viewing pleasure), but rather to ask why those spectacles of violence, death, and destruction so mesmerize us, and why we flock eagerly to see them as an apparent antidote to the tedium of our daily existence.

If we are now alive, we will die; almost as soon as we leave the realm of childhood, this fact is brought home to us increasingly by our parents, by the nightly news, by chance encounters with disasters that befall others, by deaths within our own family. Yet as long as the experience of death is denied us, it remains abstract. We read a newspaper headline: "Drop of Virus from a Monkey Kills Researcher in Six Weeks"; what are we to make of this? A young woman, Elizabeth R. Griffin, twenty-two, was working in a laboratory as an assistant in Atlanta, Georgia, when a rhesus monkey infected with the herpes B virus unexpectedly "flung a tiny drop of fluid—perhaps urine or feces—at her face. It struck her in the eye" (Bragg, 16). Six weeks later, despite expert medical care, this tiny speck of viral fluid killed Elizabeth Griffin by inducing a combination of encephalomyelitis, bacterial infections, and respiratory distress syndrome, leading to paralysis that left her unable to breathe on her own. At the time of her death, she was unable to move, though still alert, and dependent upon a respirator to help her breathe. She had hoped to become a doctor. As the newspaper account of her death noted, she "probably never thought she was at risk" (16). The poet Gregory Corso observes in his poem *Bomb* that "death's finger is free-lance" (65). Did John Hodiak expect to die on the morning of October 19, 1955, at the age of forty-one, of a massive heart attack, despite no history of heart trouble, while on his way to the studio to complete the film *On the Threshold of Space* (Parish and De Carl, 318)? When Jack Cassidy went to sleep on the night of December 12, 1976, how could he possibly know that a smoldering cigarette butt would set his Hollywood penthouse apartment on fire, leaving his body so badly charred by the blaze that it had to be identified through dental records (Parish, 8)?

When Jeff Chandler entered the hospital for routine surgery to correct a slipped disc at the age of forty-two, how could he know that serious complications arising from this simple procedure would lead to a series of internal hemorrhages, infections, and pneumonia, resulting in his death after a marathon seventy-two-hour corrective operation on June 17, 1961 (Parish, 9–10)? Rebecca Schaeffer could never have expected that an obsessed fan would shoot her for spurning his affections on the morning of July 18, 1989 (Parish, 79). Carl "Alfalfa" Switzer never expected to die in a senseless and violent gun battle over a $50 debt on January 21, 1959, after appearing in dozens of *Our Gang* comedies (Parish, 82). Sharon Tate had no intimation that the members of the Manson Family would murder her and her unborn child, along with Jay Sebring, Abigail Folger, Wotjek Frykowski, and Steven Parent (who besides their relatives remembers their names now?), in a house on Cielo Drive on the night of August 9, 1969 (Parish, 82). Tyrone Power could not have known that he would collapse after filming a dueling scene with actor George Sanders for the film *Solomon and Sheba* on November 15, 1958, and die of a heart attack shortly thereafter (Parish, 148). Dick Shawn had no idea that he would die in the midst of performing a comic monologue in which he saw himself as one of only five hundred survivors of an apocalyptic nuclear conflict, in front of an audience at the University of California, San Diego. "And I would be your leader!" Shawn shouted, and then fell motionless to the stage, dead of a massive heart attack (Parish, 153–54).

Bruce Lee died at the age of thirty-two on July 20, 1973, after taking a pain killer which apparently caused swelling of the brain (Parish, 189). Sal Mineo was murdered in the parking garage of his apartment complex by an assailant who later bragged that he had killed Mineo because it had been "easy to do" (Parish, 76). Ramon Novarro was beaten to death by two male prostitutes in his house in Hollywood Hills on October 31, 1968 (Parish, 78). Capucine, whose last major theatrical feature was Blake Edwards's *Curse of the Pink Panther* (1983)—the film was also actor David Niven's final project—jumped to her death from her apartment building on March 17, 1990, following years of depression at the state of her dwindling career (Parish, 216). Brandon Lee, the son of Bruce Lee, was killed in a freak accident on the set of *The Crow* on March 31, 1993 (Parish, 240). Rock Hudson died of complications due to AIDS on October 2, 1985 (Parish, 132). Hounded by the House Committee on Un-American Activities in the early 1950s, John Garfield died of cardiac arrest at the age of thirty-nine on May 20, 1952 (Parish, 121). Marilyn Monroe died under mysterious circumstances, ostensibly from an overdose of sleeping pills, on August 5, 1962, setting off a series of rumors surrounding possible other causes for the death, rumors that have persisted to this day (Parish, 194). Singer and actor Rick Nelson, who grew up performing in his parents' television show *The Adventures of Ozzie and Harriet*, and who appeared with his wife Kristin Nelson not only in the teleseries but also in a bizarrely anachronistic feature film, *Love and Kisses* (1965), directed by his father, died in a plane crash with the members of his backup group, the Stone Canyon Band, on December 31, 1985 (Parish, 38). This list of untimely, brutal, capricious deaths could continue indefinitely; each of these fatalities received wide press coverage, and many have passed into the realm of contemporary folklore, to be repeated and embellished with each retelling.

But what of the 183,000 (the number has been rounded off for the sake of actuarial convenience) people who drowned on April 30, 1991, in Bangladesh? As Annie Dillard notes in her article, "The Wreck of Time," this figure is so large as to be almost unfathomable. Dillard quotes serial killer Ted Bundy as being perplexed by the media frenzy surrounding his arrest and trial. Bundy couldn't fathom the reason for all the fuss: " 'I mean, there are *so* many people,' " Bundy complained to the police. Dillard then reels off a series of appalling statistics: "Two million children die a year from diarrhea, and 800,000 from measles. . . . Stalin starved 7 million Ukrainians in one year. Pol Pot killed 1 million Cambodians, the flu epidemic of 1918 killed 21 or 22 million people" (Dillard, 51, 54). And she asks, implicitly, does any of this *mean* anything to us? Since none of this is happening to us, can we connect in any way with the suffering and torment of these millions of unnamed, unknown, noncelebrity deaths? Marilyn Monroe's death is remembered. James Dean, Jimmy Stewart, Robert Mitchum, Elvis Presley—all are remembered. What about the millions who died in the Holocaust, or Ted Bundy's victims, or the victims of John Wayne Gacy, or Stalin, or Mao Tse-tung? No one except the members of their immediate families knows their names; perhaps, in the case of Stalin or Mao Tse-tung, destruction was so complete that no one was left to tell the tale of loss. As Dillard notes,

"The atom bomb is nothing to be afraid of," Mao told Nehru. "China has many people. . . . The deaths of ten or twenty million people is nothing to be afraid of." A witness said Nehru showed shock. Later, speaking in Moscow, Mao displayed yet more generosity: he boasted that he was willing to lose 300 million people, half of China's population.

Does Mao's reckoning shock me really? If sanctioning the death of strangers could save my daughter's life, would I do it? Probably. How many others' lives would I be willing to sacrifice? Three? Three hundred million?

An English journalist, observing the Sisters of Charity in Calcutta, reasoned: "Either life is always and in all circumstances sacred, or intrinsically of no account; it is inconceivable that it should be in some cases the one, and in some the other.' " (Dillard, 56)

What the cinema does, what photography and popular culture hope to accomplish in these circumstances of dire necessity, is nothing less than the retrieval of the dead, and the reentry of their phantom presences into the realm of the living. In *Love and Kisses*, Rick and Kristin Nelson will be forever married, forever young, living down the street from their parents, who are only a phone call away in case of emergency. In making this film, Ozzie Nelson sought not only to recapture his own youth as a band leader but also to preserve in stasis the image and tactile presence of Rick and Kristin—a wedding present of cinematic immortality for the young couple. Within a few years, Rick and Kristin were divorced; Ozzie died, then Harriet. The film lives on. What happened to the dream of being forever young, forever in demand, always the object of the public's adulation? In one sense it is gone, but in another the dream exists so long as the film exists, or the pressbook exists, or stills of the film can be accessed and viewed.

The house used in *Love and Kisses* was a standing studio set at Universal; the film was made quickly and cheaply, utilizing whatever existing facilities were available, saving most of its production budget for the use of Technicolor processing as an added incentive when advertising the film for Rick and Kristin's public. The same house featured in *Love and Kisses* (at least the living room, staircase, and central dining area—the kitchen was a set constructed specifically for the film, designed to promote the use of Tappan ovens, as noted by the *Love and Kisses* pressbook) had been previously used in numerous theatrical motion pictures and television shows, including an extremely cheap Universal horror film entitled *The Thing That Couldn't Die*, which was shot for a mere $150,000 in fourteen days (January 1–15, 1958). Thus the space appropriated by Ozzie Nelson for *Love and Kisses* represents a doubly phantom zone, a location in which any action becomes possible.

In *The Thing That Couldn't Die*, Gideon Drew (Robin Hughes), an ancient sorcerer, is ritually beheaded as punishment for practicing black magic. Drew's head is buried separately from his body in a small locked chest, so that he can never use his magic to rise from the dead and wreak havoc on the living. However, in the film's narrative, a young woman, Jessica Burns (Carolyn Kearney), discovers the location of the body several hundred years later. Pressured by greedy family members who think they have found a chest of buried treasure, Jessica allows the body to be exhumed. For the rest of the film's running time, the decapitated head of Gideon Drew seeks to be reunited with its body so that full reanimation may be effected. Drew enlists the members of the living who dug him up in this quest, and then disposes of them when they can no longer be of service. For most of the film, Drew says not a word; he controls those around him through the power of his gaze alone. One look into his eyes is sufficient to elicit complete obedience. In this, the gaze of Gideon Drew mirrors the gaze of the television screen within the domestic sphere, the gaze that controls us and refuses to let us look away. We may flip the dial all we like, but for most of us, turning off a television is a seemingly impossible task. As long as the television remains on, we remain in the zone of hypersurveillance it constructs. Directed by Will Cowan, *The Thing That Couldn't Die* was made during a peculiar time at Universal, in which the studio was ridding itself of back inventory both in terms of physical properties and of actors whose services were under contract to the studio.

When I began making *The Thing That Couldn't Die*, some interesting situations occurred. With the times being as they were in early 1958, it was the function of all the department chiefs to clear themselves of contract individuals. This picture, as were most horror films, was not regarded highly. The chiefs of casting approached all the contracted talent on the lot and suggested they do a part in this picture. Jill St. John was one, among others. They, or their agents, would turn a picture of this budget away which resulted in a suspension, and the studio was no longer obligated to pay them. So what *The Thing That Couldn't Die* did was "clean out" the contract ranks. William Reynolds, Andra Martin, and Jeffrey Stone were all contracted Universal talent and accepted. Carolyn Kearney was a newcomer and was tickled pink about doing the film. At the time *The Thing That Couldn't Die* was nearing completion, Universal had dismissed a large chunk of [the studio's workers]. All of the writers were gone, and [scenarist] David Duncan remained on the staff as a sole survivor and was given very little time to complete the screenplay.

I can clearly remember driving to the studio on the last day of shooting, still undecided on how to direct the finale. So actually the last few minutes of *Thing* where the casket is brought back to the house and the headless body emerges was somewhat ad-libbed. On the last day of shooting, all of the department chiefs had been present to see what I had come up with for a climax! We shot *Thing* in about 14 days and entirely within the Universal lot. The rolling hills which are seen in the film are actually the Universal back-lot property with the Santa Monica and San Gabriel Mountains in the distance, looking toward Burbank. The ranch house used in the picture can be recognized as the old "Ma and Pa Kettle" facade. It had been seen in countless other Universal productions throughout the years and is still standing as part of New England Street on the Universal tour route. (Parla, 24)

When tourists come to the Universal lot, then, and see the New England Street, or the ranch house facade used in the *Ma and Pa Kettle* series, or perhaps, if they are lucky enough to be on the VIP tour, some of the standing studio sets, or the scenery docks, they may encounter the living room used in *Love and Kisses*, *The Thing That Couldn't Die*, Jack Arnold's *Monster on the Campus* (1958), Douglas Heyes's *Kitten with a Whip* (1964), and numerous other Universal films of the period or television shows of that era. What will they see? What personages will they associate with these abandoned locations of the cinematic dream apparatus? The same haunted house set used in the teleseries *The Munsters* was used not only in the movie *Munster, Go Home!* (1966, dir. Earl Bellamy) but also in the slapstick comedy *The Ghost and Mr. Chicken* (1965, dir. Alan Rafkin). Who will studio visitors remember when and if they see the facade of the house: Fred Gwynne as Herman Munster, or Don Knotts as Mr. Chicken?

For these sets are locations of public memory and shared spectacle, some more famous than others, but all of them occupying the same physical and psychic space. Film sets are merely what Cowan observed: they are "facades." There is no substantive reality behind them. Those who trade in the manufactured fantasies of the cinematograph know this and embrace each captured moment as precious because they know (now more than ever) that whatever is photographed by the eye of the Dominant cinema, the lens of the Mitchell or Panaflex camera, will in all likelihood be preserved forever. Once, when film studios had only theatrical distribution as an avenue for the exhibition of their product, they were extremely careless with the negatives, trims, and stills of their works. Now, in the digital age, when hundreds of still images can be stored with excellent resolution on a single compact disc, and new cable networks, satellite broadcast networks, and other methods of media dissemination compete for our attention, Hollywood has become much more diligent in the care and preservation of its films. Whole new markets have opened up. Jeff Chandler's many program films for Universal (George Sherman's *Sword in the Desert*, 1949; Delmer Daves's *Broken Arrow*, 1950;, Joseph Pevney's *Foxfire*, 1955, and *Away All Boats*, 1956; Jack Arnold's *The Tattered Dress*, 1957; Russell Rouse's *Thunder in the Sun*, 1959; and many others) have now become a staple on American Movie Classics; leased from Universal at an attractive price, run and rerun by AMC, they offer hours of escapist entertainment for millions of televiewers at a fraction of what new programming would cost.

Love and Kisses is screened alongside *Broken Arrow* without missing a beat; both films are Universal product, now locked away in carefully monitored film vaults, along with the output of Columbia, Warner

Brothers, Twentieth Century Fox, MGM, and the other majors; even Monogram and Producer's Releasing Corporation (PRC) films, once the lowest of the low in then-contemporary cinematic product, are now screened next to Edmund Goulding's *Grand Hotel* (1932) on the Turner Classic Movies cable channel. Thus, Buster Crabbe once again ventures into the cardboard and plaster jungles of studio Africa in Sam Newfield's *Nabonga* (1944), to confront a young Julie London and her pet gorilla in the colonial landscape of 1940s escapist entertainment cinema. Kane Richmond, Sam Flint, Marguerite Chapman, Hans Schumm, and Tristram Coffin continue the struggle between Nazi Fifth Columnists and American espionage agents in the endlessly repeatable twelve chapters of William Witney's 1942 Republic serial *Spy Smasher*. *Ozzie Nelson and His Orchestra* seem as fresh and appealing as they did when they stepped in front of the cameras at the Warner Brothers studio in early 1940 under the direction of Jean Negulesco (who would later direct such films as *How to Marry A Millionaire*, 1953, and *Daddy Long Legs*, 1955) to appear in an eponymous one-reel musical short. John Abbott still stalks scenarist Leigh Brackett's phantasmal African locales in director Lesley Selander's *The Vampire's Ghost* (1945) searching for new victims without rest, perpetually undead. The Southern United States still teams with poisonous snakes and reliable character actors in Jean Renoir's 1941 *Swamp Water*; Desi Arnaz is still on *Holiday in Havana* (1943, dir. Jean Yarbrough).

Lee de Forest can still explain the basics of *Electron Theory* as capably as he did in a ten-minute short film produced in 1948; James A. Fitzpatrick still roams the globe in search of spectacle without human agency or suffering in his one-reel travelogues *Alluring Alaska* (1941), *Along the Cactus Trail* (1944), *Exotic Mexico* (1942), *Historic Maryland* (1942), *Mexican Police on Parade* (1943), *Old Natchez on the Mississippi* (1940), or any other of the many "Traveltalks" he produced for MGM in the 1930s and 1940s. "Joe McDoakes" still "wants to be" a *Detective* (1948), a *Muscle Man* (1949), in *Politics* (1948), and *On the Radio* (1948) as well as *To Be Popular* (1948), and *To Get Rich Quick* (1949), always without success, in Richard L. Bare's popular World War II series. John Nesbitt's *Passing Parade* series is still on display, presenting sanitized and yet titillating curios of semihistorical speculation in such short films as *Grandpa Called It Art* (1944), *Stairway to Light* (1945), *Whispers* (1941), and *Trifles That Win Wars* (1943). Tom and Jerry endlessly chase each other through the halls and rooms of an anonymous, de-peopled house, forever inflicting bodily injury on each other, yet returning in the next scene invariably intact. Constance Bennett is still a *Smart Woman* (1948, dir. Edward A. Blatt) who seeks to defend her former husband when he is unjustly accused of murder; the Bowery Boys stumble from one low-rent escapade into another with reassuring predictability and increasing familiarity.

As time passes, Sean Connery will be forever faced with the nemesis of *Dr. No* (1962, dir. Terence Young), the Beatles will frolic through a variety of international landscapes in Richard Lester's 1965 *Help!*, John Phillip Law and Dyan Cannon will still inhabit Jacqueline Susann's *Love Machine* (1971, dir. Jack Haley, Jr.), and Jean-Pierre Léaud will remain forever the young Antoine Doinel in *Love on the Run* (1979, dir. François Truffaut), the fifth and final installment of Truffaut's semiautobiographical series. Yet this cycle, like all the others, awaits only the rewinding of a reel of film, or a cassette tape, or the repositioning of a low-intensity laser to repeat the experience anew. Before one knows it, one is confronted with the final freeze-frame of the young Léaud in Truffaut's *The 400 Blows* (1959), an image that promises stasis and closure even as it beckons toward an endlessly repeatable future. Elvis Presley still sings *Love Me Tender* (1956, dir. Robert D. Webb) and *Viva Las Vegas* (1964, dir. George Sidney), partying the night away with a succession of forgotten costars in a seemingly endless series of fifth-rate musicals. Cesar Romero, Hillary Brooke, John Hoyt, Hugh Beaumont, and Whit Bissell will forever seek *The Lost Continent* (1951, dir. Sam Newfield). Ronald Colman (in 1937, for director Frank Capra) and Peter Finch (in 1973, for director Charles Jarrott) will continue to search for the *Lost Horizon*. On television, *The Beverly Hillbillies* continue to exult in their newfound wealth; Joe Friday tracks down his man in *Dragnet*; Lucille Ball gets involved in yet another ill-advised scheme in *I Love Lucy*; Jim Backus still wonders why *I Married Joan*; Captain Braddock stills heads up the *Racket Squad*.

All of it is documented, and all of it demands to be shown again, ceaselessly repeated, compelling our attention through the simple agency of physical existence. Every film sitting in a can anxiously awaits its totemic audience; liberated on the screen, its claim on our memory and collective consciousness is made all the more urgent by the passage of time since its last revivification. Now cleaned up through digital processing and videotape transfer, every surviving *frame* of film now supremely important because the possibility of commercial exploitation has been restored to it by the profusion of new distribution technologies, the films of the past, present, and future are created solely for our consumption, as companions when we can't sleep, reassuring and comforting parades of icons seeking to bring some semblance of order to our chaotic, uncertain lives.

And all of it is sponsored, by one product or another. A dazzling array

of appliances, toys, cars, denture adhesives, CDs, home videos, deter-
gents, cereals, instant coffees, and other consumer products have revived
these films for our contemporaneous contemplation. While feature films
have become the endlessly recyclable fables of our twentieth-century
televisual consciousness, the advertisements that have resuscitated these
fables have become our communal, universal religion. It is not the product itself that is important, but rather the image of life that it presents—a
world of immediate gratification, free from debt or monthly payments,
where all is consumption, friendship, warmth, the good cheer of the
shopping mall, manufactured to lull us into believing that the objects we
purchase will alter our lives. We purchase one object, then another, but
soon we realize that nothing brings satisfaction. Like the fables that sur-
round and support them, the commercials we are force fed—ten-,
twenty-, or thirty-second sermons at the rate of thirty to forty per viewing hour—instruct us in how to behave, what to spend, how we should
look, what sort of life we should aspire to. Each commercial is a complete
and intact belief system, beholden only to itself. Kitchens are always
sunny and "lemon fresh" unless they are melodramatically filthy, and
thus ripe for transformational cleaning. Cars always arrive safely at their
destinations, evading all obstacles (digital boulders, sheep, or falling tim-
ber particularly) with grace and style. Planes never crash. Families can
always come "home for the holidays." All visits to the hospital end with
the patient being discharged; life is seemingly endless, constantly renewable, as long as you have an available balance on your credit card. This is
the fantasy world we all wish to inhabit, the zone of perpetual immortality and excitement without risk. At the end of the day, we can leave the
homeless shelter and go home to the palace, secure in the knowledge that
we have only been slumming; it's time to return to the world where we
truly belong. The world of the Dominant cinema has become our new
sacred domain; if we are admitted through the gates of the Dominant cinema into the realm of digital immortality, we become icons to be venerated, whose images can be reanimated and reconstituted even after
death.

Perhaps this is why Princess Diana so courted the media, in particular
photographers, who sought to possess her image. Even as the charitable
work in which she was engaged consumed more and more of her time in
her last months, Diana also had her eye on a different sort of immortality, or doing a Princess-Grace-in-reverse shift. Shortly before the opening
of his 1997 film *The Postman*, director-star Kevin Costner announced that
he and Diana had been involved in a project which would have been a

sequel to *The Bodyguard* (1992, dir. Mick Jackson). In an uncredited news item distributed nationally by various wire services, Costner outlined the details of his and Diana's participation in the aborted project, in a brief news story ironically entitled "Di Would Have Been Next Body to Guard."

Princess Diana was negotiating before her death to star opposite Kevin Costner in a sequel to the movie *The Bodyguard*, the *New York Post* reported Tuesday.

Diana would have played a role loosely based on her life, with Costner as the bodyguard she falls in love with, Costner told *Premiere* magazine. . . . The actor told *Premiere* he had begun negotiating with the recently divorced princess more than a year ago, the *Post* said. She said, "Look, my life is maybe going to become my own at some point. Go ahead and do this script, and when it's ready I'll be in a really good spot," said Costner, who played Whitney Houston's bodyguard in the first film.

Costner said he received a second draft of the movie script just three days before Diana's Aug. 31 death in a Paris car crash. "I picked it up and the first 30 pages were totally her," he said. "It was dignified, sexy, smart, funny—and I couldn't finish. I stopped. It broke my heart." ("Di Would Have Been Next Body to Guard," 4A)

The fact that the project had moved beyond the planning stage into a second draft indicates not only Costner's seriousness but also Diana's involvement in the project, a film that would have been a stunning marketing coup for whoever produced it, marking the penultimate shift from Princess to Star, as opposed to Grace Kelly's abandonment of Hollywood (and Alfred Hitchcock) for the precincts of the principality of Monaco. What might have come of this project we will never be able to know, but if Diana did indeed actively pursue the possibility of starring in *The Bodyguard II*, then we can correctly assume that she sought some other fame beyond the transient flash of the paparazzi's intruding cameras.

Diana in her last months sought to create a space where she could unerringly control her own image, even if it was within the confines of a rigidly structured, generic fiction narrative. Being a film star would allow Diana to seek both a new career and perhaps a new image. This new Diana would then be disseminated without commercials or voice-over "news" commentary to thousands of theaters, and subsequently home television screens throughout the world. Diana would thus be able to re-create herself in a new and definitive way, free from any sort of third-person editorial intrusion. For her entire public life, Diana's image and voice had been mediated by the exigencies of a press that both hounded and flattered her.

As an international film star, as in the Barbara Cartland romances she so loved as a child, perhaps Diana could have created an image of herself living "happily ever after," devoid of care and want, a friend of the poor and sick, the ultimate celluloid construction of deposed Royalty. For in all her contacts with the press, Diana was certainly a willing coconspirator in the skillful construction of the image she knew her millions of admirers wished to see. As Max Frankel noted in an essay that appeared shortly after Diana's death,

> Far from being just a pretty face, Di told tales of betrayal by an unfeeling husband and disdain from an unsympathetic mother-in-law—to whom she was nonetheless bound by her own ambition for her beloved children. Far from just a sexy mannequin, she was a foxy fighter, an avenging angel, who repaid an adulterous husband in his coin and schemed to drag him with her out of the royal line of succession. When dumped on by the House of Windsor, she dumped right back, matching phone tap with phone tap, interview with interview and Charles's flaunting of an old love this summer with a new love of her own. (Frankel, 53)

Charting Diana's fall from public grace in the aftermath of the divorce, and then her public redemption through the medium of charitable work and a series of carefully stage-managed interviews to sympathetic members of the press, Frankel then cites Viktor Frankl, a renowned psychiatrist who died at the ripe old age of ninety-two, two days after the car crash that claimed Diana's life. As Max Frankel notes, Viktor Frankl's view of reality was forged during his internment in the Nazi concentration camps, a period of his life that he miraculously survived, and from which he drew a much deeper understanding of the human condition and our shared capacity for suffering and empathy. Intimate with death on a daily basis, Frankl despised the scandal and mundane brutality of contemporaneous journalism, summing up his reasons for the public's desire for tales of disaster and destruction in a paragraph well worth citing here:

> "The dullard newspaper reader sitting at his breakfast table is avid for stories of misfortune and death. . . . His pattern is like that of

every addict: his hunger for sensation requires a nervous jolt to satisfy it; the jolt to the nerves engenders a more intense hunger, and
so the dose must be constantly stepped up. What such a person
really gets out of these vicarious deaths is the contrast effects: it
seems as though other people are always the ones who must die.
For this type of person is fleeing what most horrifies him: the certainty of his own death—which his existential emptiness makes
unbearable to him." (quoted in Frankel, 53)

It is this desperate quest to bring meaning to our lives that drives us to
conspicuous consumerism, to purchase videos we know we will never
play, CDs we will soon store and forget, new video/audio equipment
that will soon become obsolete, generic romances, horror novels, and
action-adventure thrillers that we can read and then throw away, all
because we know that "the certainty of [our own] death" is both
inevitable and capricious, something that we cannot control, a spectator
sport for us while we remain alive, but a fact of our human existence that
is both unalterable and unknowable. It is this that we seek to run away
from, but that is impossible. The disasters and deaths of the century have
become part of the social fabric of our lives, the collective myths by
which we share our human community and gauge our mortality. The
Hindenburg, the *Titanic*, the *Challenger* disaster, TWA Flight 800: these
moments of unexpected horror and destruction both fascinate and repel
us, because of the very randomness of their occurrence. It could have
happened to us, but it didn't this time. Maybe the next time will be different.

Andy Warhol's work mirrors the artist's own obsessive meditation on
the mechanisms of violent death, particularly in the paintings and films
Warhol created during his most prolific and influential period, from 1962
to 1967. In his first paintings, images of death are insistent and pro-
nounced. In *Suicide* (1963), a man jumps from a building into a black-and-
white abyss; Warhol catches him in midair, hurtling toward oblivion. In
Ambulance Disaster Two Times (1963), we witness a spectacularly grisly collision between an ambulance and a passenger car, silk-screened twice on
a 124 x 80" section of canvas. *Saturday Disaster* (1964) documents in dupli-
cate another violent, anonymous vehicular accident. *White Car Crash
Nineteen Times* (1963) serially repeats yet another image of highway carnage across the breadth of a 144 x 83" canvas, until the image loses its concrete specificity and dissolves into a curiously abstract yet disturbing
composition. *Green Burning Car 1, Nine Times* (1963) features the seemingly

nexplicable image of a man impaled on a telephone pole in the aftermath of a car crash, his neck clearly broken, in the left foreground of each of the painting's nine identical images. *Optical Car Crash* (1962) repeats one image of a car crash more than thirty-five times on one canvas, to create an inchoate blur of violence and destruction.

Warhol seemed driven to create these perversely fascinating canvases which, in turn, enthrall the average viewer posited by Viktor Frankl. That's why pop art was "pop"; it was designed for mass consumption. Warhol continued his fascination with the iconography of random death in a series of paintings during the early 1960s, with such works as *Foot and Tire* (1963), *Bellevue II* (1963), yet another canvas entitled *Suicide* (1963), *Tuna Fish Disaster* (1963), in which two women ("Mrs. McCarthy and Mrs. Brown") are poisoned by cans of tainted tuna fish, *Lavender Disaster* (1963), a serial repetition of the image of an empty electric chair patiently awaiting to embrace its next victim, *Atomic Bomb* (1963–64), and *Red Race Riot* (1963), all canvases full of sinister fascination with the unpredictable exigencies of human existence. As critic Michael Fried wrote at the time, "of all the painters working today, in the service—or thrall—of popular iconography, Andy Warhol is probably the most single-minded and the most spectacular" (quoted in Bourdon, 134). Starting with Warhol's relatively early canvas *129 Die in Jet* (aka *Plane Crash*, 1962), "death had become a dominating theme in his art" (Bourdon, 142). Warhol himself acknowledged this fact when he told critic Gene Swenson that "I realized that everything I was doing must have been death. It was Christmas or Labor Day—a holiday—and every time you turned on the radio they said something like, '4 million are going to die.' That started it" (quoted in Bourdon, 142). While others saw this as a cautionary statement, Bourdon notes, Warhol "interpreted the figures as goals to be met. He believed that the forecasted number of fatalities lured motorists into wanting to flesh out the statistics" (142).

Yet Warhol also acknowledged that by re-creating each of his images, the immediacy of those scenes of disastrous carnage diminished, and viewers were able to maintain a comforting distance from the spectacle they witnessed. "When you see a gruesome picture over and over again," Warhol told Swenson, "it doesn't really have any effect." He added that he hadn't even started the Elizabeth Taylor series of canvases until "she was so sick and everybody said she was going to die" (quoted in Bourdon, 142). According to Bourdon, "Warhol did not feel sorry for the car-crash victims he portrayed, but he thought 'people should think about them sometime . . . it's just that people go by and it doesn't really matter to them that someone unknown was killed, so I thought it would be nice for these unknown people to be remembered by those who ordinarily wouldn't think of them' " (143). Thus Warhol implicitly acknowledged that it was the media, and the media solely, that made the differentiation between an important and an anonymous death. The oft-quoted statement by Joseph Stalin that "a single death is a tragedy, a million deaths is a statistic" (Dillard, 52) does not even apply here. The sole rule of thumb is celebrity: is the victim famous? If not, then even an individual death becomes a statistic, a statistic that in itself is endlessly repeatable to the point of dissolution, to be contemplated by anonymous viewers as a totemic glyph of desire and disaster.

When Warhol began making films, this same fascination with the mechanics of death and violence spilled over into his new work. After such early silent films as *Sleep* (1963)—in itself, the contemplation of a near-death state for an extended period of time—and *Empire* (1964), a phallic eight-hour meditation on the Empire State Building, Warhol moved into sync-sound filmed theater with the S/M-influenced *Vinyl* (1965) and the marginally released *Suicide* (1965), a project that Andy had been pursuing since one of the Warhol Factory's satellite associates, the choreographer Freddy Herko, jumped to his death from the apartment of a friend while listening to Mozart's *Coronation Mass* on October 27, 1964. As Bourdon notes, "Several of Andy's friends heard him lament on various occasions that he had not been there to film it" (191). By mid-1965, Warhol talked constantly of how exciting it would be to make a movie of someone actually expiring on the screen. He told his suicidal friends—and there were many of them—to call him immediately if they ever got serious. Warhol was elated when he came across a young man who had slashed his wrists about two dozen times. Andy talked him into describing the various attempts on his life as the camera focused on his wrists and hands. But in reliving his past, the man became increasingly distraught and subsequently threatened to sue if the film was even shown in a theater (Bourdon, 200).

And so the project was reluctantly shelved. Yet the specter of violent death continued to haunt the Factory; various members of Warhol's core group died of overdoses, suicides, or in mysterious accidents. Gene Swenson, who interviewed Warhol on his early death and disaster paintings, was himself killed in a car crash in 1969 at the age of thirty-five (Bourdon, 163). Andy was shot and seriously wounded by Valerie Solanas on June 3, 1968, putting an end to much of the artist's fascination with death, which he could no longer view at a distance. Paul Morrissey took over the actual production of Warhol's films, converting them into more conventional narrative works. Warhol himself turned to a series of celebrity portraits of the rich and famous to help pay the rent on his studio and support his staff. His work became increasingly bland and market-driven, and the artist himself more and more removed from the world that surrounded him. Many of his original staff members left the Factory, and the rest of Warhol's career as a painter (with the exception of his late *Shadows* series in 1979 and his collaborations with the late Jean-Michel Basquiat) became a series of commissioned portraits and Polaroid photo sessions, interspersed with evenings out at Studio 54, in the hope of attracting a new and wealthy patron to underwrite his work. Death experienced firsthand was no longer an abstraction; it had now become part of Warhol's interior psychological landscape.

Warhol's obsessive fascination with the specific details of death and disaster led him to cultivate a social circle in which catastrophe was almost inevitable, a world in which death was a desired object, to be courted and pursued. "Now and then someone would accuse me of being evil—of letting people destroy themselves while I watched, just so I could film them and tape record them," Warhol later commented. "But I don't think of myself as evil—just realistic" (Warhol and Hackett, 108). In his fascination with icons of disaster, Warhol achieved his first aim of memorializing the anonymous. With his own near-fatal shooting, he experienced the consequences of violent disaster firsthand. Yet despite the cautionary tale that Warhol's early work represents, we continue to be drawn to precisely the same images that Warhol first used in his work as a painter. These banal yet compelling images of lives snuffed out in random automobile accidents, machinery mangled with human flesh, anonymous suicides leaping out of windows, two cheerfully smiling women killed by a can of tuna fish constitute the bulk of Warhol's strongest work as an artist, an artist whose found images, serially repeated, constituted an extended, segmented meditation on the mechanisms of disaster and the endless process of remembering the dead. The Warhol of the early 1960s would have seized the TWA 800 disaster as an iconic glyph of lasting cultural and social significance. It is perhaps sadly fitting that one of Warhol's closest late collaborators, Jed Johnson (director of the Warhol film *Bad*, 1971), was one of the victims of that ill-starred flight, on his way to Paris to buy some antiques.

The famed dead are our new saints, totemic figures whose posthumous presence, though figurative, both sanctifies and certifies the transient reality of our earthly existence. Italian crèche artist Giuseppe Ferrigno recognized this fact when he created, not as popular novelties but rather as sincere tributes, crèche figurines of Princess Diana, Mother Teresa, and Gianni Versace, arguably 1997's most notable celebrity causalities. As writer Frances D'Emilio noted of Ferrigno's figures,

> Ferrigno and his son Marco, the fifth and sixth generation in his family to hand-fashion crèche figurines, are keeping to a nearly 400-year-old Neapolitan tradition in creating pieces that are closely tied to the day's events, not just the timeless Christmas story. . . . "They were figures held in high regard by Italians, Diana in particular," Marco Ferrigno said. "She was a normal person who became a princess, a fairytale that became reality. Everyone secretly dreams for that. . . . This year, the Ferrignos have some 350 orders to fill for clay and wire sculptures of Diana, Mother Teresa, and Versace. (D'Emilio, C1).

Nor do cultural historians see this as blasphemous, or even unusual within the highly religious culture of Neapolitan society. As D'Emilio documents, the practice is both widespread and an accepted part of contemporary discourse: " 'In Neapolitan crèches, the sacred is central enough, but popular culture is identified with very strongly,' said anthropologist Alfredo Luombardozzi, at Rome's National Museum of Traditional and Popular Arts" (ibid., C1). Diana Spencer, Gianni Versace, and Mother Teresa have become, without benefit or need of the traditional canonical process, instant media saints. When we put them in our Christmas crèche, along with the more traditional figures of Mary, Joseph, the baby Jesus, and the three Wise Men, we are implicitly acknowledging that both memory and the values of contemporary society are mediated by death. With the removal of the "real" beloved object from the sphere of the living (even if we have never actually seen or met them, unmediated by television or the print media, while they were alive), we must create new copies of them to venerate, particularly since the absence of the original creates a vacuum of representation. Diana is no longer with us. Hence, we can no longer take pictures of her, capture her likeness on film, preserve the external essence of her being in a photographic or video image. In contemporary celebrity culture, Diana herself became above all other considerations the template from which endless copies of her image could be created, much in the manner of Warhol's serial silk screens. Pursued in life, is it not sadly appropriate that, as the wreck of Diana's car was lifted from the underpass of the Pont de l'Alma long after her still-living body had been extracted from the wreckage, the members of the international press were still snapping away in a frenzy? The twisted hunk of Diana's Mercedes thus became a sort of ghastly, strobe-lit sculpture, given artificial life through the agency of the literally thousands of strobe-light flashes that illuminated it in the dark.

And yet as Diana ascends into pop sainthood, other versions of her relationship with the press continue to circulate, projecting Diana as an active seeker-after of her own celebrity, who, as Rushdie noted, knew exactly how to manipulate her image for the desired effect. As media critic Frank Owen related in his essay "Death and the Media Maiden," two of the most aggressive photographers who pursued Diana during her years with the Royal Family have a distinctly different view of the public image Diana so carefully cultivated. Commenting on a book written by Mark Saunders and Glenn Harvey, two paparazzi who specialized in capturing spontaneous images of Diana and other members of the Royal Family, Owen reports on what they had to say about Diana Spencer:

> In sharp contrast to the picture of Di as a saintly figure, Saunders and Harvey depict her as a royal fruitcake. . . . They nicknamed her "the Loon," and her hysterical outbursts on the street directed at the press became known as "Loon attacks." They portray a woman barely in control of her emotions, a walking contradiction. One minute, she's bitterly complaining about press intrusion, the next she's holding secret meetings with favored writers, or tipping off photographers when she takes her sons on outings to amusement parks, or attending a closed meeting with Red Cross officials with a camera crew in tow.
>
> That Diana actively courted fame, there can be little doubt. Her medium was, and remains, the camera. What the authors called her "instinctive desire for publicity" was well illustrated on the night that Prince Charles confessed to adultery on national television. Seizing the media moment, Diana turned up at a high-profile party modeling an exact replica of an outfit Charles's mistress Camilla Parker-Bowles had previously worn, right down to the pearl choker. Surely she was aware that next morning's tabloids would feature pictures of herself and Camilla side by side. . . .
>
> The most shocking episode in the book is the time the Princess turned from hunted to hunter and attempted to ram the photographers' car during a high-speed chase. "I could see Diana's face in the rear view mirror," Saunders writes. "She looked possessed. She

was driving with only one hand, with the other gesturing wildly at me. Her car remained just millimeters from me. . . . At about 120 mph, I lost her and managed to slip into the middle lane. Diana sped past, mouthing obscenities as she went." (Owen, 51)

But Owen also locates an even more disturbing aspect to the media frenzy surrounding Diana's death. Citing British cultural theorists Fred and Judy Vermorel, Owen notes that many fans of the various icons of popular culture "dream about seeing their idols maimed, or crippled, or dead. . . . An academic study that examined the rumors of Paul McCartney's death that swept the world in 1969 concluded that the base of this tall tale was 'an eerie and embarrassed longing that the story be true' " (Owen, 51). Owen then compares Diana's funeral to the 1985 Live Aid Concert at Wembley Stadium in Britain, which both Charles and Diana attended. "The funeral service . . . at Westminster Abbey looked a bit like a replay of Live Aid, with Elton John performing his retooled version of 'Candle in the Wind' and Live Aid veterans like Sting, George Michael, and Richard Branson in attendance" (Owen, 51).

Who would dare to disrupt such a solemn, celebrity-studded pageant of remembrance? The Vermorels have created a useful phrase to describe this sort of compulsory, group-mandated mourning: "consensus terrorism . . . whereby goodwill is hijacked and the public conscripted into an aggressive campaign that allows no dissent" (Owen, 51). The endless procession of memorial tributes to Diana have the same air of compulsory mourning about them as did her funeral; even the Queen was pressed, apparently somewhat against her will, into joining the public spectacle of bereavement. At first reluctant to address her subjects, Queen Elizabeth was finally, according to Donald Spoto, badgered into a public profession of sorrow by her son Charles, the Prince of Wales. As Spoto recounts, "At the age of forty-eight and perhaps for the first time in his life, the Prince of Wales stood up to his mother. Threatening that if she did not say something to the nation, [Charles announced that] he would forthwith take his sons and proceed on his own. . . . On Friday, September 5, 1997, Her Majesty Queen Elizabeth II addressed the nation and the world; this was only the second time in her forty-five-year reign that she had spoken to her subjects, outside of the traditional Christmas greeting (the first had been during the Gulf War)" (Spoto, 183–84). And so even the members of the Royal Family were forced to bow to the demands of "consensus terrorism," to assist in the enshrinement of Diana Spencer into the precincts of the pop pantheon. The dominant posthumous view of Diana is that she was "a living saint. With her death, a cult has become a global religion that brooks no heresy" (Owen, 51).

When Jacqueline Kennedy died, her public image had been commingled not only with the Kennedys and the "Camelot" years in Washington during the early 1960s but also with her marriage to Aristotle Onassis, a relationship for which many of her formerly adoring admirers never fully "forgave" her. Thus her passing was marked with a respectable modicum of grief, but nothing like the outpouring of public approbation that accompanied the death of her first husband, or James Dean, or Marilyn Monroe, or even Elvis Presley, all of whom died relatively young, seemingly at the peak of their careers, leaving (except in Presley's case) only iconic images of well-coiffed, sleek perfection to be recycled and venerated by the members of their public. Diana's death presented a similar occasion for mass mourning: like Richie Valens, Buddy Holly, and the Big Bopper, she died capriciously, violently, creating a suitably televisual spectacle in the wake of her passing. And this disaster, make no mistake about it, is what the public awaits. Maurice Blanchot commented "that there is no awaiting the disaster is true to the extent that waiting is considered always to be the awaiting of something waited for, or else unexpected. But awaiting—just as it is not related to the future anymore than to an accessible past—is also the awaiting of awaiting, which does not situate us in a present" (117). And thus the public, eager to devour stories of rape, murder, race riots, automobile and plane wrecks, train derailments, wars, strikes, and other occasions of violence, seeks closure to the romance of a "fairy tale" wedding not in the phrase "they lived happily ever after" (which is, after all, only a point of beginning rather than a conclusion), but rather in the bathos and melodrama of disastrous events, precipitous declines, divorces, scandals, and societal raptures. Diana's life afforded both the press and public all of these narrative elements; it is perhaps for this reason most of all that she has been the object of such conspicuous public commemoration.

But what of the anonymous victims of equally anonymous disasters? If they are not memorialized in print, video, or other manifestations of the popular culture (as in Warhol's paintings), what is their share of the public's memory? What of the four hundred men trapped in the St. Paul Coal Company Mine in Cherry, Illinois, on November 13, 1909, all of whom died? Or of Daniel De Grosse, fourteen, who was struck and killed by an automobile near his home in Matawan, New Jersey, on the same day? Who recalls the sinking of the Canadian Pacific liner the *Empress of Ireland* in the St. Lawrence River on May 29, 1914, after she was hit in a dense fog by a Danish coal ship, the *Storstad*? The *Empress of Ireland* sank to the bottom of the St. Lawrence in a mere fourteen minutes, at a cost of 954 lives out of the 1,387 persons on board; no one remembers her today, no legend is attached, no films are made of the disaster. What of the 1,800 men, women, and children who died when an excursion boat capsized in the Chicago River on Saturday, July 24, 1915? One Harry Miller, a deckhand on the *Eastland* who survived the incident, told of watching a mother trying to save her son and daughter, and at length, exhausted, she saw her daughter drown because she could no longer hold her in her grasp. Most of the passengers were women, children, and babies on their way to a picnic. A diver pulling bodies from the wreck of the *Eastland* was so appalled by the carnage that he tore off his diving suit and began screaming with rage, running across the hull of the boat. He was finally subdued by the other rescue personnel and taken to a local hospital. Why has this awful event faded from our collective memory, while the *Titanic* disaster is constantly exhumed, reconstructed, and presented for profit, not only in a series of films but also as a Broadway musical?

Who remembers the explosion of the French Line steamer *Mont Blanc* in the harbor in Halifax, Nova Scotia, on Thursday, December 6, 1917, after it collided with a Belgian Relief steamship, the *Imo*? Loaded with munitions, the *Mont Blanc*'s explosion killed two thousand people, leveled two square miles of the city, and caused a tidal wave in the docking area in which hundreds of dockhands were swept away. On Friday, March 19, 1937, in New London, Texas, the London Consolidated High School exploded as the result of a gas leak, killing five hundred teachers and students in a matter of seconds. W. C. Shaw, the superintendent of the school, had just left his son inside the building and was standing fifty feet away from the school when it exploded without any warning. "It's unbelievable," Shaw told a reporter on the scene. "There wasn't much noise. The roof just lifted up, then the walls fell out and the roof fell in. It was all over in a minute; no, less than that; half a minute. . . . I don't believe over a hundred children got out and a lot of them were so badly hurt they won't live. We haven't found our own boy, Sam. We're afraid he's gone, too" (Berger, 1). Who remembers any of these people today, the living or the dead, victims of a disaster more than half a century ago, a disaster that took less than "half a minute" to claim five hundred lives?

What of the 1,400 dead in Ecuador as the result of an earthquake on Saturday, August 6, 1949? Or the more than one thousand dead in another earthquake in San Salvador on Monday, May 7, 1951? Or the victims of the Gresford Colliery Disaster in North Wales, England, on Saturday, Sep-

tember 22, 1934, in which 260 men died as the result of a gas explosion? As
Michael Wynn Jones noted in his commentary on the mine explosion, "It
was, after Hulton and Senghenydd, [England's] worst mine disaster of
the century, and—if only for a moment—it *reminded* [emphasis mine] the
whole country of the appalling facts of contemporary mining life: that
each year in British mines between 800 and 1,000 men were being killed
and as much as five times as many injured" (111). But how long did the
memory last? For how long did the general public remember? Or did
their eyes stray down the front page of *Reynold's Illustrated News*, which
offered one account of the disaster, to an advertisement masquerading as
a news item entitled "I Have Lost 20 lbs of Fat"? Did anyone think that
these two items were incongruous? Did anyone stop to consider these
lines of text in the advertisement: "It is no good covering your eyes from
the truth. In this year of 'grace' you must cultivate the lithe, free-from-fat
figure if you want to win admiration—or to hold admiration already
won" (1). Who could possibly care about such matters in the face of this
intolerable human suffering? Who would respond to such an advertisement? Who could have realized that a bus boy's match would accidentally start a fire at the Coconut Grove nightclub in Boston on November
29, 1942, a blaze in which 492 people would die? Who remembers the
BOAC "Comet" disasters, in which a series of British-built airplanes dis-
integrated in midair for no apparent reason on May 2, 1952, January 11,
1954, and April 9, 1954? Finally, after the remaining planes in the Comet
fleet had been grounded and exhaustive tests had been run, it was discovered that long-flight metal fatigue—instantaneous, and without
warning—had caused all three planes to crash. After it exploded in
midair, the wreckage of TWA Flight 800 was painstakingly reassembled
in a deserted airplane hangar. Almost all the bodies of the passengers of
that ill-fated flight were recovered from the ocean. At least two computer-generated animatics were produced by the National Transportation Safety Board and the FBI which purport to portray and, to an extent,
explain the reasons for the jet plane's explosion. Yet no one is certain that
a definitive explanation has been reached. Did the fuel tank explode, as a
number of investigators speculate, because of some stray spark caused by
faulty wiring? What will bring the victims back? What totems did they
leave behind? The next time we get on a plane, will it happen to us? Or
something new and equally inexplicable, an incident that is beyond
memory's recall because all those who witnessed it are no longer alive?

What were the last thoughts of the thirty-nine young skiers who died
at the Val d'Isere Youth Hostel resort in the French Alps, when an

avalanche interrupted their breakfast on the morning of February 10, 1970? Or of the citizens of Iran on Monday, April 11, 1972, when an earthquake struck the ancient town of Shivaz, burying it under a heap of rubble, leaving at least two thousand Iranian citizens dead? Or of the people of northern Pakistan on Monday, December 30, 1974, when an earthquake struck at nine towns in the country, killing an estimated 4,700 men, women, and children in a matter of minutes? What warning did they have? What were their final seconds of existence like? We can never know; this is the zone of the dead, not the living, and those who died took their experience with them to the grave.

No matter how many times we play back the "black box" tapes of downed jetliners, or how many times we view the videotaped assassination of Lee Harvey Oswald by Jack Ruby, or how many times we watch the Zapruder film of the John F. Kennedy assassination, or the videotape of Sirhan Sirhan shooting Robert Kennedy in the hallway of a hotel, no matter what details Ted Bundy discloses on the murders he, at length (indeed, just hours before his execution), admits that he committed, *we will never understand*. We are alive, they are dead. It is beyond our comprehension. We understand that evil exists, but we do not understand how this evil disguises itself within the compass of mainstream society; we are still surprised when it becomes manifest, erupting into frenzies of murders, rapes, mutilations, and serial killings. A photo exists of Rosalyn Carter innocently posing with serial killer John Wayne Gacy at a Democratic fund-raiser, utterly unaware of the atrocities Gacy has committed—and will keep on perpetrating until he is caught. As Blanchot notes, "If it weren't for prisons, we would know that we are all already in prison" (66). Constantly under surveillance, protected only by an authority that will always arrive too late, we seek escape in a myriad of diversions and momentary escapes from the artifice of our existence.

One of Diana's favorite sweatshirts bore the slogan "I'm a Luxury Few Can Afford." Can we doubt for a moment that we live in a medieval plague state, where the dominant media seeks to assuage our unrest with satellite images of Mars, endless coverage of various forms of civil unrest, hours of royal and military pageantry ceaselessly run and rerun, then stored in a vault for future consumption—who knows what context tomorrow will add to the events of the day? Why, in February 1953, did future horror film actor Bryant Halliday and his partner Cy Harvey open the Brattle Theatre near Harvard University in Cambridge, Massachusetts, reviving for the first time the collected films of Humphrey Bogart in a week-long festival that captured the public's imagination, initiated the present-day Bogart cult, and generated gratifying returns at the box office (Stevenson, 67)? Was it because the films of the early 1950s, created in an atmosphere of anti-Communist hysteria fueled by the HUAC black-list, lacked both verisimilitude and resonance for the young Harvard students? Was it not easier then, as it is now, to return to the safety of their shared cinematic past, chanting dialogue along with the actors in Michael Curtiz's *Casablanca* (1942) as if it were a history lesson, a manual of arms, a series of instructions in how to conduct one's self in the face of protracted antagonism?

At length, however, classicism fails. The lessons have been learned. It is no longer enough, finally, to resurrect the successful films of the past. In the search for new texts to memorize, those filmmakers who operate on the fringe of cinematic expression are dragged into the center of the critical discourse, bringing to light such films as Ray Danton's *Crypt of the Living Dead* (1973), Barry Mahon's *Cuban Rebel Girls* (aka *Assault of the Rebel Girls* and *Attack of the Rebel Girls*, 1959; Errol Flynn's last film, which he also wrote), Larry Buchanan's *Creature of Destruction* (1967), Jacques Tourneur's *The Giant of Marathon* (1959), Arthur Dreifuss's *The Love-Ins* (1967), Richard Harbinger's *The T-Bird Gang* (1959), Bert I. Gordon's *Food of the Gods* (1976), and Russ Meyer's *Faster Pussycat! Kill! Kill!* (1965). Good or bad, these films serve as an anchor for our collective consciousness, an index of the gap between ambition and competence.

As the present becomes more and more intolerable, films are not made, they are remade. Sydney Pollack re-creates Billy Wilder's 1954 *Sabrina* in 1996, with Julia Ormond in the role first realized by Audrey Hepburn, Greg Kinnear in the role first played by William Holden, and Harrison Ford standing in for Humphrey Bogart. Will anyone notice the difference? The animated teleseries *The Flintstones* becomes an eponymous feature film in 1994 (Brian Levant's *The Flintstones*) with Elizabeth Taylor as Fred Flintstone's annoying mother-in-law and John Goodman as Fred—humans substituting for characters originally created as a series of barely animated drawings. Peter Brook's *Lord of the Flies* (1963) becomes Harry Hook's *Lord of the Flies* (1990), this time in color and Americanizing the protagonists from the British schoolboy originals of William Golding's novel into a pack of spoiled television addicts marooned on a desert island. All the old stories, the old romances and melodramas, the epics and the small intimate dramas will be recycled again for a new audience, inured to the lure of soft black-and-white imagery, eager for color, spectacle, images of disaster and destruction, hyped-up violence and digital stereo soundtracks that blast the viewer out of her/his seat. All is televisual. The Holocaust has become programming for the cable television networks; Hitler, Goebbels, Himmler, and their minions continue to goose-step through the streets of Berlin and Paris on A&E and the History Channel. Millions of Jews, Poles, and Gypsies are once again shipped off into the night in rows of boxcars, in newsreel compilations and reenactments, to face the horrors of Buchenwald and Auschwitz anew, all in the name of spectacle and suffering. Programming is required; programming is delivered.

And at the Christmas season, if you live in an apartment with no windows, or perhaps you have windows but don't care for the view, you can now pop in a videotape that "turn[s] your TV into a Christmas wonderland . . . just pop this video into your VCR and gaze at the frosty snowflakes falling softly against the evening sky . . . warm to the glow from the flickering flame of the candle as it slowly burns down . . . watch the colorful ornaments and lights sparkle on the festively decorated tree . . . and see the snow slowly gathering in the corner of each windowpane . . . have a white Christmas no matter where you live . . . make your TV a window on Christmas" ("Turn Your TV into a Christmas Wonderland," 15). These images of safety, icons of family and friends, have become digitized glyphs for holiday consumption. Your window has become obsolete; now all that you see, all that you view is a digitized image of snow, a tree, a candle, and on the soundtrack "your favorite holiday music, as this video creates a nostalgic, old-fashioned Christmas that will touch your heart" (15). And at only $12.95 plus $3 postage and handling, you'll want to order copies for your friends so that they too can sit in front of their television sets, gazing into the digital night. Best of all, the tape is only forty-nine minutes long. When it's over, we can make some cocoa and pop in the tape of the wedding, or the funeral, of Diana Spencer, Princess of Wales (take your pick). And when *that's* over, we can rewind it, replay it, and then store it on the shelf, next to our other videocassettes and CDs, the detritus of our shared imagistic past, our images of safety and desire.

2

MANUFACTURING IDENTITY IN THE COLD WAR ERA

the televisual gaze

With the national application of broadcast television in the early 1950s came the birth of the televisual advertisement, and with the 60-second spot came the need to tell one's story quickly, efficiently, and without wasting a second of precious, purchased airtime. As television progressed, the 60-second spot gave way to the :30, the :20, and the :10, and now to the :03, which blasts a single image in the viewer's face for a fragment of time ("Coke!"; "CBS!"), just long enough to make a psychic imprint on the viewer's consciousness. With the need for speed came the "instant read icon," an image that would be universally understood within the boundaries of a specific culture to convey certain meanings: the housewife in the kitchen by her spotless sink, yellow sunlight filtering in through the curtains; the hard-hat construction worker eating from his lunch pail on the job; the authoritative man of medicine in his book-lined study or operating room, stethoscope around his neck; the wide-eyed children whose perfect smiles and even features promote toothpaste, breakfast cereals, toys, bicycles, and video games. The "Caesarean vision" of this sort of image production is that all these images are shorn of any additional resonance or context beyond that of the surface image, in which exterior features replace interior motivation. The young housewife in her kitchen is no doubt white, middle-class, facing a problem no more serious than a clogged sink; the construction worker, a member of the lower middle class, is concerned with the contents of his lunch box.

The figure of the "doctor" wants to reassure us that a certain nostrum will immediately cure our ailments, or else sell us life insurance, hospital insurance, or recommend a certain practitioner for medical care. These are images we see everyday, for the most part in advertisements. Just like Versace and Princess Diana in the manger, they have become an unquestioned part of our visual memory. They are glyphs we read superficially, instantaneously, yielding only that image that the dominant televisual culture wishes to endow us with. There is no need for characterization. Here is the hero, this is the heroine, here are the antagonists, here the kindly grandfather and grandmother, or the benevolent uncle or aunt.

This autosuggestion apparatus ensures that we will confine our reading of the images presented to us to a very narrow range, one from which we deviate only at our peril. For behind these images there is only a vast emptiness, a significatory void that disavows all meaning, all interpretation. The surface is all. More disturbingly, these same "instant-read" constructions have now permeated all levels of our imagistic culture, even to the practice of the supposedly independent cinema, which seemingly seeks to question these premanufactured images.

Such 1997 films as *Afterglow* (Alan Rudolph), *Fast, Cheap, and Out of Control* (Errol Morris), *The Ice Storm* (Ang Lee), *Live Flesh* (Pedro Almodóvar), *The Myth of Fingerprints* (Bart Freundlich), *Office Killer* (Cindy Sherman), *Taste of Cherry* (Abbas Kiarostami), and others traffic in the same easy conceits, the same reliance on visuals-as-narrative, and seek to find a space for themselves within the commercial cinema as competition within the marketplace—adversaries in name only to the spectacle offered by such mainstream films as John Woo's *Face/Off* (1997) or Taylor Hackford's *The Devil's Advocate* (1997). Independent cinema in the early 1960s was shorn of narrative, dealt in images that were often obscure and hard to decipher, and for the most part avoided the strangling standardized format of the feature film, preferring shorter works of disparate lengths to reach their intended audience. Today's distribution system, controlled by conglomerates who in turn own the theater screens on which the films of the Dominant cinema are projected, allows no space for the filmmaker who wishes to work outside the system.

Such supposedly alternative film festivals as Sundance and Slamdance (and perhaps, soon, "Slavedance," in honor of our communal enslavement to the deification of mass-media visual entertainment) continue to function as nothing more than proving grounds for young filmmakers seeking to align themselves with the majors and to create multimillion-dollar films with international saturation distribution. Above all, the images we are confronted with, urging us to buy, to donate, to cry, to laugh, to feel outraged, sympathetic, frightened, or overjoyed, must move *faster*. We have no time for time in the cinematic present; all is motion, all is change. As computers and digital imaging systems increase in speed and decrease in size, speed of imagistic transaction is the most urgent requirement. As James Gleick notes,

> No matter how fast a movie goes these days—or a situation comedy, a newscast, a music video or a television commercial—it is not fast enough. Vehicles race, plunge and fly faster; cameras pan and

shake faster, and scenes cut faster from one shot to the next. Some people don't like this. "Shot-shot-shot-shot, because television has accustomed us to a faster pace," says Annette Insdorf, a Columbia University film historian. "Music videos seem to have seeped into the rhythms of creativity. It's rare these days—it's rare in 1997— that films afford the luxury of time." (Gleick, 54)

Television, particularly, has seized the initiative for greater speed in its program presentations to the viewing public. As Gleick notes, a research unit within NBC-TV, tagged NBC 2000, is looking for new ways to cut down on fades, dissolves, and other transitional devices within the programs they broadcast, "the barely perceptible instants when a show fades to black and then rematerializes as a commercial. Over the course of a night, this might save the network as much as 15 precious seconds, or even 20" (54). Theatrical motion picture director Barry Levinson (maker of *Diner* [1982], *The Natural* [1984], *Bugsy* [1991], and other glossy commercial films) notes that "I don't know that we [the viewer] demand[s] more content—we demand more movement. We're packing more in, but the irony is that it isn't more *substance*" (Gleick, 54; Levinson's emphasis). The by-product of this process is the degradation of each individual shot, or image. The "blenderization" of cinema has kicked into full gear, fueled in part by new editing systems such as the AVID. Rather than actually cutting film with tape splicers, today's editors download all the raw material for a film onto digital disks, making the creation of rapid cuts, dissolves, intercuts, crossfades, and other hyperreal transitions increasingly easy. The days when an editor physically cut pieces of film together are long gone. Today, the digital culture makes editorial hyperstructure a near prerequisite for contemporary audiences, who comfortably occupy the phantom space of blue-screen digital compositing without complaint. Time is important; advertising the finished product is equally essential.

Trailers drive the theatrical process; these are the motion picture previews that we see in a theater before the "feature presentation" of the film we have actually chosen to view. The importance of trailers in the marketing process is enormous. Bernard Weinraub interviewed one Hollywood advertising director who was refreshingly blunt concerning the function of the contemporary theatrical trailer:

"It's the first impression everyone gets of a movie," said Oren Aviv, senior vice president of creative advertising at the Walt Disney Studios, "and the audience gets a real taste and representation of the film. Audiences make up their minds right away. You have one shot at it. If you don't win them over, it's hard to win them back." (Weinraub, 2)

Even films based on the classics of literature have to pass this "instant demand" test, as Mark Gill, head of Miramax's Los Angeles office, notes of the company's marketing plan for Iain Softley's *Wings of the Dove* (1997), loosely based on the novel by Henry James. Far from being a meditation on the constraints of society and conscience, Miramax has positioned the film through its trailers as "a sexy thriller. And if we had sold it as a traditional frock drama we'd be worse than dead right now. You do these things to create a sense of urgency about a film to get people to say, 'I want to see that film now.' That's really your job. You're asking people to go out of the house and spend money and that doesn't happen easily" (quoted in Weinraub, 2). It "doesn't happen easily" because, as Geoffrey O'Brien asserts, "the 20th century draws to a close amid a glut of product and a pervasive loss of surprise. . . . What [contemporary films] have in common is their acceptance of sudden, drastic change as a permanent possibility" (1997:110–11). There is no stable ground on which to stand, no place to operate from that isn't already compromised. We seek in the new that which is not new precisely because, in the hail of ultraviolent strobe cuts that engulf us, we paradoxically search for spaces of safety, repose, and respite. Most viewers still go to the movies to escape, to avoid the certitude of their predictable existences. But the contemporary cinema only offers the illusion of constant change. Behind the tapes, mattes, and video imaging, the stories have evaporated in a haze of pixels. It wasn't always this way.

After the establishment of the Hollywood studio system as an international institution during the early years of this century (particularly during World War I, when the United States flooded European nations with Hollywood product when local production was severely inhibited by the war effort), Hollywood incorporated the technologies of sound, color, and vertical integration (ownership of studios, distribution systems, as well as a worldwide network of theaters) to achieve a lock on global viewing patterns which remains, for the most part, unchallenged. World War II came and went, signaling a shift from Depression-era musicals to propagandistic war films and patriotic home front paeans, but the basic formula of the cinema remained the same. Through the many series films produced in the 1920s, 1930s, and 1940s in Hollywood, audiences built up an identification with the process of going to the movies, seeing a double bill, a newsreel, some shorts, and a travelogue, along with some previews, and then returning home—to a space devoid of manufactured moving images and dominated by radio, books, newspapers, and magazines. But with the end of the Second World War and Stalin's institution of the "Iron Curtain," paranoia began to seep into the public discourse, and with it, the disruptive specter of television, postponed by the war effort but now entering the domestic sphere. In such films as Edward Dmytryk's *Crossfire* (1947), Elia Kazan's *Gentleman's Agreement* (1947), R. G. Springsteen's *The Red Menace* (1949), Gordon Douglas's *I Was a Communist for the F.B.I.* (1951), Edward Ludwig's *Big Jim McLain* (1952), William Cameron Menzies's *The Whip Hand* (1951), William Wellman's *The Next Voice You Hear* (1950), Harry Horner's *Red Planet Mars* (1952), and Leo McCarey's *My Son John* (1952), all filmic genres were pressed into the service of either defining or delimiting social shifts within the fabric of American society.

In *Gentleman's Agreement*, magazine writer Gregory Peck finds himself ostracized from "polite society" when he pretends to be Jewish. *The Red Menace* and *I Was a Communist for the F.B.I.* both traffic in outrageous, nearly hysterical anti-Communist propaganda, conflating Chicago-style gangster tactics with quotes from Marx and Lenin. John Wayne tracks down a wily Communist cell-leader (Alan Napier) in *Big Jim McLain*; the ex-Nazi, now Communist, mad scientists in *The Whip Hand* seek to use a small town on the rural East Coast of the United States as a base for international germ warfare. God's voice is heard on the radio (but never by the film's audience; as spectators, rather than participants in the action, we are entitled only to transcriptions of Holy Writ) in *The Next Voice You Hear*; while in *Red Planet Mars*, God sends messages from Mars to hasten the collapse of the Soviet Union. *My Son John*, Robert Walker's last film (which had to be finished with trims from Alfred Hitchcock's *Strangers on a Train*, 1951), casts Walker as an undercover Communist agent intent on the overthrow of the United States, who is deterred from his mission only by a fatal car crash.

But even as the climate of social paranoia increased, Hollywood faced an even greater problem than the HUAC hearings or the supposed Communist influence on the film industry. Television, initially free, and with minimal commercial interruptions during its first decade of existence, was providing a convenient and essentially cheaper alternative to theatrical motion pictures. Various strategies (CinemaScope, Natural Vision 3 D, Cinerama) were tried in an attempt to lure paying customers back into the theaters, but despite all industry efforts, an atmosphere of malaise and unease pervaded all aspects of the industry. Television could provide entertainment for the entire family in the privacy of their own home; as television sets become ubiquitous, block "viewing parties" gave way to the current isolationist model of the individual person and/or family unit, done in the home with the viewer engrossed in an intimate, even solitary experience.

British television producers also tried to fill the American need for product, with some interestingly reverse-colonial results. In the late 1950s and early 1960s, British producer-writer-director Ralph Smart created a number of teleseries for the British ITC (Incorporated Television Company, Ltd.) organization, beginning with the series *Robin Hood* (starring Richard Greene, which was also shown on American television), and *William Tell*, which was a modest success. But his most important contributions to British television history are arguably his last two major hits for British ITC: *H. G. Wells' The Invisible Man* and *Secret Agent*. Smart was born in Sydney, Australia, but was educated in London and began scripting program pictures for British International Pictures, including several films for the British comedian Will Hay. Returning to his native Australia in 1939, Smart made training films for the Royal Australian Air Force and then produced two feature films, *The Overlanders* (1946, dir. Harry Watt) and *Bush Christmas* (1947), which Smart also directed. Later, Smart worked for producer Sydney Box's Gainsborough Films in London during the late 1940s, and then Sir Lew Grade's famous film and television production unit, where he began to produce television programs in earnest.

In 1958, Ralph Smart created a new British teleseries, *H. G. Wells' The Invisible Man*, ostensibly based on the character created by Wells. But Smart's version had very little to do with the 1933 classic James Whale film from Universal, or even with any of its many sequels for that company. In direct contradiction to the source material, the hero of Smart's series, Dr. Peter Brady (whose identity was never revealed by Smart as a publicity gimmick; the actor was "voiced" by performer Tim Turner), lives in the lap of bourgeois luxury in the English countryside near Elstree with his sister, Diane Wilson (Lisa Daniely), and her daughter Sally (Deborah Watling). Unlike the protagonist of Wells's narrative, Brady becomes invisible by accident, while working on an experiment into the qualities of refracted light on a guinea pig. For the most part, the "invisibility" special effects are handled by wires holding various objects such as car keys, test tubes, guns, and the like; "matte" photography is used very sparingly. Quite often, first-person camerawork from Brady's point-of-view lends artificial presence to his "invisible appearance" on screen; Brady's asynchronous "voice" and his transparent "look" thus replace any other personal physical characteristics.

These "special effects" in H. G. Wells' The Invisible Man are quotidian in the extreme; they are not the focus of the series' narrative thrust, which operates on the principle of the denial of spectacle. As the series progresses, Brady's invisibility becomes increasingly mundane, and absolutely public. At one point, Brady lectures to his students at Oxford University in a partially invisible state, pointing to the blackboard with empty sleeves to press home a point, adroitly picking up a piece of chalk with his invisible hands. Consequently, I would argue that what interests producer-writer Ralph Smart much more that these feeble parlor tricks is the series' vision of the flagging hold of the British empire on global politics, and concomitant ways in which an invisible emissary can be used to retain British dominion abroad.

In the "origin" episode of H. G. Wells' The Invisible Man, entitled "Secret Experiment," Brady's sudden invisibility is explained away as the result of a freak nuclear accident. The authorities are immediately suspicious of what Brady will do with his newfound powers and imprison him. Brady escapes and drives to the home of fellow scientist Dr. Crompton (Michael Goodliffe), seeking assistance in his quest to return to a normal existence. In Smart's version of Wells's tale, it is Crompton who attempts to fill Brady's head with delusions of power and megalomaniacal grandeur. Brady, however, refuses to be tempted. Crompton knocks Brady unconscious, drives to Brady's lab, and steals the notes for Brady's experiment in the hope that he, too, can become invisible. Brady, however, comes to in time to alert the police, who aid in Crompton's capture, and social order is restored. The authorities, in return, promise not to confine Brady in the future, but rather to use his special skills in various "hot spots" around the world, wherever the interests of the empire are threatened.

Thus, in subsequent episodes of the series, Brady is dispatched by Cabinet Minister Sir Charles (first played by Ernest Clark, and replaced by Ewen MacDuff) to one mythical Middle Eastern, Eastern European, or African country after another, to foil gunrunning schemes, attempted revolutions, atomic weapons smuggling, and the like, all with the consent and cooperation of the British authorities. In one episode, "The Gun Runners," American B actor Louise Allbritton uncovers a gun-smuggling operation in a wayward British colony; Brady tags along invisibly, to successfully assist her in uncovering the scheme. In another episode, "Man In Power," the young prince of an unstable Mideast monarchy is called home from his studies at Oxford (where Dr. Brady is one of his tutors) after his father is assassinated by a corrupt military dictatorship. Brady again acts as an invisible agent in service to the empire, unmasks the traitorous general responsible for the attempted coup, and ensures the young monarch is properly crowned. In both episodes, much is made of the "moral obligation" these smaller countries have to uphold the political dominion of the West; if they are not directly colonies, then their interests are certainly seen as being allied with those of Great Britain and the United States.

In one of the most prescient and/or paranoid episodes of *H. G. Wells' The Invisible Man*, entitled "The Big Plot," parts to produce a nuclear bomb are discovered in the wreckage of an otherwise ordinary aircraft crash. Confronted with the evidence, Brady immediately leaps to the extraordinary conclusion that an international gang of terrorists plans to plant nuclear devices in every major capital of the Western world, and extort vast sums of money from capitalist countries to underwrite the activities of the Soviet regime. Further, Brady theorizes that these activities are being carried out under cover of an international "peace" organization. As subsequent events will prove, his bizarre theory is correct on all counts; the narrative thus reads something like an updated version of Hitchcock's *Foreign Correspondent* (1940). Indeed, a newspaper article of the period ("TV Film 'Could Cause Hatred,' " in the *Chronicle* [London] for November 17, 1959) noted that the series was seemingly designed to heighten international political paranoia. The Labour Peace Fellowship, an organization campaigning for world disarmament, noted that the series' plotlines were "calculated to foment hatred against Russia" and went on to call the series "a danger to East-West relations" in general.

In yet another episode of the series, "The Rocket," the decadent gambling habits of a defense plant employee lead to blackmail and a plan to hijack an experimental rocket fuselage for illegal export behind the iron curtain. Brady intervenes, the rocket is recovered, and order is restored. In all cases, Brady's invisibility is readily pressed into service for benefit of the empire. "I want you here right now, Brady—and invisible!" barks a cabinet minister at one point. Clearly, Brady's invisible agency in service of the colonial British empire is seen as one of Whitehall's last lines of defense against the crumbling of the status quo. Finally, in the episode "The Shadow Bomb," Brady and his cohorts have successfully created a land mine triggered by changing patterns of light, using a series of photocells; during an experiment, a technician is trapped next to a live bomb, and only the Invisible Man (who casts no shadow) can rescue the man from violent death. As soon as the rescue is effected, the technicians triumphantly test the bomb, which will then be exported to British colonies all over the globe to further enforce the aims of the British empire.

The insistent "othering" of Third World social discourse which takes place in these episodes is both ubiquitous and phantasmal; the sets for *H. G. Wells' The Invisible Man* consist of little more than some windows with latticework screens, a few columns covered with gauzy fabric, overhead fans swirling lazily in the apparently oppressive heat, and costumes lifted from a Maria Montez film of the 1940s. No Third World actors are ever used; instead, such British stalwarts as Dennis Price, Andrew Kier, Michael Ripper, and Honor Blackman step in for the citizens of various Mideastern or Eastern European countries.

Producer Ralph Smart subsequently expanded upon this vision of colonial empire in his subsequent and even more successful series, *Danger Man* (*Secret Agent*), an espionage drama featuring Patrick McGoohan as John Drake, in much the same role (defender of the empire) as Peter Brady. *Danger Man* began as a series of thirty-nine half-hour shows, debuting on UK television on September 11, 1960. After a successful one-year run, the series was revamped into an hour-long show beginning in the United Kingdom on October 13, 1964. It was the hour-long series that was exported to the United States under the title *Secret Agent*. Both series were unusually successful for British television productions, attracting network interest in the United States against competing Hollywood product. *H. G. Wells' The Invisible Man* ran for thirty-nine half hours on the CBS network from November 4, 1958, to September 22, 1960, as part of the prime-time evening block; *Secret Agent* ran for forty-five hour-long episodes in CBS prime time from April 4, 1965, to September 10, 1966. Both series have since been successfully syndicated throughout the world. Thus, ostensibly disguised solely as entertainments, these two teleseries effectively promulgated the social aims of colonial Britain in the late 1950s and early to mid-1960s.

Interestingly, McGoohan himself followed up on the latter series with his own creation, *The Prisoner*, in which the character of John Drake from *Secret Agent* finds himself detained in a military compound called "The Village," as his superiors attempt to extract from him information which Drake may or may not have passed to the Russians. This seventeen-hour series has become something of a cult favorite, owing in large measure to its aggressive op and pop art design strategies, its liberal use of "Swinging

London" iconography, and its elliptical, semi-Beckettian dialogue, which relies almost entirely upon puns, impersonations, and Pirandellian situations which are seemingly never resolved. McGoohan produced, starred, cowrote, and even directed several of the episodes, which ran as a summer replacement series on CBS from June 1, 1968, to September 21, 1968, and has been screened in syndication and on home video cassettes ever since; in view of McGoohan's intense personal involvement with the series on all creative levels, it stands to reason that much of the series' content is highly personal in nature and constitutes an attempt by McGoohan to reclaim, and thus reframe, his fictive alter ego.

But as with *H. G. Wells' The Invisible Man* and *Secret Agent*, although perhaps more transparently so here, the political and social subtext of *The Prisoner* was certainly uppermost in McGoohan's consciousness. Indeed, what intrigues one here most is the trajectory of the empire's involvement and the rerepresentation of British colonial interests within these three successive teleseries. Ralph Smart initially projected his vision of the phantom colonial empire in *H. G. Wells' The Invisible Man* as an almost reflexive action; he later called it into question in *Secret Agent*, and McGoohan refined Smart's revisionist stance still further with the nightmarish vision of *The Prisoner*. In *H. G. Wells' The Invisible Man*, the empire is seen as protector of not only its own interests but also the interests of Third World countries existing both within and outside the British government's direct sphere of influence. This assumption is never questioned, either overtly or parenthetically; the domain of empire is seen as both secure and inevitable. Peter Brady is viewed as the invisible agency of benign colonial rule.

In *Secret Agent*, foreign governments on all sides (Western and Eastern European, African, Mideastern) are seen as corrupt and crumbling, due to inefficiency and cynicism within and without. Equipment doesn't work, cars break down, messages are intercepted, missions frequently fail or go awry, and lives are inevitably forfeited. Often, John Drake poses as a drunken agent down on his luck to lull his adversaries into a false sense of security, and just as often, he is double-crossed by his own superiors if they feel it is in the best interest of maintaining the status quo to do so. He dresses shabbily, sweats a lot, drinks too much, and isn't averse to using force and/or coercion to achieve his desired ends.

Loyalty has become dispensable; John Drake's identity ("to everyone he meets, he stays a stranger," the title song reminds us) is at once fluid and nonexistent. Cash and drugs are routinely used as bargaining chips in negotiations with the other side; nothing is as it seems, particularly

Drake's own shifting presence within the frame. By the time of *The Prisoner*, secret agent John Drake (a direct continuation of the character created by Smart) has become a perceived threat to the government that is supposed to sponsor and sanction his actions; he has become the enemy the collapsing empire seeks to suppress. Thus may we track the trajectory of the interests of the empire's invisible agency in defense of itself—from the forthright acknowledgment of the "other," which must be contained, to the unsatisfactory knowledge that the "other" has become one of our own emissaries.

Then, too, with *The Prisoner*, the lure of the processed image has replaced the requirements of narrative structure. While *H. G. Wells' The Invisible Man* and *Secret Agent* were both shot in black and white, often intercutting newsreel footage of riots, explosions, foreign locales, landmarks, and airports to achieve a crudely Vertovian verisimilitude, *The Prisoner*, filmed in garish color and awash in late sixties' British fashion and interior design (very much like Joseph Losey's underrated *Modesty Blaise*, 1966), is shot entirely within an interior/exterior studio which strives to achieve above all other qualities a definite air of unreality, a sense of the resolutely false above all other material and/or physical considerations, much like the eternally sunny backyard set of the American teleseries *The Brady Bunch*.

If Dr. Peter Brady is able to restore order to a toppling Mideast regime within the space of thirty minutes through the use of a few sleight-of-hand tricks, John Drake, in both *The Prisoner* and *Secret Agent*, feels the empire crumbling beneath him, with no one to trust and nothing concrete to believe in. In just the short space of a decade, then, these three closely related teleseries have charted in microcosm the fading interests of the British empire as a force within global social, economic, and political discourse with an unsparing economy that is both unsettling and resolutely cataclysmic.

The collapse of the safely inscribed world of Dr. Peter Brady, in which semibenevolent British government officials sanction clandestine intervention into foreign affairs with a wink and a nod, has led to the world of John Drake as a rogue agent whose ends justify any means, and finally to John Drake as the prisoner of the colonial government he once sought to serve. As one immediate sign of this, Drake in *The Prisoner* is stripped even of his name; he is referred to simply as Number Six, and the ruler of The Village is called Number One. Most of *The Prisoner*'s narrative thrust concerns Number Six's quest to find out the "identity" of Number One; when, in the last episode, his quest is successful, he finds out that Number One has no identity at all; he is simply another cipher in an enormous, meaningless, impersonal organization.

The empire never existed in the first place. There is no going back to the cozy country house in which Dr. Peter Brady constituted his artificial nuclear family using his sister and her daughter, while all the while remaining a resolutely chaste bachelor, a respected member of the ruling class, a scion of British rule. Now, there are no sides, there are no reliable regimes, there are no rules. The modish spectacle of *The Prisoner* seeks to elide the emptiness of its postcolonial vision, but for all the eye-popping sets and swirling colors that fill the frames of *The Prisoner*, for all the jagged cutting and narrative uncertainty with which McGoohan invests his numbered (not named) characters, the content of the entire seventeen hours of the series can be summed up in a few words: all is collapsed, all is nothing, we live in the domain of the eye, and the always now. Time and space have been rendered meaningless by the domain of The Village; the world of the empire has contracted from a sphere of global influence to the confines of a Pinewood soundstage. Spectacle rules, character is nonexistent. This new regime of visual dominance and narrative poverty has indeed, as *Secret Agent*'s theme song prophesied, "given you a number/and taken 'way your name."

Smart's two teleseries were among the most successful commercial properties exported from England for American network programming; together with a plethora of home-grown Hollywood product, family audiences were being entertained in their home for free, with only a few commercial interruptions per hour to annoy them. Cable television was unknown; local TV stations, particularly in major cities such as New York and Los Angeles, were soon programming old movies as part of their regular fare, and the studios became justifiably alarmed. How could they get the family audience to go out to a movie? What would drag them away from a medium that was convenient, pervasive, and, above all, essentially free (after the purchase of a television set)?

The theatrical motion picture finally responded with the only weapon in its arsenal that would keep the least attentive viewer involved: overwhelming hyperspectacle, accompanied by an appropriately thunderous sound track. In the 1950s this meant such films as Henry Koster's *The Robe* (1953), Cecil B. DeMille's *The Ten Commandments* (1956), and Joseph M. Newman's *The Big Circus* (1959); Twentieth Century Fox had announced in early 1953 that, henceforth, all of the studio's films would be shot in CinemaScope, even their travelogues and black-and-white B features. Today, with numerous narrowcast cable channels competing for audience attention, the strategy remains much the same. Such carefully designed "spectacle-as-content" films as Barry Sonnenfeld's *Men in Black* (1997) reduce even a talented thespian like Rip Torn to little more than a shuffler of glyphic cue-cards, rattling off what little information the audience needs to keep the film's narrative in motion, even as Tommy Lee Jones and Will Smith rush desperately from one cataclysmic spectacle to the next, with, predictably, the fate of the world hanging in the balance. And, despite some recent advances in this area, today's Dominant cinema structure is still overwhelmingly sexist and racist.

Tim Burton's *Batman Returns* (1992) and Joel Schumacher's *Batman and Robin* (1997), to cite just two possible examples, contain not a single character of consequence who is other than a Caucasian male. In *Batman Returns*, Catwoman's (Michelle Pfeiffer) disruption of Gotham City is seen as essentially an aberrational activity, which ends when she dies in the embrace of Max Schreck (Christopher Walken) in a gesture of self-sacrifice and synthetic martyrdom. In *Batman and Robin*, we are asked to empathize with Arnold Schwarzenegger's Mr. Freeze, but we never take him seriously in the role—he is always, above all other considerations, the internationally salable action star as figurative commodity. Contemporary viewers have thus been trained by Hollywood to see films as entertainment and escapism, rather than as potential agencies for social change.

In the 1950s, Hollywood's stranglehold on the film production process was all-consuming, far more so than it is today. Women, particularly, were denied a voice within the cinema, even as they were commodified daily in the numerous films ground out in the Hollywood production assembly line. And yet several isolated cases of resistance within the Hollywood system existed even during the Cold War era, such as the cinema of Ida Lupino. Literally alone among her peers, Ida Lupino sought to create in her films a new space for women within the realm of the cinema, and not incidentally a new role for herself as a creator of images rather than a participant in the shadow plays of the Hollywood cinema. Immediately, Lupino realized that she liked directing more than acting, because it gave her more freedom to create herself. In the early 1950s, this was no small feat, and Lupino accomplished it with modesty, grace, and a self-deprecating air entirely belied by her skill as a filmmaker.

Lupino enjoyed a long career as a film actress and, perhaps more importantly, as a film director. Because of the sexism that formerly riddled the film industry—and, to a large degree, that still prevails—Ida Lupino's directorial career is an unusual case. At the time she was working she literally had no close competition. Although she often made light of her directorial accomplishments, Lupino was obviously driven by a very real need to direct. Otherwise, it seems unlikely that she would have relinquished a secure career as a leading lady to do so. Indeed, her work as a director is, for many observers, Lupino's most significant contribution to the literature of motion pictures. As Annette Kuhn notes, "The output of The Filmakers [Lupino's independent production company] emerges in retrospect as the high point of Lupino's long career" (4).

Lupino's first film as a director, *Not Wanted* (1949) was to be directed by Elmer Clifton. However, he suffered a heart attack early on during the filming, and Lupino served her directorial apprenticeship by completing the production. The next year she began to tackle themes that the screen had handled only in a condescending, male-supremacist manner: rape in *Outrage* (1950), the effects of polio on a female dancer in *Never Fear* (1950), social climbing in the world of professional sports in *Hard, Fast, and Beautiful* (1951), and the mechanics of male violence in *The Hitch-Hiker* (1953). In addition, Lupino directed and starred in *The Bigamist* (1953), in which Edmond O'Brien finds himself married to two women, due to his own weakness of character and a Langian series of uncontrollable events. After this film, produced by the Filmakers (which she co-owned and operated with her then-husband, Collier Young), Lupino went over to television where she directed many episodes of *Kraft Suspense Theater*, *Panic*, *Alfred Hitchcock Presents*, *Mr. Adams and Eve* (in which she co-starred with then-husband Howard Duff), *The Fugitive*, *Thriller*, *The Untouchables*, and other early teleseries.

By the time she was given another shot at feature direction, it was to handle the nearly all-woman cast in *The Trouble with Angels* (1966). It was clearly sexism that got her the assignment: hire a woman to direct a film with women. Nevertheless, she did an excellent job; under her direction, Rosalind Russell delivered her last really fine performance, and Lupino got good work from Hayley Mills in the leading juvenile role. At the same time, she kept busy as a director of series television, directing episodes of *The Ghost and Mrs. Muir* and *Gilligan's Island*. As an actress, Lupino continued working until 1977, when she appeared as an aging star on an episode of the TV series *Charlie's Angels*. But her real talent was behind the camera, not in front of it. As a cinematic stylist, Lupino is on a level with Douglas Sirk in her gracefully sweeping crane/dolly camera work, and her lighting and direction of actors recalls the noirish tendencies of Robert Aldrich and Don Siegel.

To better understand Lupino's work as both actress and director, and thus the magnitude of the project she undertook in reshaping herself as a director during the repressive 1950s, one must consider the events that shaped her life. Stanley Lupino, Ida's father, was a star of the British "West End" theater and often wrote the plays he appeared in. Ida Lupino's second cousin was Lupino Lane, a music hall star of great prominence in the United Kingdom. Ida's mother, whose maiden name was Connie Emerald, also had a theater background; years later, when forming her first film production company, Ida Lupino would name it Emerald Productions (though it soon after became known as the Filmakers).

Lupino's first screen role came about in a rather unusual fashion. Director Allan Dwan was searching for a young ingenue for his 1933 British production of *Her First Affair*. Ida's mother, Connie, read for the part, but Dwan thought she was too mature for the role. Instead, he turned to Ida, who had accompanied her mother to the audition, and asked Ida to read for the part. She was immediately cast in the film, and Ida Lupino's cinema career was truly launched. Thus began a period of intense activity for the young actress.

In her initial screen appearance, Ida Lupino was billed as "the English Jean Harlow" and was forced to dye her hair platinum blonde. Lupino protested but to no avail. Other inconsequential British films followed, including Bernard Vorhaus's *Money for Speed*, George King's *High Finance*, Hanns Schwarz's *Prince of Arcadia*, Bernard Vorhaus's *The Ghost Camera*, and Maurice Elvey's *I Lived with You*, all made in 1933, but Lupino wanted to leave England and try her luck in Los Angeles. In late 1933, Lupino signed a contract with Paramount Pictures and sailed for the United States to appear in the title role of the 1933 production of *Alice in Wonderland*, a role that actually went to Charlotte Henry. For when Lupino appeared at the Paramount Studios in Los Angeles, the production executives immediately realized that there was something rather aggressive, assured, and adult in Lupino's demeanor, and they scrapped their plans to develop her into a juvenile.

Instead, Ida Lupino went straight into a series of hard-boiled roles in such films as Henry Hathaway's *Come on Marines* (1934) and Marion Gering's *Ready for Love* (1934), although her fledgling career was almost fatally sidetracked by a little-publicized bout with polio in late 1934. With characteristic tenacity, Lupino fought off the disease through sheer strength of will and continued to act in a series of predictable program features, including Benjamin Stoloff's *Fight for Your Lady* (1937), Peter Godfrey's *The Lone Wolf Spy Hunt* (1939), Benjamin Stoloff's *The Lady and the Mob* (1939), and the first film that gave her a chance to display the considerable range of her abilities, Alfred L. Werker's film of *The Adventures of Sherlock Holmes* (1939), the debut film in that long-running series.

Ida Lupino's first big acting break came in William Wellman's 1940 production of *The Light That Failed*, a role that Lupino fought for over the objections of Wellman, costar Ronald Colman, and her advisers, who assured her that the unsympathetic cockney girl she played in the film would alienate audiences. Instead, Lupino walked away with the film and emerged as a major star as the year drew to a close. Signing with Warner Brothers, Lupino commanded star billing in such gritty classics as Raoul Walsh's *They Drive by Night* (1940) and *High Sierra* (1941), Michael Curtiz's *The Sea Wolf* (1941), and Charles Vidor's *Ladies in Retirement* (1941). Ida Lupino received the Best Actress award from the New York Film Critics Association for her work in Vincent Sherman's *The Hard Way* (1942), but in truth she was becoming disenchanted with her career as an actress. Never a team player, Lupino had quarreled with Humphrey Bogart during the production of *High Sierra* and vowed after the film's completion that she would never work with the actor again. As Bogart's star continued to rise, Lupino held firmly to her decree, although Warner tried to pair the two in a number of subsequent productions. Thus, in a sense, Lupino worked against her commercial success as an actress by refusing to work in projects she did not believe in, and refusing to work with actors who failed to respect her personally, or professionally, as she felt Bogart failed to do.

In 1944 Lupino appeared in a brief bit in Delmer Daves's *Hollywood Canteen*, taking time out to film a brief theatrical commercial urging women war workers "to stay on the job, and finish the job, for victory," before portraying Emily Brontë in Curtis Bernhardt's *Devotion* (1946). But as she consolidated her success as an actress, Ida Lupino began to think of her next career move. Ida Lupino wanted to direct, and she set about to put her vision on the screen with typically unwavering energy. "Believe me, I've fought to produce and direct my own pictures. . . . [I] always nursed a desire to direct pictures" (48), she told Robert Ellis in a 1950 interview. Clearly, Lupino's films formed a personal statement for her. Although Lupino continued to make glossy romance, suspense, or costume films for Warner Brothers (and for other studios, under a loan-out arrangement that was lucrative for Warner but not for Lupino), including Raoul Walsh's *The Man I Love* (1947), Peter Godfrey's *Escape Me Never* (1947), Jean Negulesco's *Road House* (1948), and S. Sylvan Simon's *Lust for Gold* (1949), by early 1948 Lupino had laid the groundwork for her later career as a director.

As noted earlier, Lupino's first production company was named Emerald Productions. Ida Lupino had been married from 1938 to 1945 to actor Louis Hayward, but shortly after her divorce from Hayward, Lupino met and fell in love with production executive Collier Young, who was then working for Columbia Pictures. Ida Lupino and Collier Young were married in 1948, and shortly thereafter, Lupino, Young, and Anson Bond (owner of Bond's Clothing) then formed Emerald Productions. Bond soon decided that film production was too risky, and his share of the partnership was bought out by screenwriter Malvin Wald. With this change in partnership, Emerald Productions became simply the Filmakers, and Ida Lupino was ready to realize her dream as a director of theatrical motion pictures.

The Filmakers lasted as a production entity from 1949 to 1953, during which time the company made eight feature films. Lupino directed six of the eight features. Collier Young served as the company's president, Lupino was vice president, and Wald functioned as the business manager. The first production of the Filmakers was Elmer Clifton's *Not Wanted* (1949), the story of an unwed mother (Sally Forrest) who gives up her baby for adoption, then regrets it and kidnaps another child to replace the child she has lost. Lupino cowrote the film's screenplay. While the film is often unduly melodramatic, it is still important as a pioneering examination of what was then considered a taboo social problem, and the film is also noteworthy as Ida Lupino's maiden voyage as a director. The film's nominal director, Elmer Clifton, a Hollywood journeyman whose career reached back into the days of silent films, had a heart attack seventy-two hours after the start of principal photography.

Lupino stepped in to direct, and brought the film in on time and under budget, as Clifton essentially watched from the sidelines. Up to her death in 1995, Lupino maintained that her first assignment as a film director was simply a matter of necessity and budgetary constraints, and that there was simply no money in the budget to hire a replacement director. This may or may not be true, but had Lupino wished to, she certainly could have found another reliable Hollywood professional to take Clifton's place, such as William Beaudine, Sam Newfield, or the then-up-and-coming Anthony Mann. *Not Wanted* was made for the very small studio Eagle Lion Productions, which had formerly been known as Producer's Releasing Corporation, arguably the cheapest studio in Hollywood. If Lupino had needed a replacement, Eagle Lion could have supplied a director on a moment's notice.

However, Lupino had been studying the craft of direction for several years, most assiduously during a period when she had been "on suspension" for refusing to star in a program picture that she felt was beneath her dignity as an actress. In "Me, Mother Directress," an article that Lupino wrote for the Director's Guild of America's in-house magazine, *Action*, Lupino described how she began to pick up the skills that would successfully guide her through her directorial career: "For about eighteen months back in the mid-Forties I could not get a job in pictures as an actress. . . . I was on suspension . . . when you turned down something you were suspended. . . . I was able to keep alive as a radio actress. I had to do something to fill up my time. . . . I learned a lot from the late George Barnes, a marvelous cameraman" (1967:15). *Not Wanted* cost only $154,000 and was shot in less than thirty days, but it still did not make back its negative cost. Nevertheless, the film was enormously influential among those viewers who went out of their way to see it, and although Lupino refused to sign the film (giving Clifton full credit), it remains a remarkable directorial debut.

The next production of the Filmakers was *Never Fear*. The film starred Sally Forrest as a young dancer who is stricken with polio. Through sheer determination, the young woman recovers, and the film seems obviously influenced by Lupino's own brush with the disease. The film, shot at the Kabat-Kaiser Institute in Santa Monica, California, as a whole has an earnest, documentary air in its construction, which did not, however, sit well with the public. The Filmakers distributed *Never Fear* through a tenuous States Rights system of theatrical bookings, as they had with *Not Wanted*. Even when retitled *The Young Lovers* to gain additional attention at the box office, *Never Fear* failed to earn back its production costs. However, the film caught the eye of Howard Hughes, who had recently purchased RKO Studios, and who was looking for suppliers of low-budget feature films to fill out his distribution schedule. Hughes agreed to distribute the Filmakers' next three features and put up financing of $250,000 per film as part of a negative pickup deal. The Filmakers would have total control over the content and the production of the films, and Hughes would distribute them through RKO. Thus, Lupino's company had worked its way into an ideal situation—guaranteed distribution, creative freedom, and "up-front" financing. Lupino's next three films, happily, would be both commercially and critically successful.

Outrage was Lupino's first film under the RKO deal. Coscripted by Lupino, the film was the first major Hollywood production to deal with rape in a sympathetic, nonsensational manner (the same cannot be said, for example, of Mervyn LeRoy's *They Won't Forget* [1937] or Stephen Roberts's *The Story of Temple Drake* [1933]), and was Lupino's first solid success at the box office. The film starred Mala Powers as the rape victim, although, due to the censorial climate of the period, Lupino could only refer to the crime as a "criminal assault" in the screenplay. In sharp contrast to earlier, male-centrist films dealing with rape, Lupino stages this film almost entirely from the viewpoint of a sympathetic, undeniably feminine omniscient observer, and stages the rape itself offscreen, thus depriving the audience of any scopophilic "pleasure" they might have derived from witnessing the horror of the event because the action is implied, rather than directly stated. In this film, for the first time, Lupino demonstrates her mastery of the mobile camera, with a number of impressive crane and dolly shots, and indulges in noirish low-key lighting, placing most of the events for the first half of the film in a netherworld of ominous shadows.

Hard, Fast, and Beautiful showcased Lupino's continued progress as a director, as a filmmaker who was essentially growing up in public with the creation of her previous films. Although *Hard, Fast, and Beautiful* was another low-budget production, shot in thirty days for a total of slightly less than $200,000, Lupino was able to secure the services of actress Claire Trevor for a pivotal role in the film, which again featured Sally Forrest as one of the principal characters. Not a few critics, including Francine Parker and Ronnie Scheib, have commented on the close physical resemblance between Forrest and Lupino. *Hard, Fast, and Beautiful* is another film based upon actual events, and these critics have come to the conclusion that, through Forrest, Lupino may be casting "herself" as the protagonist in these films.

The plot of *Hard, Fast, and Beautiful* is straightforward. Claire Trevor appears as Millie, a ruthless maternal figure who coerces her daughter, Florence (Sally Forrest), into becoming a professional tournament tennis player. In this quest, Millie is aided by an unscrupulous promoter (Carleton Young), who also attempts to seduce Millie and wreck her marriage to her long-suffering husband, played by Kenneth Patterson. Robert Clarke appears as Florence's boyfriend, and it is through his continual criticism that Florence begins to question the validity of her pursuit of sports stardom. At the film's conclusion, Florence refuses to continue on as a tennis champion, thus forfeiting her title, in order to care for her ailing father. In this, Lupino restates her own desire to remain subservient—at least superficially—to the existing patriarchal order. As she observed in her article, "Me, Mother Directress,"

Any woman who wishes to smash into the world of men isn't very feminine . . . Baby, we can't go smashing. I believe women should be struck regularly—like a gong. Or is it bong? If a woman has a man who loves her, she better stick close to home. I've turned down jobs in Europe because I'd have to leave my husband and my daughter and my cats. I couldn't accept those jobs unless I was a guy. (1967:15).

The promoter immediately shifts his sights to a rival tennis player, and Millie is rebuffed by her husband and her daughter. The final shot of the film shows Millie at night, alone, sitting in the now-empty bleachers of the championship tennis court, her plans for vicarious stardom smashed. What raises this somewhat melodramatic narrative above the level of a standard program picture is, as in all her work, the visceral intensity that Lupino brings to the production. By shooting on location, as she did in *Outrage* and *Never Fear*, Lupino gives *Hard, Fast, and Beautiful* a documentary look that makes Florence's bid for tennis stardom all the more real. In addition, Lupino is not averse to detailing the grubby mechanics of sports exploitation: endorsements, product promotions, publicity stunts, and merchandising tie-ins. Remembering that Lupino made these films in the early 1950s, we should not be surprised that contemporary critical commentary was overwhelmingly negative. Bosley Crowther, for example, writing in the *New York Times*, called Lupino's directorial style "overwrought," and an extension of "her own jittery screen personality" (16). As time passes, the film looks anything but "overwrought"; indeed, it seems restrained in its criticism of the marketing of sports personalities. At seventy-nine minutes in length, the film is compact, epigrammatic, and suitably brutal. In her examinations of unwed motherhood, rape, parental exploitation, and the debilitating effects of polio, Lupino was certainly ahead of her time and served as both an entertainer and a social commentator.

The Hitch-Hiker was reportedly Lupino's favorite of all her films. Based on the case of one William Cook, who murdered six innocent people during a hitchhiking "thrill kill" spree, *The Hitch-Hiker* is a mere seventy-one minutes long and was shot for the most part on location in the California desert. Once again, Lupino was tackling a controversial theme, although the film did have a harrowing precedent in Felix Feist's 1947 film *The Devil Thumbs a Ride*, in which Lawrence Tierney played a psychopath who goes on a similar rampage. As a woman directing in Hollywood, Lupino was still something of a curiosity to the press, and

UPI sent a reporter and photographer to the Baja desert to photograph Lupino in action.

Stills taken during this visit reveal the Spartan working conditions endured by Lupino and her cast and crew. Lupino is dressed in dungarees, sneakers, and a check flannel shirt topped with a baseball cap, her hair tied back in a bun. The crew, entirely male, look on with professional detachment as Lupino explains a typically complex shot to stars Edmond O'Brien and Frank Lovejoy. There are a few reflectors (to enhance the use of natural daylight in the film), but the camera equipment used is modest, outdated (a 35mm Mitchell camera), and somewhat bulky. Trash cans full of soda pop on ice are in evidence, as a small compensation for the brutal desert heat, but on the whole, the film is obviously being shot under extremely difficult circumstances. Yet all the participants look as if they are having an excellent time on the film, laughing, joking, and working very, very quickly.

Lupino was beginning to feel that her role as a social critic was somewhat limiting and later declared that during the making of *The Hitch-Hiker* she realized that suspense was her niche. As the psychopathic killer who terrorizes O'Brien and Lovejoy, William Talman is remarkable as Emmett Myers, an escaped convict with a paralyzed right eye, which remains open whether Myers is asleep or awake. *The Hitch-Hiker* is certainly Lupino's most purely visual film, and also her most intimate. Once again working with an essentially triangular situation (Myers's terrorizing of O'Brien and Lovejoy echoes the conflict between Carleton Young, Sally Forrest, and Claire Trevor in *Hard, Fast, and Beautiful*), Lupino stages *The Hitch-Hiker* in a series of starkly lit close-ups, wideshots that emphasize the inhospitality of the desert terrain, and lighting strategies that favor shafts of light in the darkness of the desert night, or else slightly overexposed shots to convey the heat of the desert during the daytime.

Still, during production of the film, Lupino was criticized for her usurpation of what was considered a traditionally male occupation, and she felt compelled to give an interview during the filming which appeared under the heading "Ida Lupino Retains Her Femininity as Director." In part, Lupino stated that "I retain every feminine trait. Men prefer it that way. They're more co-operative if they see that fundamentally you are of the weaker sex even though [you are] in a position to give orders, which normally is the male prerogative, or so he likes to think, anyway. While I've encountered no resentment from the male of the species for intruding into their world, I give them no opportunity to think I've strayed where I don't belong. I assume no masculine characteristics, which can often be a fault of career women rubbing shoulders with their male counterparts, who become merely arrogant or authoritative" (1953:4). It is also worth noting that *The Hitch-Hiker* was made by Lupino and the Filmakers Company after her divorce from Collier Young, and represents a return to the director's chair after a two-year hiatus. Though filming of *The Hitch-Hiker* went smoothly, and all seemed well on the surface (Collier Young even appears in a cameo in the film as a sleeping "Mexican peon"), there is an atmosphere of real violence in the film—not only in the subject matter but also in Lupino's relentless pacing, hyperkinetic camera setups, and her intense use of oppressive close-ups to heighten the film's suspense.

The Bigamist was the last of Lupino's films under her RKO deal, which was not renewed. For the first time, Lupino appeared in a film that she directed. The production is surrounded by considerable irony, inasmuch as it was Joan Fontaine's involvement with Collier Young (and Lupino's corresponding association with actor Howard Duff) that precipitated the divorce between Lupino and Young. Young and Fontaine were then married, as were Lupino and Duff. The film was distributed by the Filmakers group after RKO passed on the complete film. Without the necessary national distribution mechanism afforded by a major studio, the film failed to obtain adequate bookings, and the Filmakers went out of business.

While a number of critics consider it the most accomplished of Lupino's early films, *The Bigamist* remains a problematic entry in Lupino's directorial career for most viewers. The acting is superb, but visually the film fails to excite. Nevertheless, in its examination of social standards in the early 1950s, the film gives us an uncomfortably claustrophobic vision of the constraints forced upon both women and men during this period. Yet it would be impossible not to notice the lack of visceral energy in *The Bigamist*. Lupino's career as a theatrical director was about to be abruptly terminated, and she was about to enter television direction in earnest, both to make ends meet and also to provide herself with a creative outlet in a medium that required exactly those directorial skills that Lupino so obviously possessed: speed, and the authority to deal with actors despite tight shooting schedules.

The end of her career as a theatrical feature film director led to Lupino's work in television, which began after a directorial lapse of five years. During this period, Lupino acted in a series of conventional melodramas, including Joel Newton's *Jennifer* (1953), in which Lupino, costarring with new husband Howard Duff, becomes involved in a murder in an old, forbidding mansion; *Private Hell 36* (1954), a Don Siegel crime film, again with Duff; and Lewis Seiler's *Women's Prison* (1955), in which she played a sadistic prison warden, opposite crusading prison doctor Duff. Her best film as an actress during this period is arguably Fritz Lang's *While the City Sleeps* (1956), and she also appeared in Irving Rapper's *Strange Intruder* in that same year. In addition, Lupino and Duff costarred in the mid-1950s TV sitcom *Mr. Adams and Eve*, which was a substantial ratings success; Lupino directed several episodes of the series.

In late 1958, David Niven, one of the partners in the Four Star Television Company, creators of the television series *Four Star Playhouse*, asked Lupino to direct several episodes of the series, in addition to appearing in other segments of the series. The arrangement was successful on all counts and led to episodes of other television series, including *On Trial* ("The Trial of Mary Seurat," 1959), *Alfred Hitchcock Presents* ("Sybilla," 1960; "A Crime for Mothers," 1960), *Have Gun—Will Travel* ("The Trial," 1960; "Lady with a Gun," 1960; "The Gold Bar," 1961), *Dick Powell Theatre*, *Thriller* (the Boris Karloff anthology series; Lupino directed all the 1961 episodes of this program), *Hong Kong*, *The Untouchables*, *Mr. Novak*, *The Virginian*, *Kraft Suspense Theatre*, *Dr. Kildare*, *Bewitched*, *Gilligan's Island*, *The Fugitive*, *The Rogues*, and a number of other series. In all these assignments, Lupino quickly consolidated her reputation as a no-nonsense director who used effective camera coverage combined with astute direction of actors to complete her television episodes on time and often under budget. On *The Untouchables*, for example, she had only six days to complete a forty-eight-minute program, under strict IATSE (International Alliance of Theatrical Stage Employees) union conditions, which meant no night shooting and no overtime. Lupino's half-hour shows, whether drama (*Have Gun—Will Travel*) or comedy (*Bewitched*), had to be shot in two to three days. In all cases, Lupino rose to the challenge.

Most previous studies of Lupino have failed to consider her television work, yet a careful examination of her series projects reveals that her directorial sensibility is still apparent, although muted, to some degree, by the inevitable television treadmill. There is little to say, for example, about Lupino's work on *Bewitched* or *Gilligan's Island*, but her work for *The Untouchables* and *Thriller* is often adventurous and individualistic. Barbara Scharres comments on the fluidity of Lupino's camera work in an episode of *Thriller*, describing the complexity of a single shot in this hour-long telefilm.

In one continuous close-up shot [the actress] reaches for the sponge, her hand hovers over it in a moment of indecision, she reaches instead for the chocolates; just when you think she's safe, her hand darts back to the sponge, grabs it, and she is electrocuted. Comedy, suspense, and a tour-de-force display of Lupino's wittiness come together in one shot. In contrast to the often static camerawork of Fifties and Sixties television, Lupino made extensive use of the moving camera. (4)

Executing a shot like this can be difficult enough under the most relaxed production circumstances, but to attempt something of this order within the physical context of a six-day television show is quite remarkable. Still, Lupino viewed her television work with a healthy dose of pragmatism. In an interview with Dwight Whitney, Lupino commented that

> directing keeps you in a constant state of first-night nerves. . . . You may be terrified but you mustn't show it on the set. Nothing goes according to Hoyle. . . . Reshuffle your schedule . . . Keep your sense of humor, don't panic. I sometimes wonder how anything gets on film. And yet, if I don't work, it's Panic Manor. (16)

Perhaps one of the most difficult assignments that Lupino tackled in television direction was her work on one episode of the Universal television series *The Virginian*, a ninety-minute *weekly* series starring James Drury. *The Virginian* is noteworthy as the first feature-length television program and is considered by many to be the forerunner of today's made-for-television movies. With typical cost consciousness, the Universal executives decreed that each episode of the series had to be completed in ten days, an unheard-of schedule for a major studio feature film. In addition, most of *The Virginian* had to be shot outdoors, as opposed to today's nighttime soap operas (*Dallas, Knot's Landing*), which use "interior" scenes of confrontation interspersed with a few "exterior" establishing shots. As a final difficulty, Lupino found herself being used by Universal as an attraction on their studio tours during production of *The Virginian*. In 1967, Lupino recounted her experience working on *The Virginian* and briefly discussed the straightforward manner in which she prepared for shooting:

> I would never think of indulging in what has come to be known as the woman's right to change her mind. As soon as I get a script I go

to work on it. I study and I prepare and when the time comes to shoot, my mind is usually made up and I go ahead, right or wrong. If I get a script in time, I prepare on a week-end. I go out on the back-lot or to the sets on Saturday and Sunday, when it's nice and quiet, and map out my set-ups. I do that every time it's at all possible.

I went out on the backlot at Universal awhile back to prepare a *Virginian*, but I had forgotten those studio tours, you know, twelve thousand people traipsing all over the place over the week-end. There I was on the set, dripping wet in the killing heat, wearing no makeup, looking like a witch searching for an old house to haunt, and these tours started coming through. The bright young know-it-all guide would happily tell his eager charges, "And there, ladies and gentlemen, is the famous actress-directress Ida Lupino preparing for *The Virginian*." I tell you, I wanted to die. (1967:14)

Lupino became known primarily as an action director, one who could handle fights, murders, and scenes of violence and destruction. In *Have Gun—Will Travel*, for example, her first episode for that series ("The Trial," 1960) included, according to Dwight Whitney, "a rape, eight murders, and a sandstorm" (16). Lupino was also surprised to discover that the star of the series, Richard Boone, displayed a very cavalier approach to his role. On the first day of shooting, Boone called her over and told her (as recounted by Whitney), "Doll, I don't care what you do. Just don't ask me to rehearse" (16). Faced with these difficulties, one would expect Lupino to simply shoot the program in the most efficient manner possible—which she did—but even under these decidedly unfavorable circumstances, Lupino gave every ounce of her considerable stylistic energy to the project. Other memorable projects from Lupino's television work include "What Beckoning Ghost?" (from the series *Thriller*, 1961), "The Man in the Cooler" (for *The Untouchables*, 1962), "Heart of Marble, Body of Stone" (for *Breaking Point*, 1963), "To Walk in Grace" (for *Dr. Kildare*, 1964), "Love in the Wrong Season" (for *Mr. Novak*, 1963), and a number of other programs.

Lupino's last theatrical feature was the much-underrated *The Trouble with Angels* (1966). The film was almost universally dismissed upon its initial release, and yet Lupino orchestrated a beautifully restrained performance from Rosalind Russell as the Mother Superior and created a work of considerable depth and feeling within the confines of a rather blandly modern Columbia program picture. Indeed, a number of observers have compared the film to Leontine Sagan's *Maedchen in Uniform* (1931). While

no one can argue that *The Trouble with Angels* is an altogether less ambitious and more compromised production than that film, *The Trouble with
Angels* still displays Lupino's grace under pressure as a director. Lupino
has the ability to make a personal statement within the confines of a
decidedly commercial enterprise. Although the film was a commercial
success, Lupino found the critical reception of the film difficult to take,
and so she went back to acting on a full-time basis. In 1971, Lupino acted
in Bernard L. Kowalski's exploitation film *Women in Chains*, but she
rebounded with a role in Sam Peckinpah's *Junior Bonner* (1972), in which
she played Steve McQueen's mother. In a 1991 interview with Graham
Fuller, Lupino remembered working on the film:

> I played Steve McQueen's mother, but I was only twelve years
> older than him, and he complained to Sam. He said, "What's going
> on here? How can I look at Ida and think of her as my mother?" I
> said, "That's good, because when I look at you, I'm not thinking of
> you as a son." We went to the races together, Steve and I, and we
> won five races and came back with a small fortune. One of the
> horses was called Ida's Pet, and it went on to become quite famous.
> Sam was angry—he said, "The next time you go racing make sure
> you take me with you." (118)

Junior Bonner was followed by acting assignments in a series of routine
films, including Robert Fuest's *The Devil's Rain* (1975), in which she
appeared opposite a young and then unknown John Travolta, Bert I. Gordon's *Food of the Gods* (1976), and a 1977 "guest star" appearance on the
television show *Charlie's Angels*. After this, Ida Lupino retired from the
screen, and in 1984 she moved from the Brentwood house she had lived
in with Howard Duff (whom she divorced that same year) to a smaller
residence in Van Nuys, California. As she entered the final period of her
life, she watched her old films on late-night television and thought of her
long career. At the time, Lupino told interviewer Graham Fuller that "I
sit up every night watching lots of films, from midnight till six or seven
o'clock, and I see some wonderful films at that time." In some interviews,
Lupino has dismissed her work as a director as the result of sheer economic necessity. Just before her death, however, Lupino admitted to
Fuller that she got "more satisfaction out of directing than acting . . . I
enjoyed it much more (118)."

The perpetual paradox of the motion picture medium is the inherent
compromise between artistry and finance required of its practitioners.

Ida Lupino's position as a film director is remarkable for a number of reasons. She was a woman working in Hollywood at a time when both the cultural climate and the incipient sexism of the industry mitigated against her efforts; she was an actress who turned to direction when her career in front of the camera failed to satisfy her needs as an artist; she directed films and television shows of a surprisingly violent nature during a period when television was known as the "safe" medium; and she was unafraid to tackle impossible schedules and production budgets on a routine basis, creating work of dignity and originality under exceedingly difficult circumstances. Unavailable for decades, Lupino's works as a director have recently been the subject of a revival, and her films have now been digitally remastered for public consumption and are finally receiving the attention they deserve (Koestenbaum, 182).

Now I would like to turn to the case of another 1950s auteur who sought to create a personal statement in his work in a much more modest fashion, but whose despairingly bleak vision of American society in the fifties accurately limns the claustrophobic atmosphere of Cold War Hollywood cinematic discourse, in which every move was suspect and deviations from either standard generic practice or the social norms of the era were viewed with the greatest suspicion. In this case, the actor-director is male, but when one considers his vision of what the construction of "masculinity" required in 1950s cinema, Richard Carlson's films as a director offer a disturbing commentary on the requirements of 1950s genre fiction and the narrow confines of the socially approved roles that could then be offered to a "male lead" in the Dominant cinema. Much like Lupino, Carlson sought to break out of the mold that was so profitably confining him. The film he chose to make for his first project as director, *Riders to the Stars* (1954), tells us much about the commercial straitjacket that leading men in the 1950s were forced to wear, just as Ida Lupino grew tired of the succession of shrews, ingenues, and slick career girls forced on her during her acting career at Warner Brothers.

In 1953, when Richard Carlson's commercial appeal as an actor was at its peak, with such genre films as Curt Siodmak's *The Magnetic Monster*, Jack Arnold's *It Came from Outer Space*, Budd Boetticher's *Seminole*, William Cameron Menzies's *The Maze*, and Douglas Sirk's *All I Desire* (all 1953), Carlson also created a feature film that was more of a personal project, serving as both actor and director on the film *Riders to the Stars*. Apart from his apprenticeship as an actor to such competent directors as William Cameron Menzies, Robert Stevenson, Frank Lloyd, Compton

Bennett, Andrew Marton, Arthur Lubin, and others, Carlson had been writing articles and scripts for a number of years prior to the production of *Riders to the Stars*, and all this experience proved to be extremely useful to him. Interestingly, Carlson is not cast as the lead in the film, but rather in a subsidiary role as a somewhat weak and disillusioned university professor, Dr. Jerry Lockwood. This in itself was something of a gamble for the actor, who had established himself firmly with the Cold War era American public as the stereotype of the calm, rational, yet heroic man of science who inevitably fends off the forces of science run amok, or alien invaders, with a steady manner designed to impress and reassure the average filmgoer.

As a character, Carlson's Jerry Lockwood in *Riders to the Stars* is certainly a departure from this model. Jerry Lockwood is (as events will demonstrate) unlucky in love (his proposal of marriage is brusquely rejected, twice, by his nominal fiancée); he is a coward (one of his objectives in marrying is to avoid the space flight assignment handed to him by the government, as no married pilots are eligible); he is apparently an ineffective lecturer, abandoning his lectures at a moment's notice; he is indecisive and perhaps even a national security risk (at the last possible minute before the flight, he still can't decide whether or not to go, much to the chagrin of his superiors); and in the climax of the film, having accepted the assignment, Jerry "snaps" in outer space under the strain of traumatic stress syndrome (triggered by unpleasant memories of service during World War II) and, for all intents and purposes, commits suicide.

This does not exactly conform to the heroic paradigm Carlson portrayed as the steadfast, reasonable astronomer or physicist in his other, more conventional genre films of the fifties. Further, unlike the world of narrative values inhabited by the characters in *It Came from Outer Space*, *The Magnetic Monster*, or *The Creature from the Black Lagoon* (1954), in which the disruptive force of an alien menace is introduced solely to be vanquished, and thus, through its demise, further enhance the dominion of the status quo, *Riders to the Stars* exists in a world of Cold War paranoia, in which the protagonists are constantly being surveilled, scrutinized, tested, questioned, and quarantined. The "real world" as seen in *Riders to the Stars* is an unhappy place, filled with fear, failure, disillusionment, and treachery. Only nominal lead William Lundigan (as the stalwart astronaut Richard Stanton) is allowed any degree of personal space or satisfaction within the film, as both the son of Dr. Donald Stanton (Herbert Marshall), the eminent scientist–father figure whose presence dominates the film, and through his romantic relationship with Jane Flynn (Martha Hyer), Dr. Stanton's assistant, who falls in love with Richard Stanton as the film's narrative progresses, once again marginalizing the attempted advances of Carlson's Jerry Lockwood, who is thus thrice scorned in his pursuit of love.

For all these reasons, *Riders to the Stars* is both an anomaly among science fiction films of the 1950s and an obviously personal project for the director and costar, who was clearly putting his screen image severely on trial with such a deviant, doom-laden narrative. But as we shall see, Carlson's key collaborators on the project, editor Herbert L. Strock, scenarist Curt Siodmak (both of whom had also directed deeply dystopian science fiction and/or horror films), and producer Ivan Tors (also no stranger to the science fiction genre), brought their own set of concerns to the completed project, thus making *Riders to the Stars* the product of the combined visions of four genre specialists determined to make something unusual and offbeat in the guise of a conventional science fiction thriller. If every motion picture (or book, or painting, or any work of art) can be seen at some level as a political act, surely this was particularly true in the ultra-paranoid Eisenhower 1950s, at the height of the Cold War and the movie and television blacklist. To create an even mildly personal work in such highly charged circumstances is not an easy task. I wish to examine how the four key players—Carlson, Strock, Tors, and Siodmak—managed to effectively create and distribute such an alienated (and alienating) film, despite the cultural obstacles engendered by such an enterprise.

Richard Carlson was born on April 29, 1912, in Albert Lea, Minnesota. After graduating summa cum laude from the University of Minnesota, Carlson tried teaching for a time, but after receiving his M.A. degree, Carlson abandoned academe for work in theater. A string of repertory and Broadway acting assignments, coupled with jobs as a writer and director in summer stock, led to Carlson's debut as a motion picture actor in Richard Wallace's *The Young in Heart* and Alfred E. Green's *The Duke of West Point* (both 1938). Initially cast as a juvenile because of his baby-faced good looks, Carlson toiled through a wide variety of genre program pictures, including Frank Lloyd's *The Howards of Virginia* (1940), George Abbott's musical *Too Many Girls* (1940), the Abbott and Costello comedy *Hold That Ghost* (1941, dir. Arthur Lubin), Richard Thorpe's steamy jungle melodrama *White Cargo* (1942), opposite Hedy Lamarr, Budd Boetticher's thriller *Behind Locked Doors* (1948), Compton Bennett and Andrew Marton's *King Solomon's Mines* (1950), and numerous other predictable genre films. But true stardom eluded Richard Carlson. Relegated to supporting roles in A pictures and interchangeable leads in B films, by 1950 Carlson was frustrated with the direction of his career and sought a new avenue of expression in his work.

This new direction came in the unlikely shape of yet another B science fiction thriller, Curt Siodmak's *The Magnetic Monster* (1953), a United Artists release produced by "science fact" buff Ivan Tors, with a screenplay by Tors and horror/science fiction veteran Curt Siodmak, and editorial supervision by Herbert L. Strock. In accepting this acting assignment, Carlson would not only alter the direction of his career permanently, he would also set himself on the road to being a director less than twelve months later with *Riders to the Stars* and become embroiled in a creative partnership with three of the most successful and idiosyncratic science fiction auteurs of the 1950s. Curt Siodmak, brother of director Robert Siodmak, had a long and successful career as a writer behind him before he wrote the script for *Riders to the Stars*. Single-handedly or in collaboration, Siodmak scripted many of the classic horror films of the 1930s and 1940s, including George Waggner's *The Wolf Man* (1941), Arthur Lubin's *Black Friday* (1940), Robert Siodmak's *Son of Dracula* (1943), Jacques Tourneur's *I Walked with a Zombie* (1943), and Fred F. Sears's *Earth vs. the Flying Saucers* (1956). All told, Siodmak scripted, coscripted, and/or directed over thirty feature films from 1929 to 1967, becoming in the process one of the most dependable genre scenarists in the science fiction and horror field.

Herbert L. Strock, the editor on *The Magnetic Monster*, had a long career as a film publicist and film editor. Strock drew the editor's assignment in *The Magnetic Monster*, but soon wound up taking over the director's chair from Siodmak when the producer of the film, Ivan Tors, felt that Siodmak was failing to get the right visual flavor for the piece. Then, too, much of the visual material used in *The Magnetic Monster* was stock footage lifted from a 1934 German film, *Gold*, directed by Karl Hartl. However, Siodmak retained sole directorial credit for *The Magnetic Monster*. Strock, as an editor, knew exactly how to shoot new footage to match the existing scenes. In subsequent years, Strock would direct the violent science fiction horror film *Gog* (1954), followed by *Battle Taxi* (1955), *I Was a Teenage Frankenstein* and *Blood of Dracula* (both 1957), *Rider on a Dead Horse* (1962), and *The Crawling Hand* (1963). As a director, Strock moves through his material with brutal efficiency. Perhaps his most accomplished film, *Gog*, which he was directing even as he was completing editing on *Riders to the Stars*, involves a series of gruesomely detailed murders at a remote scientific laboratory buried deep in the desert of New Mexico. Strock's participation in *Riders to the Stars* extended beyond the editor's room; he also directed a few scenes in the film as well.

Ivan Tors, born in Budapest on June 12, 1916, wrote plays in Europe in the early 1930s before moving to the United States. During World War I, he served with the Air Force, as well as the Office of Strategic Services, and gradually worked his way into filmmaking as a scenarist. His first credits as a screenwriter or coscreenwriter include Clarence Brown's *Song of Love* (1947), Robert Z. Leonard's *In the Good Old Summertime* (1949), Compton Bennett's *That Forsyte Woman* (1949), and Jack Donohue's *Watch the Birdie* (1950). But in the early 1950s, he took a turn toward the science fiction genre, and as a producer (and occasionally cowriter) he created *The Magnetic Monster*, *Riders to the Stars*, and *Gog*. By the early 1960s, however, Tors had moved away from the bleak, dehumanized future depicted in these films for more mainstream projects, particularly the television series *Flipper* and *Gentle Ben*. Similarly light theatrical feature film productions followed, including James B. Clark's *Flipper* (1963), based on Tors's TV series. Tors then turned to direction himself, completing *Rhino!* (1964), *Zebra in the Kitchen* (1965), and other similar projects before his death in 1983.

On *The Magnetic Monster*, Tors, Carlson, Siodmak, and Strock began a brief but productive relationship. Although *The Magnetic Monster* itself was neither a commercial nor critical hit, the film did recoup its production cost and proved to be a good training ground for the four men. The finished film was released on February 6, 1953, in trade screenings for critics and exhibitors. At seventy-six minutes, *The Magnetic Monster* was brief enough to be relegated to the bottom half of the double bill at movie theaters (a distribution concept that collapsed with the concomitant demise of the B film). With a budget of a mere $105,000 (Weaver, 307), the film made back its initial investment.

Directing *The Magnetic Monster*, Strock was impressed with the way Carlson handled himself on the set: "He was an actor with a photographic mind—he would merely look at a script, ask you what it was about, and then learn the lines that you wanted to put on film immediately" (Weaver, 315). Carlson's celebrity as an actor reached an all-time high after the release of the lavishly budgeted *It Came from Outer Space* on May 18, 1953. Produced in 3-D, stereophonic sound, and a 1.85:1 widescreen format, *It Came from Outer Space* was indisputably an A feature, with a much more thoughtful script than the usual 1950s alien invasion film, in part because the film was based on a short story by science fiction writer Ray Bradbury. The public responded favorably, and overnight Carlson was catapulted from B films and second leads into indisputable star status. In *It Came from Outer Space*, Carlson once again played the reliable, reasonable scientist who, despite the incredulousness and inefficiency of the authorities and townspeople, deals with the "invasion" of an alien being who has crash-landed on Earth by accident and seeks time only to effect repairs to his spaceship for the voyage home. *It Came from Outer Space*, tastefully directed by Jack Arnold, became a genre classic, and Carlson's career was truly launched.

For Richard Carlson, his newly won stardom meant that, for the first time, he would have some say over the films he agreed to appear in. But working in the 1950s, Carlson, it seems, had the sense to realize that no *major* studio would take a gamble on him as a director, even if he agreed to star in the film, and even if the film disguised itself as a straightforward science fiction thriller. Thus it was that producer Ivan Tors put together a package involving an original script by Siodmak, Tors as producer, Strock as editor, and Carlson as director and actor. Given the credentials of all involved, and Carlson's marketability as a star commodity, Tors struck a deal with United Artists to distribute the film. Production, however, had to proceed at a brisk clip; Carlson had other pressing feature film commitments, and on *Riders to the Stars* he would be performing two roles rather than just his usual presence in front of the camera.

Yet from the start, Carlson acquitted himself admirably in both departments. "He was very capable," Strock remembered. "Carlson directed *Riders to the Stars*—with my assistance—and I edited and was associate producer on that picture. We went to the U.S.C. [University of Southern California] Centrifugal Force Department, and we actually photographed Bill Lundigan in a centrifuge and spun him around and got the effects that we wanted from him" (Weaver, 315). But *Riders to the Stars* was very much a personal film for Carlson. As a result, the film went slightly over budget and over schedule. Recalls Strock, "He was not sticking to planning. He was into color and into perhaps a larger production than he expected, he needed help and he asked me . . . 'Would you come down and direct the scenes that I'm in?' I did. . . . I liked Dick quite a lot" (Weaver, 317). The production of *Riders to the Stars* was also not without its serious mishaps. During filming, one of the special effects technicians, Maxwell Smith, was seriously injured at his home while building the model rockets used in the film. Recalls Strock, "[The accident] was due to a leaky oxygen or hydrogen tank in his living room, that blew off his right arm and cut a hole in his left leg. He did recover—we all ran out and gave blood" (Weaver, 317). But despite all the problems and delays, *Riders to the Stars* was completed in less than a month and previewed to the public on January 14, 1954, to commercial and popular critical success, although few actually recognized the film's genuinely subversive social content.

From the beginning of the film, it is obvious that rather than a conventional horror film, or even a standard science fiction thriller, *Riders to the Stars* is the work of an elegist, a mournful acknowledgment of humankind's frailty and mortality. As the film opens, an experimental rocket is returning to earth, tracked by two teams of government scientists. When the rocket's payload crashes in the desert, the two teams track it down, retrieve it, and deliver it to the laboratory of Dr. Donald Stanton (Herbert Marshall). In this opening sequence, Marshall's noirish voice-over establishes the dominant mood of paranoia that pervades the film: "Our government has given us an urgent, top-priority directive. Find out if man can ever survive in space. If he can, our men must be the first . . . the security of the whole world may depend upon it." The problem facing Dr. Stanton and his colleagues is that continual bombardment by cosmic rays during flight has effectively crystallized the solid steel frame of which the rocket is made, thus rendering it hopelessly fragile and subject to disintegration at the slightest stress.

Dr. Jane Flynn (Martha Hyer), a member of the team, theorizes that meteors travel through space endlessly without disintegrating; they must, she feels, have some sort of natural protective shield which prevents their destruction. Donald Stanton seizes upon this idea and, through military channels, summons a group of scientists and pilots to a secret location in the desert, to train for a flight into space. Their objective is simple: they hope to capture meteors in space before they themselves are burned up by friction in the earth's atmosphere, and to bring the samples back for analysis. At the film's end, when only one of three pilots finally chosen for the mission returns alive, the scientists discover that a natural coating of "pure carbon" shields the meteors from destruction. Space flight will now be possible. While the plot is of course preposterous, I would argue that in itself it is really of little importance to Carlson as director and actor. What is of most concern to him in *Riders to the Stars* is the human and social cost of scientific progress.

As the Pentagon/FBI dragnet ordered by Dr. Donald Stanton sweeps into action, twelve finalists are selected for the mission. Dr. Richard Stanton (William Lundigan) is among those chosen, though he remains unaware that he will be working for his father until the midpoint of the film's narrative. Young, confident, intensely patriotic, and unmarried (this last attribute has been deemed essential for the success of the mission), Richard Stanton is the personification of the 1950s science fiction genre hero, and he accepts the assignment after just a few questions, almost immediately agreeing even though he is given only the slightest possible information by the FBI agents who seek him out.

Next, the scene shifts to "Science Hall" at an unnamed Midwestern University, where Dr. Jerome Lockwood (Richard Carlson) is conducting a seminar on theoretical mathematics when the FBI contacts him. Pale, nervous, obviously ill at ease, Jerry Lockwood is superficially another archetype of fifties sci-fi—the impractical academic. Yet in his diffident manner and his lack of self-assurance, Jerry also seems suspect, untrustworthy, and weak. Unlike Richard, Jerry accepts the assignment with great reluctance, initially declining the commission with the comment that "this sounds not at all attractive to me." Jerry finally accepts the papers from the FBI, but offers no assurance of his cooperation. Unlike Richard, Jerry hesitates and calls his fiancée, Susan Manners (Dawn Addams), a fashion model, to seek her advice. Cutting short his lecture, Jerry hurriedly drives to the photo studio where Susan is working on a magazine shoot for a car advertisement.

At the photo studio, Jerry seems even more abstracted and unsure of himself than in his classroom. And, as it turns out, his apprehension is justified: Susan, not surprisingly, is more interested in her career than Jerry's sudden proposal of marriage. If she agrees, Jerry tells her, he'll turn down the mission. But Susan refuses to commit to Jerry, accurately noting that "whatever you're getting into must be pretty bad if you're willing to get married to get out of it." When Jerry suggests they meet later that evening to discuss the matter further, Susan turns him down entirely. As a final insult, she offers to drive him to the bus station in the morning when he reports for duty: "That way," she tells him, "I can use your car while you're gone." Without another word, Susan returns to the photo shoot, leaving Jerry shattered.

In a blitz of stock footage, the twelve finalists arrive at the Snake Mountain Proving Grounds. Disembarking from a depressingly beat-up Trailways bus, the men are met by Dr. Drayden (George Eldredge), who starts them almost immediately on their course of instruction. Unbeknownst to the men, they have already been under surveillance by an FBI agent on the bus, who abruptly disqualifies one of the candidates, an astrophysicist named McBride, because of "undue anxiety . . . he's not for us." Further pressuring techniques (lengthy and overly personal questionnaires, uncomfortable waiting rooms, a distinct lack of solid information as to the nature of their assignment) eliminate several others, among them Sidney Fuller (James Best), who cracks up in the waiting room due to incipient claustrophobia.

As they are dismissed, the failed candidates leave the waiting room with ashen faces; each has displayed some socially unacceptable character trait which makes him suspect in the eyes of the government. Oddly, for this section of the film, *Riders to the Stars* seems more interested in those who fail to measure up than with those who will ultimately be chosen—several candidates are rejected for chain smoking, a "belligerent attitude," or other mildly deviant behaviors. Additional testing the following day in a high-speed centrifuge cuts more potential astronauts; the documentary brutality of this footage (which, as Herbert L. Strock noted, was *not* faked) further underscores the inhumanity and social hostility of this experimental enterprise. Grueling footage of William Lundigan on the USC centrifuge is intercut with motion picture X rays of his heart and lungs during the procedure, further heightening the hypersurveillant nature of the film.

At length, just four candidates remain: Lockwood, Stanton, Walter Gordon (Robert Karnes), and David Wells (Ken Dibbs). Wells drops out during a final briefing, denouncing the project (rather accurately) as "a suicide mission." When the elder Dr. Stanton insists that the mission is vital to national security, in order to prevent "a space platform operated by a dictatorship [that] would make slaves of all free people," Wells rejects this as "cloak and dagger stuff. Here we go again, boys! War! Killing! Every invention seems to have the same end! One thing I learned in the Army—never volunteer." With this last comment, Wells stalks off, leaving Stanton, Lockwood, and Gordon, who immediately agree to participate in the mission. But, in a penultimately neat paranoid touch, before Wells can leave the building he is warned against telling anyone of his visit to the base, on pain of imprisonment. "Don't worry," snarls Wells, "I know all about the Espionage Act . . . and the Articles of War!" as he slams the door behind him.

What is most remarkable about this entire sequence from *Riders to the Stars* is the detailed attention given by Carlson and Siodmak precisely to those who will *not* be allowed to take part in the rocket flights. It is almost as if the director and scenarist are more interested in the mechanics of Foucaultian surveillance and elimination through "social deviance" than in the exploits of the nominal heroes of the film. Indeed, up to this point, none of the three final candidates has received much screen time or anything like the typical "star buildup." Rather, what interests Carlson, Siodmak, Strock, and Tors is the terrible toll taken upon individual freedom and personal dignity to serve the demands of the state, demands that are seen as both capricious and inherently dangerous.

As the pilots prepare for their mission in the final days before the flight, Jane Flynn and Richard Stanton fall in love. But their incipient genre romance is overshadowed not only by Harry Sukman's relentlessly melancholic score but also by fellow astronaut Walter Gordon's isolationist, monosyllabically detached behavior (Gordon declines all offers of coffee, cigarettes, or idle conversation) and the increasing angst of Jerry Lockwood, who becomes even more withdrawn and insecure after his fiancée Susan sends him a "Dear John" letter (duly intercepted by base personnel) terminating their engagement. Jerry is unceremoniously brought before a tribunal of Air Force and FBI brass, brusquely told of the contents of Susan's letter (which Jerry has not yet read) and told that perhaps "his emotional problems might jeopardize his performance." Further, Dr. Delmar (Laurence Dobkin), the project's resident psychiatrist, theorizes abruptly and without any preamble that Jerry's "real subconscious motive in accepting this mission might be suicide."

Shocked by the directness (and perhaps, in light of subsequent events, the accuracy) of this accusation, Jerry momentarily affects intense anger (in an extreme close-up), but rapidly regains control of his emotions and becomes once again the artificially placid scientist of Carlson's more conventional genre films during this period. Keeping his emotions under control, Jerry argues his case and persuades the project directors to keep him on. Sounding like Ronald Reagan delivering a State of the Union address, Jerry declares dramatically in conclusion that "I want to fly that rocket!" His superiors are impressed and agree to keep Jerry on the mission. Yet, as he leaves the conference room, Jerry is now more unstable and alienated than ever. Rejected in love, distrusted by his superiors, unhappy in his work as a university professor, and now pegged as a suicide risk, Jerry Lockwood is certainly not a prime candidate for such a dangerous undertaking. But perhaps because of their need to complete the mission, or perhaps because they have been misled by Jerry's superficially calm exterior, the project managers allow him to continue on his fatal trajectory, which will climax with his violent death in space.

On the day of the flight, the astronauts and the other members of the mission team, who have practically been living on cigarettes and coffee for the entire film, admit to being "a little edgy." In perhaps the most wholly conventional scene in the film thus far, Richard Stanton and Jane Flynn passionately kiss before takeoff, pledging their love to each other,

Jane praying for Richard's safe return to earth. The three rocket ships blast off, each with one astronaut, and the mission is under way. The results, far from being triumphant, are overwhelmingly tragic. Astronaut Walter Gordon tries to scoop up a meteor that is too large to fit in his spaceship's holding tank; his meteor and the ship collide, and there is a terrific explosion. Gordon's hideously charred body, burned alive within its thermally protected space suit, is jettisoned into space. As Jerry Lockwood looks through his view finder, Gordon's ghastly remains float into his field of vision, in an image deeply surprising and disturbing for its graphic specificity. Indeed, the lingering close-up we see of Gordon's skeletal, blood-soaked face, grinning obscenely at us within the confines of his still-intact space helmet, seems more redolent of 1980s "splatter" films than 1950s mainstream sci fi.

Seeing this, Jerry goes into shock, ripping off the belts that restrain him and the hoses of his life-support system, screaming "I'm bailing out!" imagining himself back in World War II as a fighter pilot. In a trance, Jerry keeps repeating his last name over and over, as if it were a protective mantra that will return him home safely ("Lockwood . . . Lockwood . . . Lockwood . . .") until finally, as his discarded space helmet floats uselessly around the cabin, he realizes his true situation. But it is too late. Kicking frenziedly in the air in a desperate attempt to reach the control panel, Jerry accidentally trips a series of switches that trigger the booster rockets of his craft. The ship accelerates off course and careens into the distance of space, until Richard Stanton alone is left to complete the mission.

At length, Stanton locates a meteor of appropriate size, captures it, and returns to earth, where he crash lands because the fuel on his reentry rockets has been depleted through preflight miscalculations by the engineering staff. In the rather obligatory and hastily executed conclusion of *Riders to the Stars*, young Richard Stanton miraculously emerges from the crash unscathed and is reunited with Jane, while Richard's father, Donald, retrieves the meteor from the ship's hold. A coating of "pure carbon" has protected the meteor during its flight through interstellar space; the elder Dr. Stanton now confidently theorizes that the same protective coating will enable rocket ships to someday travel to "the moon, and beyond."

It should be obvious to even the most casual observer of genre films that *Riders to the Stars* is an anomaly, a harrowingly depressing and unsparing film whose canonical exclusion from the list of 1950s science fiction "classics" can be easily explained. Unlike even Herbert L. Strock's

Gog, which came out shortly after *Riders to the Stars*, and which is even more vicious and brutal in its execution of cast members in a variety of scientific "accidents" (again at a remote laboratory outpost located in the desert), Carlson's film effectively deconstructs his own carefully crafted persona as a conventional cinematic hero, portraying him indelibly as an unstable psychotic pushed over the edge by a scientific and educational establishment that cares nothing for the individual and is interested only in progress at any cost. The grim and shabby offices of the scientific laboratory, the methodically dehumanizing experiments, the lack of warmth and compassion in the film are too pervasive to be anything but premeditated. That same year, Carlson was starring in one of the fifties' most hyperparanoid television series, *I Led Three Lives*, based on the memoirs of one Herbert J. Philbrick, who was an FBI informant, a member of the Community party, and "an American husband" with a wife and children. While the series was extremely popular during its initial run, Carlson never again reached the height of genre stardom he had achieved between 1953 and 1954.

Carlson directed several other features, including the noirish Western *Four Guns to the Border* (1954), the crime drama *Appointment with a Shadow* (1958), which featured an alcoholic reporter as its protagonist, *The Saga of Hemp Brown* (1958), a routine Rory Calhoun western, and *Kid Rodelo* (1965), a downbeat, angst-ridden western that Carlson both directed and starred in. But by 1968 he was reduced to a virtual cameo in Byron Haskin's *The Power*, for Carlson's name was now firmly associated in the public's mind with genre science fiction and little else. In one of his last starring roles, as an alcoholic pianist driven to murder in Bert I. Gordon's *Tormented* (1960), Carlson perhaps presented himself, at last, as he really was—sad, introspective, probably too intelligent for an industry that deals in types rather than whole beings. This sadness beneath the surface of Carlson's persona gives *Riders to the Stars* a double resonance, as a guide to the man behind the manufactured image and an indication of how deeply he distrusted the mechanisms that had thrust him into the limelight in the first place.

In sum, in the careers of Ida Lupino and Richard Carlson, two actor-directors who were also "insider outcasts" in the social fabric of 1950s Hollywood, we see the dream machine of the cinematograph exposed for what it is: a disseminator of celluloid fantasies and instructions, designed both to pacify and satiate the viewer, but always with the enticement of something newer, fresher, more potentially liberating on the horizon—in the next film we see, or the next installment of any one of the film series franchises now proliferating within the industry. What sort of a community does Hollywood then theorize for the viewers of the Dominant cinema? What visions will the state afford us, now that the tale has been told too often and the narrative structures that once sustained the cinema have collapsed?

3

THE INDUSTRY OF TRANSCENDENCE

theorizing a community

Contemporary Dominant cinema discourse operates on two inherently false assumptions, as codified by Jean-François Lyotard in his study *The Postmodern Condition*: "first . . . that it is possible for all speakers to come to agreement on which rates or metaprescriptions are universally valid . . . [and second] that the goal of dialogue is consensus" (65). In short, the cinema of the spectacle seeks an artificial common ground among its viewers, inviting them to vicariously participate in a shared system of values based on violent change and constant action. Yet as Lyotard notes, "Consensus is only a particular state of discussion, not its end. . . . Consensus has become an outmoded and suspect value. . . . We must thus arrive at an idea and practice of justice that is not linked to that of consensus" (65–66). Lyotard specifically refers here to what he terms "language games" (66), but his comments are equally applicable to the structure of the Dominant cinema and its increasingly overwhelming "image games" as practiced by Hollywood in the late 1990s. More and more, what Hollywood seeks in its current imagistic product is the universal approval of all potential viewers, regardless of class, race, or gender—a homogeneity that is as artificial as it is inherently impossible to construct.

This superficial "agreement" of social and cultural interdependence is foregrounded particularly by the Disney corporation's attempts to extend its products and merchandising projects into the domain of the private sphere, with increasing success. Entertainment areas such as Disneyland, Walt Disney World, and EPCOT Center are precisely what they appear to be—all-inclusive environments in which the values of a specific corporation and its attendant totemic constructs are literally paraded in front of the consumer-viewer as the only possible cultural universe one can inhabit. Mickey Mouse, Donald Duck, Goofy, Beauty and the Beast, Aladdin, the Little Mermaid, Hercules—all of these totemic icons, either created by Disney or appropriated from myth or popular culture, form the central imagistic cluster of the world of Disney. Now, in its instantly produced community of Celebration, Florida, the Disney group seeks to restructure nothing less than the fabric of American social existence, by artificially forcing consensus on those who enter into the community's zone of influence and control.

As Michael Pollan notes, "It may be Disney's boldest innovation at Celebration to have established a rather novel form of democracy, one that is based on consumerist values. For many of the people I met there the measure is not self-rule but corporate sensitivity to their needs" (58). Just as Disney has sought to redesign and thus redefine Manhattan's Times Square with its extensive renovation of the 42nd Street area, replete with shops selling Disney merchandise, yoked together with appropriately chosen restaurants and entertainment complexes, in Celebration, Disney's social architects seek to create not only an artificial and rigidly enforced form of social consensus but also a return to the overwhelmingly white-dominated social culture of early twentieth-century America. Celebration was spun off from some ten thousand acres of land surrounding Walt Disney World in Florida that the company in the early 1980s determined would never be used for the amusement park itself. "By de-annexing the 10,000 acres and populating them with taxpayers, Disney could please local governments and smooth the approval process for future theme park projects, like its new Animal Kingdom," Pollan notes (59).

But this new social experiment, a return to the Main Street of Walt Disney's youth at the beginning of this century, comes with numerous rules and regulations attached, all of which a potential home buyer must contractually agree to before moving to Celebration. These include the proscriptions that "all visible window coverings must be either white or off-white. A resident may hold only one garage sale in any 12-month period. A single political sign (measuring 18 by 24 inches) may be posted 45 days prior to an election" (Pollan, 78), and so on. But the greatest internal controversy that Celebration has experienced thus far surrounds its "school of tomorrow . . . a model for education into the next century" (Disney brochure, as cited in Pollan, 63). This kindergarten through twelfth grade facility opened in the fall of 1996 and offered to its students a nonjudgmental environment in which "tests are few, and there are 'narrative assessments' instead of grades. ('This is a place,' the principal said, 'where nobody fails.')" (Pollan, 63).

When a group of some thirty parents gathered together to object to these pedagogical practices, Disney responded with a full-scale public-relations blitz, including the creation of a Dream Team—"a parents organization that lent moral support to the teachers, who were thought to be demoralized by the controversy" (Pollan, 63). But perhaps most tellingly, those parents who objected to the curriculum of Celebration School were rapidly ostracized by the other members of the community, the self-styled "positive" parents who found nothing wrong with the way in which their children were being taught. Dissenting parents became social outcasts within the newly constructed community. As one disillusioned resident put it, "Those of us who weren't sprinkled with pixie dust were ostracized . . . and it was orchestrated by Disney. We were treated in a very ugly manner . . . instead of facing up to problems . . . they hold pep rallies!" (Pollan, 76).

What is finally most ominous about the disagreement swirling about Celebration School and, by implication, the value system it seeks to impart to its students, is that the new corporate/domestic culture created by Disney within this surreal, experimental community brooks no dissent. As Pollan notes, "Large unscripted public meetings where residents might speak freely have been scrupulously avoided; in their place, Disney has held 'focus groups' about the school" (76). At length, a small group of families decided that the loss of personal freedom and expression wasn't worth the hyperreal vision of small town America that Celebration seemed to afford to its residents: they packed up and left. Although the Disney Corporation at first sought to force the departing families to sign "an agreement promising never to reveal their reasons for leaving Celebration" (Pollan, 76), eventually the disgruntled homeowners were allowed to sell their property and depart, no strings attached.

But for those who remain, Celebration has proven that while it may offer the ultimate "gated community" to its residents, the vision of domestic harmony it presents comes at the price of individual expression. As Lyotard posited, for Disney and the overwhelming number of residents of Celebration, the goal of dialogue truly is consensus. Without universal agreement, there is no unified field. This is the same sort of viewer homogeneity that Dreamworks SKG, Paramount, Universal, MGM, and the other major studios seek to create in their own telecultural imagistic "communities"—an environment that offends no one and seeks to please everyone. But such an objective is only realized when all the edges of normative societal discourse have been rounded off, when consensus is seen not only as a goal but as the only possible result of all interaction between the viewer and the major studios' product.

Appearance, as the white or off-white houses and generally uniform look of Celebration informs one, is all. A distressing dialogue between Hollywood icon Sharon Stone and actress Lili Taylor throws this into sharper focus. Admiring Stone's business acumen in getting roles in a series of big-budget films, starting with her breakthrough performance in Paul Verhoeven's sex-and-violence-drenched thriller *Basic Instinct* (1992), Taylor notes that "I think it's neat that you've been able to combine the business and the acting so well, which is something I'm actually not doing that well with. . . . I'm having trouble getting some *independent films* [my emphasis], because either my stock's not high enough or I'm not a smart enough business woman" (Hirschberg 1997b:79). This statement in itself gives one pause in considering the current system of star commodification practiced by both the majors and the minors in Hollywood. Taylor, the star of such films as Nancy Savoca's *Household Saints* (1993), Mary Harron's *I Shot Andy Warhol* (1996), and Abel Ferrara's *The Addiction* (1995), is one of the most original and fiercely independent actors of her generation; producers and directors should be lining up to work with her. But perhaps her "look" isn't quite right. As Taylor comments, "In the scripts that I've seen, if a woman is pretty, she loses some of the depth. But I'd love to play, you know, a beautiful woman who has depth"—in response to which Stone advises, "Go to a premiere. Wear a low-cut dress . . . pull your hair off your face." In short, sell yourself to the public as a commodity—make yourself appealing to the widest possible audience. Taylor continues, "I don't want to make myself out to be this starving actress who can't get a job. It's not that way at all. But it's kind of amazed me a little bit because I thought: 'Well, this is my little family, my little independent family. I'm accepted. That's great. I'll be doing this all my life.' [But] they're playing by different rules now than when I started out" (Hirschberg 1997b:81).

Indeed they are. As critic Neal Gabler notes,

> It is possible that Hollywood has never been as esthetically divided as it is now. As I write, the films reaping the critical hosannas are *Boogie Nights*, *The Ice Storm*, *Telling Lies in America* and *The Full Monty*, all of which have been released by indies and all of which are smallish pictures that appeal to audiences seeking intellectual, emotional or esthetic stimulation. Meanwhile, the films reaping the top grosses include *I Know What You Did Last Summer*, *The Devil's Advocate*, *Kiss the Girls* and *The Peacemaker*, all of which have been released by major studios and all of which appeal to audiences interested in action and cheap thrills. A film like Warner Brothers's *L.A. Confidential*, a moody, modern noir that manages to combine intelligence with action, is now the rare exception. (Gabler, 76)

Gabler's explanation for this binaristic split in viewership is that the traditional audience base has collapsed, in part because of the rise of television, and in part because the precipitous drop in movie attendance after World War II will no longer sustain what he terms the "middle" picture, a film that is neither a blockbuster nor an exploitation programmer. As Gabler reminds us,

> From 78.8 million weekly admissions in 1946, or over four billion for the year, the number of viewers has steadily and precipitously declined all the way down to 58 million by 1950, 25.1 million by 1960, to a low of 15.8 million in 1971. At the same time, the percentage of recreational dollars spent on the movies was taking a similar nose dive. (Gabler, 76)

Hollywood

In this sort of economic environment, only a big-budget blockbuster can generate real grosses at the box office—a film that relies on spectacle and gloss to sell itself to the consumer. Even films such as Kevin Reynolds's *Waterworld* (1995), which went notoriously over budget and did poorly in its U.S. release, "are more likely to be profitable abroad because they have lavish production values to display" (Gabler, 77). And indeed, it is the major Hollywood blockbusters that account for an overwhelming percentage of the international exhibition dollar. Thompson and Bordwell note that "in the early 1990s, approximately 4,000 theatrical feature films were made worldwide. The U.S. majors and independents produced only 300 to 400 of these, yet these films attract 70 percent of global box office revenues" (720). In addition, home video rentals and sales accounted for an increasingly important portion of a feature film's total revenues; "by 1986, at least half of major film companies' domestic revenues came from video cassette sales" (Thompson and Bordwell, 703). And while dialogue-driven, narrative-based films can often translate poorly in overseas markets, the common language of spectacle, violence, and destruction cuts across all territorial and linguistic boundaries, surviving even the exigencies of dubbing and/or subtitling to reach the widest possible audience base. For in America, Gabler argues, the core audience which midcentury Hollywood counted on simply doesn't "exist anymore."

> In the past, the industry didn't pay much attention to its audience profile. With a constituency nearly as large as the population itself, the old Hollywood always thought in terms of *the* audience, never

an audience. It always tried to make films that appealed to the largest possible number of viewers, which is why movies were the art of the middle.

By the '70's, however, it was clear *the* audience did not exist anymore. Instead, as admissions had plunged through the '50's and '60's, the audience realigned itself so that it was no longer a cross section of the country. More specifically, the moviegoers who had deserted film were primarily those moviegoers over 40. A result was that the movies became a medium for the young.

Of all the factors affecting motion pictures, the age of the audience is probably the most salient. According to a survey conducted by Opinion Research Corporation for the Motion Picture Association of America last year, 67 percent of the audience is under 40, even though they represent just 50 percent of the population. What's more, 50 percent of the audience is between 12 and 29 years old, though they are now only 30 percent of the population. And even these figures understate the case, because young moviegoers go to the movies far more frequently than older ones: 26 percent of those 18 and older went once a month, compared with 48 percent of those between 12 and 17. (Gabler, 77–78)

And the young, quite predictably, demand continual action and nonstop spectacle to keep them entertained. Michael Curtiz, Dorothy Arzner, Jean Renoir, Yasujiro Ozu, Howard Hawks, Ernst Lubitsch, Fritz Lang (to name just a few directors from the classical age of cinema) were all creators of commercial projects that combined a strong narrative base with an instinctive understanding of the requirements of then-contemporary cinematic commerce. Viewed today, by a younger, less patient audience, their films seem hopelessly quaint and naive. For one thing, most films of the 1930s–1960s are in black and white, which is no longer a medium but rather a stylistic effect. Color replaced black and white as the basic vehicle for cinematic commerce in the mid-1960s.

Fueling the current switch to spectacle as a replacement for narrative is the shared assumption (by both audience numbers and filmmakers) that bigger *is* better, or, as the trailer for the 1998 version of *Godzilla* bluntly puts it, "Size *does* matter." Producer Lawrence Gordon, who specializes in spectacular blockbusters like John McTiernan's *Die Hard* (1988) and Walter Hill's *48 HRS.* (1982), sums it up with these comments, in a conversation with independent producer Christine Vachon, whose credits include Todd Haynes's *Poison* (1991), Mary Harron's *I Shot Andy*

Warhol (1996), and Larry Clark's *Kids* (1996), all low- to medium-budgeted films, which did well but not spectacularly at the box office. In response to Vachon's suggestion that Gordon might consider making smaller films, Gordon responds:

> Listen, the one thing I do know is the difference between a big movie and a small movie: sacrifice and attitude. That is all it is. It is more fun to take your time. It is more fun to have the best. It is more fun to have the most, the biggest and powerful. It is more fun. Would you rather play with a little tiny electric train or a gigantic electric train? (Hirschberg 1997a:107)

When Vachon responds that "sometimes there is a price for the bigger train set," Gordon counters that "even with straight-to-video movies, they want to know who is in it" (Hirschberg 1997a:107). Both Gordon and Vachon are, of course, right. Making a film with unlimited financial resources is a heady experience, but the film itself becomes answerable to a plethora of bankers, investment syndicates, focus groups, audience-testing sessions, and the like; it loses the opportunity to be responsible only to itself. This remains one of the central paradoxes of genre cinema. The genre film must reach the widest possible audience, and so it is subjected to every possible test of audience response.

Some contemporary mainstream directors, such as Richard Donner, Walter Hill, John Carpenter, Penny Marshall, and Martin Scorsese seek to inject their personal value systems into even the most mundane of their films, as secret codes to be deciphered by astute viewers who care to take the time to search for them. But these images are so subliminal that they won't distract the core audience seeking merely escapist entertainment. And yet, to be truly involving, the spectacle and destruction must remain, despite its scope and all-encompassing frenzy, a personal affair for the members of the coproducing audience. As Fareed Zakaria notes, "The key to a successful action movie today is righteous violence. Audiences cannot simply partake in gruesome barbarism; they must feel redeemed by it" (132). Contemporary action films often begin their spectacle/narrative with particularly cruel scenes of sadism and violence, perpetrated by the villain and/or his henchmen in the pursuit of their particular unlawful goal.

And yet, who decides what pictures we will finally see? Despite our conspicuous appetite for violence, we seem particularly obsessed, in this age of HIV/AIDS, with precisely those images we wish to see and those we do *not* wish to see. This is particularly true of Queer Cinema, which the Dominant cinema decisively rejects. Projects such as Frank Oz's *In and Out* (1997) are little more than token gestures released to a generally uncomprehending and hostile commercial audience; but even such timid approaches as this often fare poorly at the hetero-dominant box office. The far more provocative and serious work dealing with same-sex themes is left to the marginal cinema. Derek Jarman's *Queer Edward II* (aka *Edward II*, 1992), for example, is a decidedly non-Dominant cinema project, and one of the most compelling in a series of Queer activist films from the outspoken British director, whose status as an HIV-positive filmmaker afforded great urgency to his uncompromising and boldly beautiful work. Indeed, *Queer Edward II* is a brilliant example of the new filmmaking renaissance in England, which began in the early 1980s and shows no sign of abating.

In the beginnings of the new-British movement, despite Margaret Thatcher's draconian fiscal and social policies, a small but determined group of filmmakers worked throughout the decade to create films of genius and startling originality—films quite unlike those turned out by Hollywood for mass audience consumption. Often working under the twin pressures of low budgets and tight shooting schedules, filmmakers as dissimilar as Terence Davies (*The Long Day Closes*, 1992), Sally Potter (*The Gold Diggers*, 1984), Julien Temple (*Absolute Beginners*, 1986), Michael Radford (*Another Time, Another Place*, 1983), Stephen Frears (*My Beautiful Launderette*, 1985), Neil Jordan (*Mona Lisa*, 1986), Clare Peploe (*High Season*, 1987), and many others created a shared body of work that questioned the repressive milieu of Thatcherism. England in the 1980s and early 1990s was not an easy place to make films, even with the help of the British Film Institute Production Fund and Channel 4, the British television network. Films had to be made quickly and cheaply; budgets on these projects rarely exceeded $2,000,000 and were often much less: Derek Jarman's *Caravaggio* (1986) was shot in a warehouse in "London's derelict dockland" for a mere £475,000 (Jarman 1986:6).

Diagnosed in the late 1980s as being HIV positive, Jarman continued making films at a torrential pace. After his apprentice work as a costume designer for the British director Ken Russell, Jarman began his career as a director with such early works as *Sebastiane* (1976), a film about the martyrdom of St. Sebastian, and continued on through *Caravaggio*, *War Requiem* (1988), *The Last of England* (1987), *The Garden* (1990), and *Wittgenstein* (1993). In these films, Jarman fashioned a painterly, somewhat florid but always arresting visual style that depends a good deal on light, fabrics, colors, and skin textures to transform bare studio space into a magical realm. Ever the experimentalist, making films primarily to please himself rather than an imagined audience, Jarman contrived to make films that departed from the conventional syntactic structures of narrative cinema, coupled with daring innovations in technical execution as well. *The Garden* is almost wholly improvised, rather than following a finished script. *The Last of England* mixes regular 35mm film with home video Camcorder footage blown up to large-screen size. *War Requiem* featured Sir Laurence Olivier's final role, that of an aging veteran of World War II, and also mixed small-format video with 35mm theatrical imagery. *Caravaggio* startled many viewers because of Jarman's deliberate use of anachronisms (typewriters, motor scooters) in what was otherwise a faithfully accurate historical recreation.

Queer Edward II, based on the play by Christopher Marlowe, tells the story of Edward's corruption and eventual death through his love for Gaveston, his aide, as brought about by Lightborn, a Luciferian figure who murders Edward with a white-hot poker. Jarman uses Marlowe's text as the jumping-off point for a brilliant series of tableaux, in which everyone from pop singer Annie Lennox to veteran British performers Dudley Sutton and Jill Balcon assist Jarman in reinterpreting Marlowe's play. *Queer Edward II* seems closest to *Caravaggio* in many ways, but it is a deeply impassioned work, "dedicated to the repeal of all anti-gay laws, particularly Section 28," the British statute forbidding the production and/or exhibition of films, books, or plays that deal with gay or lesbian themes, no matter how serious their intent. There is a complete absence of sensationalism in the work, which emerges as a sculptural and austere meditation on the mechanics of power, love, betrayal, and violence that is as applicable today as it was in Marlowe's era.

Jarman kept a diary of the shooting of *Queer Edward II*, published by the British Film Institute in 1991, which gives fascinating insights into the production of the work and features nearly one hundred full-page stills of the cast and crew creating the film at Bray Studios, one of England's oldest production facilities. Jarman was often unwell during the production of *Queer Edward II*, as his shooting diary notes, and on a number of production days had to use the services of a "ghost director" (Ken Butler) to shoot scenes that Jarman had thoroughly "storyboarded." Early on in the diary, Jarman notes that each morning during the film's production he had to "swallow, with increasing difficulty: a cordial of Ritafer, Fansidar, AZT, Pirodoxin, one Calcium Folinate (to counteract the Ritafer) and two Carba-mazapepine" (1991:2) simply to survive. That he did survive and kept on working under such immensely difficult circumstances is a tribute both to Jarman's tenacity of spirit and the uncompromising ferocity of his vision. Before his death, Jarman managed to create one final film, *Blue* (1994), an extended meditation on his impending extinction set against the backdrop of a pale blue screen—one continual color block for the entire length of the film. It is an anguished, furious, and altogether personal film, just the sort of cinema that Dominant cinematic practice would never tolerate. Derek Jarman died in 1994.

Hanif Kureishi, once the scenarist for director Stephen Frears, made his debut as a director with *London Kills Me* (1992), an examination of the most marginalized aspects of British society in present-day post-Thatcher London. The film's determinedly undramatic approach to its material (a group of junkies wander through the bleak landscape of 1990s Britain, searching for food, drugs, and employment) assured a mostly negative critical reception. The direct antithesis of Kureishi's film is Danny Boyle's *Trainspotting* (1996), which uses freeze-frames, captions and intertitles, reverse motion, and other empty yet eye-catching cinematic tricks to transform what should have been a rather harrowing tale into *A Hard Day's Night* on heroin (*Trainspotting* contains several allusions to the Beatles and Richard Lester's exuberant 1964 comedy). *Trainspotting* received generally excellent notices and wide distribution; Kureishi's film went almost immediately to home video.

Stephen Frears, who began his career as a director with such interesting films as *Gumshoe* (1971), *My Beautiful Launderette* (1985), and *Sammy and Rosie Get Laid* (1987), attempted to enter the mainstream cinema with *Hero* (1992) and *Mary Reilly* (1996), two of his least successful films. On the other hand, Frears has continued to direct smaller, more personal films such as *Dangerous Liaisons* (1988), *The Grifters* (1990), *The Snapper* (1993), and *The Van* (1996), which have proven to be both critical and modest commercial successes. This demonstrates that, for some directors, it is possible to work in both the Dominant and the marginal cinema without a crippling degree of compromise.

Other contemporary non-Dominant cinéastes include Chantal Akerman, who created a vision at once despairing and romantic in an outpouring of features and short films which includes *A Couch in New York* (*Un divan à New York*, 1996), *Portrait of a Young Girl at the End of the 1960s in Brussels* (*Portrait d'une jeune fille de la fin des années 60 à Bruxelles*, 1994), *D'Est* (1993), *Night and Day* (*Nuit et jour*, 1991), *I'm Hungry, I'm Cold* (*J'ai faim, j'ai froid*, 1984), *All Night Long* (*Toute une nuit*, 1982), *The Meetings of Anna* (*Les Rendez-vous d'Anna*, 1978), *Jeanne Dielman, 23 Quai du Commerce*,

1080 *Bruxelles* (1975), *I, You, She, He* (*Je, tu, il, elle*, 1974), and numerous other works. Akerman remains one of the most vital and aggressively independent filmmakers and installation artists currently working in film and video.

Filmmaker Idrissa Ouedraogo has created a series of compelling visions of life within African society (mainly in Burkina Faso) in a torrent of films since the early 1980s, most recently with *Kini and Adams* (1997) as well as his earlier films *Afrique mon Afrique* (1994), *The Heart's Cry* (*Le Cri du coeur*, 1994), *Gorki* (1994), *Samba Traore* (1993), *Karim and Sala* (1991), *Obi* (1991), *Tilai* (The Law) (1990), *Yaaba* (1989), *Les Écuelles* (1983), and *Poko* (1981). Ouedraogo is only one of many African filmmakers working to create a new cultural history for African viewers and historians. Other African artists of note include Ousmane Sembene, whose many films include *Tauw* (Senegal, 1969), in which a young unemployed dockworker deals with street life in Senegal, and his day-to-day struggle for existence and dignity; *Borom Sarret* (Senegal, 1964), Sembene's first short film, about a cart-driver in Dakar and his daily rounds; and *Guelwaar* (Senegal, 1993), a political comedy in which the body of a village patriarch is buried in the wrong graveyard. Filmmaker Sarah Maldoror created *Sambizanga* (Angola, 1972), a film centering on a young woman's search for her jailed husband. Mahama Johnson Traoré directed *Njangaan* (Senegal, 1974), an important and sharply realistic exposé of authoritarianism, religious submission, and the devastating effects of colonialism, with the Koranic school standing as a symbol for Senegal's ingrained colonial structures.

Desiré Écaré created a sensual and romantic feature film, *Faces of Women* (Ivory Coast, 1985), in two parts. The first section depicts a graphically lyrical love affair between a young man and a woman in contemporary Africa; the second section deals with an aging matriarch who struggles to hold her family together, while consolidating a large commercial fishing business she has built up over the years. Typically, Écaré made this film with little financial backing. Production was begun in the mid-1970s, but lack of funds caused him to shut down production for ten years while he found the necessary backing to complete the film; hence the production's two-part structure. Ababacar Samb created the political allegory *Jom, The Story of a People* (Senegal, 1982), an inquiry into Senegal's colonialist past that is surprisingly lavish and yet deeply ferocious in its political outrage at the historical incursion of the white colonial influence. These are just a few of the films and filmmakers coming out of Africa at the end of the millennium; none of them has received widespread commercial distribution. Instead, these films are confined to the art house and museum circuit and remain largely unseen by the general public, who, through no fault of their own, often do not even know of their existence.

Jane Campion began her career with a series of student shorts, including *After Hours* (1984), *A Girl's Own Story* (1984), *Passionless Moments* (1983), *An Exercise in Discipline—Peel* (1982), and the TV film *Two Friends* (1986), before breaking through with the features *Sweetie* (1989), *An Angel at My Table* (1990; a television miniseries on the life of writer Janet Frame), and finally *The Piano* (1993), which decisively launched her on the international cinematic landscape. Since then Campion has directed an interesting, updated adaptation of Henry James's *The Portrait of a Lady* (1996), which received wide distribution and generally excellent reviews. Isaac Julien directed the highly influential Queer film *Looking for Langston* (1988), before going on to create the feature film *Young Soul Rebels* (1991), *The Darker Side of Black* (1993), and *Frantz Fanon: Black Skin, White Mask* (1996). Terence Davies directed a number of short 16mm apprentice films before directing *The Long Day Closes* (1992) and *Distant Voices, Still Lives* (1988), part of a series of Davies's group of autobiographical films, in which he examines his working-class upbringing in post-Blitz Britain.

Most of the directors mentioned above came to prominence in the late 1970s through the early 1990s; some have embraced the Dominant cinema, while others have remained relatively independent. All these directors first approached their material from a multiplicity of cultural, social, and sexual viewpoints, creating works of originality, depth, and beauty; it is both limiting and myopic to dismiss these works as "fringe" productions. The social concerns these filmmakers address vary according to their political, sexual, economic, and racial positioning within the overall discourse of film theory and history, but in each case, these films have been produced against the formidable opposition of a system of film production that seeks only to satisfy the lowest common denominator in its audience members. Perhaps this is why there is a recent resurgence of interest in the work of visual artists who deal in just those images which comprise the phantom zone of contemporary visual culture.

Underground filmmaker Jack Smith created a series of films and theatrical spectacles which heralded with cheerful glee the destruction of American popular culture, in such films as *Flaming Creatures* (1963) and gloriously "pasty" theatrical extravaganzas as *Rehearsal for the Destruction of Atlantis* (1965). Smith presents us with the collapse of spectacle, exposing the fraud and deception behind every gesture, every pose of the theatrical/cinema machine (Carr, 39–40). Smith was a pioneer of the Queer cinema, but in more recent films such as Meena Nanji's *It Is a Crime* (1996), Fanny Jacobsen and Collen Cruise's *Lost in Telespace: The Loneliness of the Long Distance Lover* (1996), Mickey Chen and Ming-Hsiu's *Not Simply a Wedding Banquet* (1997), and Warren Sonbert's brutal, posthumous film *Whiplash* (1995–1997), Smith's work of deconstructing the Dominant cinema ideology is carried forward.

Indeed, as these new works are released to the public, they bring with them revivals of ancillary works that helped pave the way for this new cinematic consciousness. The Eleventh New York Lesbian and Gay Experimental Film and Video Festival in New York City in 1997 presented not only an abundance of new work but also the revival of such important Queer films as José Rodriguez-Soltero's feature film *Lupe* (1966), a sixty-minute meditation on the career and demise of 1930s–1940s Hollywood screen star Lupe Velez, with erstwhile Warhol superstar Mario Montez in the title role. The same festival also screened an extremely rare reel of Jack Smith performing *I Was a Male Yvonne de Carlo for the Lucky Landlord Underground* (1975), in which Smith plays the role of Yvonne de Carlo in an inspired series of improvisations. Like most truly underground cinema, Smith's work, and the films, videotapes, and theatrical performances of his compatriots, teeters continually on the brink of social and financial collapse, inherently stretching to the limits the minimal resources available. The images created by these filmmakers signal the exhaustion of that which is known, a desire for new systems of transgressive reinscription, and the writing of both the sacred and the profane across the consciousness of the existing visual landscape.

Why is so much of this work marginalized? Simply put, much of the attention in film studies, and thus in exhibition/production/distribution, centers around traditional Hollywood filmmaking, which encodes in its imagistic and narrative structures rigid concepts of class, race, gender, and iconic standardization that narrate one potential story (that of the usually white, male, middle-class protagonists) over the stories of any of the other characters (men and women of color, in particular). Mas'ud Zavarzadeh's text *Seeing Films Politically* foregrounded this problem in filmic discourse with great cogency and urgency. Zavarzadeh's commentary is, for the most part, concentrated on those racial groups marginalized by current cinema discourse, but one should also examine the erasure of the feminine in filmic practice, and concomitantly, the lack of attention and distribution given to foreign films outside the major metropolitan centers, such as New York and London. But this in itself is not surprising. The Dominant cinema has long ago successfully rewritten cinema history, particularly its beginnings, to elide the fact that when it was first conceived, cinema was very far from the patriarchal form of societal discourse that has become so ingrained in our collective consciousness.

Until the early 1920s, women occupied a prominent position within the industry, directing and producing films that were both commercial and critical successes. Women were responsible for some of the earliest and most influential work in cinema history, beginning with the production of Alice Guy Blaché's film *The Cabbage Fairy* for Gaumont in 1896. Many claim that *The Cabbage Fairy* is the first film narrative directed by either a man or a woman. A reevaluation of the genealogy of the cinema must inevitably begin with the works of those women filmmakers whose films have been "erased" from cinema history. Women worked in Hollywood up until 1920 with a great deal of freedom, writing, producing, and starring in their own projects with great regularity and success, particularly for Carl Laemmle's Universal Pictures (the studio, of course, is still active today).

But after 1920, the number of women allowed to make films in Hollywood dwindled drastically. Some of the many films directed by women, both in Hollywood and abroad but yet somehow eliminated from critical and historical review, include Alice Guy Blaché's films *Black Maria* (1897), *He* (1897), *The Mummy* (1897), *Pierrot's Christmas* (1897), *Midnight* (1897), *The Legend of St. Nicholas* (1897), *Passion* (1902), *The First Cigarette* (1904), *Dreams of an Opium Eater* (1906), *The Knife* (1906), *A Child's Sacrifice* (1910), *Rose of the Circus* (1911), *The Doll* (1911), *The Violin Maker of Nuremberg* (1911), *The Detective's Dog* (1912), *Canned Harmony* (1912), *A House Divided* (1913), *Matrimony's Speed Limit* (1913), *The Pit and the Pendulum* (1913), *The Tigress* (1914), *The Monster and the Girl* (1914), *The Vampire* (1915), *The Soul of Magdalene* (1917), *Out of the Fog* (1919), *The Brat* (1919), and Blaché's final film, *Tarnished Reputations* (1920).

Blaché's films explored such syntactical strategies as cross-cutting for dramatic effect and/or ironic juxtaposition, the use of close-ups; regendering of roles (particularly in *The Detective's Dog*, in which the detective himself is tied to a log in a sawmill and rescued by his wife), location shooting, and a more naturalistic style of acting than was generally favored for the period. Blaché's career has been eclipsed by that of the better-known D. W. Griffith, Edwin S. Porter, and other male directors of the period, yet Blaché's work is of equal importance and value, both aesthetically and from a historical viewpoint. Only a dozen or so films by Blaché are known to survive; those that *do* still exist should be programmed on a constant basis in film history courses and film archives, to correct the current "historical" perspective (or lack of it) in film studies.

In Europe, Germaine Dulac produced a series of experimental films, of which the most famous are *The Smiling Madame Beudet* (1923) and *The Seashell and the Clergyman* (1934). Lois Weber directed and produced a pioneering series of socially conscious films, including *His Brand* (1913), *The Eyes of God* (1913), *The Hypocrites* (1914), *Jewel* (1915), *Discontent* (1916), *John Needham's Double* (1916), *The Hand That Rocks the Cradle* (1917), *The Man Who Dared God* (1917), *When a Girl Loves* (1919), *Forbidden* (1919), *The Blot* (1921), *What Do Men Want?* (1921), *Sensation Seekers* (1927), and *White Heat* (1934). During the 1920s, Weber was one of the highest paid directors in Hollywood, tackling issues such as birth control, women's rights, and suffrage, producing films that were entertaining (and hence profitable) as well as thought-provoking. Dorothy Arzner directed a series of excellent films for Columbia and MGM during the 1930s and 1940s, including *Fashions for Women* (1927), *Get Your Man* (1927), *Merrily We Go To Hell* (1932), *Christopher Strong* (1933; with a young Katharine Hepburn), *Craig's Wife* (1936), *The Bride Wore Red* (1937), *Dance Girl Dance* (1940; a feminist deconstruction of Burlesque shows, featuring a deeply felt performance by Lucille Ball), and *First Comes Courage* (1943; in which Merle Oberon plays an undercover Norwegian Resistance fighter during World War II).

Producer-writer-director-actress Cleo Madison made a series of brilliantly evocative two-reel films for Universal, including *A Soul Enslaved* (1916), *His Bitter Cup* (1916), *The Guilty One* (1916), and *Her Defiance* (1916), all of which were commercial and critical successes. Of all of Madison's films, only *Her Defiance* is known to survive, and it gives some indication of Madison's quadruple-threat stature as a creative artist. In that film, Madison plays a young woman who finds she is pregnant while still unmarried. She is nearly forced into marriage with a much older man whom she despises to "legitimize" the child, but rebels at the last minute and runs off to New York to have the child in solitude. After the child's birth, she works scrubbing office floors at night to bring the child up. A last-minute reconciliation with the father of the child is rather forced, but within the confines of the narrative structure imposed by audience expectations of the period, *Her Defiance* is a compact and compelling film.

Other early women directors included Ruth Stonehouse, Lule Warrenton, Grace Cunard, Ida May Park, Margery Wilson, Dorothy Davenport-Reid, Frances Marion, Kathlyn Williams, Marguerite Bertsch, and Nell Shipman; all made films worthy of our extended attention today. If we are to begin to rewrite the history of cinema and to expand the artificial, selective, sexist, and arbitrary cinematic canon that exists today, we could do a great deal worse than to consider these groundbreaking films by women who paved the way for today's feminist directors, including such disparate voices as Penny Marshall, Lizzie Borden, and Julie Dash. The career of Julie Dash offers an interesting departure point for the continuation of this discussion, in that Dash is an African-American woman who, in the 1940s or 1950s, would no doubt have been denied any chance to produce or direct a film at all. After the success of her thirty-minute short film *Illusions* (1982), about a young black woman who is employed by a mythical Hollywood film studio in the 1940s, Dash went on to produce the epic feature film *Daughters of the Dust* (1992), which created an international sensation. Since then, Dash has directed the TV feature *Subway Stories: Tales from the Underground* (1997), and it seems that she is launched on the beginning of a promising career. But how many other African-American women will follow Julie Dash's example, and perhaps more importantly, how many women will be *allowed* to do so? Hollywood still discriminates against women directors, even on the most commercial projects. Forest Whitaker directed the feminist comedy-drama *Waiting to Exhale* in 1995; why wasn't Julie Dash, or Darnell Martin (director of the ferocious comedy *I Like It Like That*, 1994) given a shot at the project?

One should also consider the films of Oscar Micheaux and Spencer Williams, two African-American filmmakers working at the fringes of the industry in the 1930s and 1940s. Their works, including Micheaux's *Lying Lips* (1939), *Swing!* (1939), *God's Step Children* (1937), *Murder in Harlem* (1935), *The Girl from Chicago* (1932), *Veiled Aristocrats* (1932), *An Exile* (1931), *A Daughter of the Congo* (1930), *Body and Soul* (1925), *Birthright* (1924), *Deceit* (1923), and *Within Our Gates* (1920), along with Williams's *Juke Joint* (1947), *Dirty Gertie from Harlem U.S.A.* (1946), *Go Down Death* (1944), and *The Blood of Jesus* (1941), are also eminently worthy of revival and reconsideration. For the most part, these films have been consigned to the phantom zone because of the unrelenting cheapness of their physical production. Working at blinding speed, Micheaux and Williams were forced to complete their features on budgets as low as $10,000, using short ends of raw stock, out-of-date equipment, and friends' apartments as shooting locations. Furthermore, the finished films would never be allowed to play white-owned movie houses. They were relegated to a string of black-owned-and-operated theaters throughout the United States, which served as the sole purveyors of non-Dominant cinema for African-Americans of the era.

To criticize the sets, lighting, acting, and production values of these films is to miss the point entirely. It is a miracle that such films as *The Blood of Jesus* or *Veiled Aristocrats* exist at all. Presenting a world in which African-Americans operate on all levels of society without interference from whites, these productions offered their audiences the vision of a time and place in which racial equality already existed. White cops bow deferentially to well-to-do African-Americans as they stride through the streets of Harlem after midnight on the way to an after-hours party; heterotopic families live in middle-class affluence, untroubled by racism or poverty. Contemporary African-American audiences were well aware that this vision was a fantasy. But these films served as a blueprint for what might some day be reality, even though the creation of the films themselves was the result of strict racial segregation in the cinema, both on and off the screen.

One manifestation of the racism, marginalization, and sexism perpetuated by the Dominant cinema is the ratings system. The ratings system functions at best as a vague series of guidelines as to the actual content of any particular motion picture, and in many cases is part of the lure that compels us to attend certain films in the first place. We expect a certain level of nonviolence from a "G" film, a commodity which now seems particularly in demand, as witness the flood of films (both live action and animated) from Disney and various rival studios in the late 1990s. These films promise a "family viewing experience," something akin to having country music icon Garth Brooks introduce Frank Capra's *It's a Wonderful Life* (1946) during the film's annual Christmas appearance on network television, in order to make the black-and-white images of Capra's film somehow more accessible and contemporary to an audience of the young and the restless.

A PG-13 rating, originally created specifically for Steven Spielberg's *Indiana Jones and the Temple of Doom* (1984), promises a certain amount of mayhem, but certainly with less intensity than the parade of graphic violence unspooled in an R-rated film, which precertifies an abundance of violence, nudity, simulated sex, and/or coarse language. An X rating (which the Dominant cinema regards as the kiss of death) signifies a film that traffics in images and/or aural constructs which societal consensus has declared to be border-line utterances. These X-rated films (other than pure sex films, which also receive an X rating) receive scant distribution and thus have little hope of recouping their production costs, even if they are labelled NC-17.

This evaluative process is ritualistically schematized and carefully catalogued, down to the last frame, noting that which we may see or not see, according to a film's given rating. Far from being a deterrent, R films apparently provide most members of the contemporary audience with exactly those elements they most prize in two hours' worth of entertainment. Wes Craven's *Scream 2* (1997) opened in late December 1997 with a weekend gross of more than $33 million, a record for a December opening in *any* genre and an all-time record for a horror film. These box office results themselves have become news. Where once viewers, or potential viewers, of a film might discuss the stars of a given work, or a film's particularly intriguing plot twists, contemporary viewers seek to have their tastes reinforced through the artificial consensus of box office returns.

Thus the Dominant cinema "theorizes" and artificially creates a community within the space of its projection/reception, creating a realm of tactile sublimity, a space within which the simulacrum of the spectacle may operate outside the zone of visual justice inherent in the staging of the hyperreal spectacle of the Dominant cinema. The facticity of this community may be gauged by the relative commercial success and/or failure of any given spectacle, a process now so commodified that the future of the spectacle is already part of its memory of history within the first days of a film's initial release.

But what of those images that fall outside the guidelines of these imagistic control structures? Some images are so graphic that they never receive distribution at all, images that we almost *never* see: the realm of the autopsy room, the operating room, the torture chamber. But as we approach the end of the century, shards of imagery from these forbidden zones have begun to leak out. In the films and videos of young, unaffiliated artists, and in ever more graphic news reportage, we are increasingly confronted precisely with that which we do not wish to see. Nevertheless, the images persist, with haunting intensity. In Rwanda, Burundi, and the Eastern Congo since 1990, the Hutu and Tutsi tribes have systematically slaughtered each other with unrelenting ferocity, causing more than a million deaths in the last decade. Indeed, the conflict has been going on for generations.

In Jean-Luc Godard's *Band of Outsiders* (*Bande à part*, 1964), two gangsters waiting to rob a house read accounts of the latest Hutu and Tutsi massacres in the daily newspapers to kill time. Nothing has changed in forty years. In a 1997 essay, James C. McKinley describes

two images [that] burn in memory after a year's worth of violence between the Hutu and Tutsi ethnic groups in Central Africa. A young Hutu woman lies in the city of Kisangani, Congo, her jaw blown off by bullets in an attack by Tutsi soldiers on a Hutu refugee camp in April. Her tortured eyes glare with fear and confusion out of the bloody bandages where her face used to be.

In a border-town hospital in Rwanda, a 4-year-old Tutsi girl struggles to stay alive, her head having been split open by a machete wielded by a Hutu militant attacking Tutsi refugees last week. How the frail child survived the raid, which left 300 other people dead, is a mystery. (McKinley, 3)

But how can these images linger in one's mind if one never sees them? What of the anonymous atrocities, starvations, and fatal illnesses that go unreported, undocumented, and unknown? McKinley's news story was illustrated by a single photograph, depicting a group of several dozen bodies floating face-down in a body of water. "During the slaughter of hundreds of thousands of Tutsi in Rwanda in 1994, bodies floated at the bottom of a fall on the Kagera River on the Tanzanian border near Rusomo," the caption informs us. In 1994? Where, precisely, is the Kagera River? Who besides career diplomats have heard of the town of Rusomo? What has happened in the region since 1994? Why has it taken this long for this particular image to reach the public? What of recent photographic evidence of Japanese atrocities during World War II, in which live Chinese captives were used repeatedly for bayonet practice, or vivisected as part of a series of gruesome and ultimately worthless medical "experiments?" Where are the images that document these acts of brutality? Why aren't they more widely distributed? Why do we either dismiss them or, paradoxically, revel in them, as phantom proof of our own increasingly fragile dominion over death?

As another example of this need to reinvent the cinematic past, the introduction of the child as a central determinist figure in the symbolic structure of fantasy films requires a degree of iconographic maturity that can be gained only through the exhaustion of all other alternatives. Frankenstein's monster and Dracula, the two most infamous literary monsters of the nineteenth century, were successfully translated to the screen as early as J. Searle Dawley's 1910 *Frankenstein* and F. W. Murnau's 1922 *Nosferatu*. In the 1930s and 1940s, Hollywood began its own love affair with these two monstrous constructs, concentrating on the image of the adult male as a marauding beast (Frankenstein's monster, sewn together from the dead bodies of men; the Wolf Man, infected by the bite of a werewolf) or a supernaturally possessed vessel of evil (Dracula, the "undead" adult male). Children were left out of this cycle of films, except as victims, because our immediate visual impression of children is one of uncorrupted innocence. In addition, the small size and lack of physical power of a child would seem to make her or him a rather benign figure, certainly no threat to adult domination.

It was only as the late fifties segued into the early sixties, with such films as Mervyn LeRoy's *The Bad Seed* (1956) (more a thriller than a fantasy film, featuring Patty McCormack as a child psychopathic killer) and American International's teenage horror cycle, featuring Gene Fowler Jr.'s *I Was a Teenage Werewolf* (1957) and Herbert L. Strock's *I Was a Teenage Frankenstein* (1957) (both, in hindsight, unexpectedly effective pieces of filmmaking), that the studios began to consider the possibilities of children as central characters in the horror or fantasy story. However, beginning with Joseph Losey's generally ignored but often brilliant 1961 film, *These Are the Damned* (aka *The Damned*), even younger children have rapidly assumed a prominent place in the literature of fantasy, horror, and science fiction films as "prime movers" of evil, inexplicable forces that seek to destroy or control the adults who ostensibly would be their superiors. One might speculate that the rapid drop in average age of attendance that began in the mid-1950s forced producers to present heroes or antiheroes who would be more readily identifiable to their increasingly younger audiences, and with Wolf Rilla's *Village of the Damned* (1960), the new age of children in fantasy films began in earnest.

Briefly, the story of *Village of the Damned* has all the residents of a small British village, Midwich, suddenly becoming unconscious for no obvious reason by what is believed to be a "gas attack" of some kind. When the residents come to, they discover over the next few weeks that every woman in the village capable of bearing a child has become pregnant, including all the younger, unmarried teenage girls. Recriminations inevitably arise, but these are quickly put aside when the children are all born simultaneously and rapidly demonstrate intelligence far beyond that of average infants. The "demon" children are generally blond or fair-haired, self-controlled to an unusual degree, and seem overtly serious when compared to the "normal" children in the film.

Further, the children are linked telepathically, and as they grow up, they demonstrate powers of telekinesis, forcing village residents who harass them to shoot themselves, set themselves on fire, or run their automobiles into walls. Along with their superior intellect, the "demon" children seem to have a singular lack of emotion: anyone who gets in their way is dispassionately destroyed. In the final minutes of the film,

George Sanders, the children's teacher, blows up both himself and the children with a homemade bomb during a physics lesson. The film's ending, however, leaves the possibility of a sequel clearly open: as we dolly back from the ruins of the destroyed schoolhouse, the eyes of the children are superimposed on the background image, seemingly floating away toward space, where presumably they originated. Based on John Wyndham's novel, *The Midwich Cuckoo*, the film created a sensation, and its public success insured both the sequel promised by the last minutes of the film, Anton Leader's *Children of the Damned* (1963), and the creation of a new subgenre in horror and fantasy films: children as messengers of destruction.

Village of the Damned is an elegant and gracefully classic piece of filmmaking, a fact brought home forcefully by John Carpenter's 1995 remake, which substituted increased doses of graphic violence for the atmospheric sense of evil that permeated Rilla's film. Several key sections of Rilla's original film seem especially striking today, as when a three-month-old "space child" correctly assembles a puzzle of blocks with blinding speed, and then psychically forces his jealous brother to return the blocks to him by the power of his gaze when the latter steals them in spite. Martin Stephens is coldly effective as the leader of the group, and the entire production has an air of quietly assured craftsmanship. *Children of the Damned*, which recapitulates the original under the direction of the less talented Anton Leader, relies on shock effects and has little substance not already covered in the first film. Interestingly, at the end of *Children of the Damned*, the new group of moppets makes peace with the world that would destroy them, promising that they will unfold "a new age of life, liberty, and human dignity" if left unmolested.

However, at approximately the same time as these two films were being shot, director Joseph Losey (best known for his films *Accident* [1967], *Modesty Blaise* [1966], *King and Country* [1964], and *The Servant* [1963], among others) was creating his own bleak vision of childhood as the realm of the monstrous. Losey's futuristic science fiction horror film *The Damned* (*These Are The Damned* in the United States) was completed for Hammer Films in May-June of 1961, shot on location in the decaying seaside resort of Weymouth, England (Caute, 141).

The film would be Losey's only film for Hammer, the first studio to introduce graphic violence to the screen, and the genesis of *The Damned* was a troubled one. Losey based the film on H. L. Lawrence's novel *The Children of Light*, working with a script by longtime collaborator Ben Barzman, but at the last minute the director substituted an alternative script by Evan Jones, enraging both Barzman and Hammer. The completed film differed considerably from the Gothic horror fare that one had come to expect from Hammer, in such films as Terence Fisher's *The Curse of Frankenstein* (1957) and *Horror of Dracula* (aka *Dracula*, 1958).

For those unfamiliar with *The Damned*, the plot deals with a group of children who are being kept at a top-secret military installation on the coast of Cornwall, all of them infected with enormous overdoses of radioactivity, yet somehow showing no ill-effects from the exposure. They are, however, lethal to anyone who comes in contact with them, and so they must live in a hermetically sealed environment, monitored by television cameras and Geiger counters. Deprived of any human contact, their education is conducted entirely through closed- circuit television. Oliver Reed, in a very early and effective performance, plays the leader of a vicious motorcycle gang (prefiguring in both style and substance Stanley Kubrick's 1971 film of Anthony Burgess's *A Clockwork Orange*) who comes upon the children by accident while on vacation at the seaside. In a fit of momentary altruism, Reed decides to help the children escape, only to die of radiation poisoning, as the children are recaptured by ominously garbed government scientists and returned to their prison.

There are numerous other subplots interwoven into the action, involving Macdonald Carey as a failed novelist and Viveca Lindfors as an unsuccessful sculptress. But the core of the film belongs to the innocently destructive children, who yearn for the human contact that is continually denied them, yet who will inevitably kill anyone they touch. Interestingly, the "failed" adults serve as an effective counterpoint to the deadly, mysterious children. While the adults are already "burnt-out cases," the children have all the time and possibilities inherent in the realm of youth. Yet the children simultaneously possess the capability of destroying, albeit unwittingly, any of the adults who attempt to help them, resulting in their complete isolation from normative human society.

Columbia Pictures, which had contracted to release *The Damned*, was not at all pleased with the results and summarily shelved it. Screened at the Spoleto Festival in 1962, it attracted some critical commentary, but was not released in London until May 20, 1963, on the bottom half of a double bill with another Hammer film, Michael Carreras's *Maniac* (made in 1962 but also held back from immediate release). The film was finally released in the United States in July 1965 under the title *These Are the Damned*, after having been cut from eighty-seven to seventy-eight minutes (Caute, 143). Although the film never achieved a wide commercial audience, it was favorably reviewed by a number of sympathetic critics, and its subterranean reputation grew. The image of these wide-eyed tots serving as the messengers of death impressed those relatively few who saw the film. Along with *Village of the Damned* and *Children of the Damned*, *The Damned* served as an influential iconic template for the production of William Friedkin's *The Exorcist* (1973), based on William Peter Blatty's popular novel, which again dealt in images of perverted childhood innocence.

Despite its enormous commercial success, *The Exorcist* has little of the distinction of the earlier films and emerges as little more than a catalogue of prosthetic effects. Regan (Linda Blair), a "possessed" nine-year-old girl, vomits large quantities of green bile, twists her head completely around in a 360-degree circle, levitates, breaks out in mysterious rashes, and intones suitably shocking blasphemies directed at the priests who would exorcise her. During this section of the film, which took many months to shoot, Regan's character becomes completely submerged in gruesome displays of technical virtuosity.

In this, perhaps, the film shares something of the same attitude toward possessed children as *Village of the Damned*, *Children of the Damned*, and *The Damned*. In all cases, the children are denied an individual personality and become merely messengers of destruction. The children are either unconcerned or unable to be concerned (as in Regan's case) with the consequences of her or his actions. Linda Blair fits the same iconographic mold as the children in the earlier films: Caucasian, conventionally beautiful, uncorrupted, seemingly cast against visual type. Further, in all four films, the adult figures are seen as essentially powerless against the forces these demonic children call forth either willingly or unwillingly. The natural order of adult dominance can only be restored through an immense sacrifice: the deaths of George Sanders in *Village of the Damned*, Oliver Reed in *The Damned*, and Jason Miller at the end of *The Exorcist*, when Miller challenges the devil to accept his soul in place of Blair's.

All three men meet their end through acts of extreme violence. Sanders is blown up along with his pupils. Reed dies of radiation poisoning. Miller is pitched headlong through a plate-glass window. In all three cases, an agonizing death is the hallmark of their sacrifice, and only their own obliteration frees the world from domination by the controlling forces of evil. Finally, in all cases, the children involved are absolved of responsibility for their actions. The children from *The Damned* are victims of government abuse. In *Village of the Damned* and *Children of the Damned*, the space-children are dispassionate automatons deprived of any measure of free will, controlled by forces they cannot comprehend.

The overwhelming spectacle-driven commercial success of *The Exorcist* nevertheless set up a series of stylistic and generic conventions that would spawn an endless series (still incomplete) of imitations, including William Girdler's *Abby* (1974), a black version of the film; Mario Bava's *House of Exorcism* (aka *Lisa and the Devil*, 1975), an Italian film starring Telly Savalas; and Gabrielle Beaumont's *The Godsend* (1979), a singularly inept English import, to name only a few of the many films that were quickly and cheaply made to cash in on the new craze.

In 1976 the production of *The Omen*, directed by Richard Donner, further refined the popular concept of the demon child as fantasy figure. In *The Omen*, Harvey Stephens plays Damien Thorn, a spawn of Hell dedicated to the destruction of his elders—this time a completely willing participant in the evil he unleashes. *The Omen* was also by far the most violently graphic of any of these films, and merged the concept of extreme depictions of human mutilation with the image of the child as Satan. Thus Damien Thorn, the young son of American ambassador Robert Thorn (Gregory Peck), serves as the "deus ex" for a series of horrifying murders. *The Omen* has the distinction of being one of the first major-studio films whose only plot is unremitting violence, with a violent murder punctuating every ten minutes of the film's running time.

Damien is responsible for a decapitation, a hanging, an impalement, and a fatal fall down a flight of stairs; in between these incidents, he is called upon to do nothing more than simply exist within the terms of the film's visual construction. His nearly nonverbal performance is limited to a few grimaces and/or blank stares. This takes the children in the *Village of the Damned* series one step further, to the point where iconography becomes acting. Damien's mere physical presence serves as an instantly comprehensible symbol of destruction. Indeed, Damien is so young he cannot even speak, and he relies upon all of his victims to do the acting for him, which they do, each dedicating their demises ("Damien, it's all for you") to his implied satisfaction.

The adults in the film again seem impotent or singularly unaware of what Damien is up to. Mrs. Baylock (Billie Whitelaw), as Damien's satanic nanny, protects the child with the aid of two large attack dogs. But only the film's fringe characters, particularly Jennings (David Warner), an eccentric photographer, and Bugenhagen (an uncredited Leo McKern), a monk locked away in a monastery in the hills of northern Italy, are allowed to effectively fight back against the child. Damien's mother Katherine (Lee Remick) is toppled from a balcony of their home when Damien bumps into her with his tricycle, and falls several floors to her near-death. Recuperating in a hospital after the accident, she inexplicably jumps from a window into the street below, conveniently plunging through the roof of a waiting ambulance.

Robert Thorn, who is shot to death in the final sequence of the film while attempting to murder Damien on the altar of a deserted church, refuses to recognize Damien's true vocation. Only after being attacked in a cemetery by a pack of wild dogs, and watching helplessly as David Warner's head is unceremoniously chopped off by a huge sheet of plate glass in a construction accident, does Robert Thorn take decisive action. In the film's last shot, we see Damien still alive in the cemetery where his father is being buried, paving the way for the sequels that followed, including Don Taylor's *Damien: Omen II* (1978), Graham Baker's *The Final Conflict* (1981), and Jorge Montesi and Dominique Othenin-Girard's *Omen IV: The Awakening* (1991), a TV movie.

The Omen paradoxically strives to transform its defects in terms of narrative structure into its strengths. Damien is evil simply because he is the son of Satan, nothing more, and the destruction that follows in his wake is the logical consequence of his existence. In direct contrast to the deaths of Sanders in *Village of the Damned*, Reed in *The Damned*, and Miller in *The Exorcist*, Gregory Peck's sacrifice at the end of the film is useless. Evil will continue to exist, and even the most extreme exertions of adult authority cannot stop it. This makes the conclusion of Losey's rather uncompromising film seem tame by comparison; in the world of *The Omen*, evil triumphs.

The Omen was almost universally reviled by the critics upon its original release, and it is easy to see why. Along with the vicious intensity of its vivid, lip-smacking depictions of horrific violence, the conclusion of the film is at once cynically commercial (insuring the future existence of the two sequels that followed it) and triumphantly despairing. In many ways, the *Omen* films represent the supreme elevation of the "child as monster," and although subsequent episodes of the *Omen* series and other films that followed strove to top the graphic effects of the original, none of them lived up to the impact of the first film. Gregory Peck's meaningless death at the end of the film effectively underscores the complete inability of the adult world to control Damien: doctors, priests, psychiatrists, teachers, parents . . . all are useless and impotent. The certainty of their destruction (as the film assumes its true structure, that of a string of grisly murders) makes one impatient with any attempt at characterization.

If Damien functions simply as an icon of evil, those who would oppose him in the film are also similarly limited. As he is indestructible, they are simply victims, and the only suspense in the film is *when* they will be killed, not *if*. Damien's would-be foes all have defects. Robert Thorn is unsure of his marriage, and unhappy and harried in his work. Jennings, the photographer, is seen as a moral cripple, interested only in getting "hot" pictures for the tabloid he works for. Bugenhagen, the monk, is a recluse who has given up on life. And because of their complete ineffectuality, the audience begins to side with Damien, in much the same fashion that Freddy Krueger and Jason have become the true "heroes" of the *Nightmare on Elm Street* and *Friday the 13th* films. Indeed, given the futility of their resistance, it almost seems as if the adults in *The Omen* are willing sacrifices, anxious to hasten their own destruction. Perhaps this is precisely because opposition to the forces of evil personified in Damien *is* useless. If death is inevitable, why not get it over with?

In the wake of *The Omen*, a flurry of demonic children swept the screen. A few of these films include the adaptation of Stephen King's *Salem's Lot* (1979), originally made as a TV movie by director Tobe Hooper, featuring a group of renegade vampire children; Fritz Kiersch's *Children of the Corn* (1984), David Price's *Children of the Corn II: The Final Sacrifice* (1993), James Hickox's *Children of the Corn III* (1994), and Greg Spence's *Children of the Corn: The Gathering* (1996), all loosely based on a story by Stephen King, in which Shirley Jackson's "The Lottery" is redone with children rather than adults; Brian De Palma's *The Fury* (1978), a film centering on the covert government abduction of a telepathic child; Robert Mulligan's *The Other* (1972), based on Thomas Tryon's best-selling novel; Piers Haggard's *Blood on Satan's Claw* (1971), involving a coven of children who are witches and warlocks; Larry Cohen's *It's Alive* (1974), *It Lives Again* (1978), and *It's Alive III: Island of the Alive* (1987), concerning the exploits of a homicidal infant; and Joel Schumacher's *The Lost Boys* (1987), in which Jason Patric, Corey Haim, and Kiefer Sutherland retell J. M. Barrie's *Peter Pan*, as a group of children become endlessly youthful vampires, terrorizing the citizens of a California beach town. Not even touched on here is the role of the child as coconspirator in fantasy films, as in the children of Steven Spielberg's *E.T.* (1982), who assist the earthbound alien in his return to his home planet; or the child in Tobe Hooper and Steven Spielberg's *Poltergeist* (1982), Brian Gibson's *Poltergeist II: The Other Side* (1986), and Gary A. Sherman's *Poltergeist III* (1988), who heralds the invasion of malevolent phantoms (through the medium of the television set) into a family's neat suburban home. These cinematic children fulfill more of an audience-participation function than anything else, and while they may be central to the construction of the films they are in, they cannot truly be called the protagonists. Why do these films remain consistently popular with audiences, even in TV remakes and straight-to-video releases? Perhaps it is because there is a naïveté in the child's imagination which allows for a certain sense of wonder. A child's perceptions of the world and its inhabitants are untutored by daily commonplace; childhood experiences are fresh, unmediated, and create in children and teenagers an immediate excitement from which adults are long removed. As long as the current movie-going audience continues to be as youthful as it is, and as long as we, as adults, continue to long for a return to a child-like system of innocent values, whether for good or evil, the child will continue to hold a place in fantasy films that fads and fancies can only temporarily mitigate.

This fascination with the domain of childhood has always been one of Hollywood's central preoccupations. As we reach the end of the millennium, the preoccupation of the young with the cinema as both a means of escape and a medium of expression has increased dramatically. The audience for contemporary theatrical films is getting younger, and with this phenomenon comes a demand for films that center on the activities and lives of teens, almost to the complete exclusion of everything else. This in itself is nothing new; every succeeding generation of filmgoers demands stories with which they can identify, in which *they* are the sole protagonists. But it seems that teenagers in the late 1990s are involved in the fantasy world of the Dominant cinema in an absolutist fashion which their predecessors shunned.

As Michael Wood of Teen Research Unlimited notes, late 1990s "teens are *so* [original emphasis] into movies. Movies are really, really hot for teens" (quoted in Weeks, 2D). As critic Janet Weeks notes, "'Teen culture could dominate film in the next few years, thanks to a growing 13-to-19 population that loves to go to the movies—loves it more than dating, shopping, and sleeping in" (D1); "loves it," in fact, even more than having a boyfriend or girlfriend, or being involved in high school sports, according to the Teen Research Unlimited report. Weeks continues: "Sometimes called Generation Y, these [teens] are the spawn of the huge population bomb known as the baby boom. These 77 million offspring born since 1978 started hitting their teen years in 1991. . . . By 2010, the teen population will crest at 30.8 million, the biggest in U.S. history" (1D). Hollywood, predictably, is more than ready to supply the films these viewers want to see.

And what do these young viewers want? Ann Horwitz, fourteen, of

Bethesda, Maryland, says she likes to go to movies because "movies create a world that isn't our world. It puts you in another place and time" (quoted in Weeks, 1D). "I like movies that have actual teens in them and that actually show real-life stuff" adds another female viewer, while Dave Fisher, eighteen, feels that "love stories and 90210 stuff [aren't] cool," while citing John Woo's 1997 film *Face / Off* as "one of the greatest movies ever. It had action right from the beginning. Fighting and violence and everything, that's always cool" (quoted in Weeks, 10). Thus, contemporary mainstream films have become the domain of video games like Quake, in which the sole object of the game's narrative is to kill one's opponent as quickly and expeditiously as possible. All is immediate, all is the eternal present. To delay means figurative death (being "out of the game"), and so action, constant and unceasing, is an omnipresent imperative. Contemporary film has become the domain of the "point and shoot" narrative, in which all is immediate desire and gratification, fueled by the love of video games and the narrative structure these games still utilize, years after their introduction in the mid-1980s. Almost without exception, such games as Mortal Kombat and its progeny require one player-participant to kill another player-participant, at the expense of narrative, character development, story structure, and all other possible concerns. The force-feed visual structure of contemporary cinema effectively parallels this, as we have seen, fusing one image into another with blinding speed and split-second cutting, so that what we view becomes a seamless mesh of grandiose destruction. Today's four major media conglomerates are poised to exploit all these varying aspects of teenage desire, whether it be for films, or CDs, or other forms of popular entertainment. In the next chapter I will examine how they effectively do this, and how their all-encompassing global structure as entertainment / news / print / music / video / cable / broadcast megastructures insures not only that there will be an endless demand for their products but that there will be an endless supply as well, available from a multiplicity of outlets, both virtual and real.

4

SUPERSTRUCTURES OF THE DOMINANT CINEMA

the alterity of symbolic capital

In late December 1997, the twentieth installment of the James Bond series, *Tomorrow Never Dies*, was released. Directed by Roger Spottis-woode, the film was begun without a completed script, yet this did not deter the $80 million production from initiating a project that would eventually encompass seventy-five sets and utilize locations in four different countries (Rogers 1997b:17). The production encountered numerous difficulties on the road to its completion, not the least of which was being denied the use of location shooting in Vietnam, thus forcing the company to substitute the back lot at Pinewood Studios in England—intercut with location footage in Thailand—to achieve the desired exotic colonialist atmosphere in the finished film (Rogers 1997b:18). Similarly, for a sequence in which Bond (reincarnated for this film by actor Pierce Brosnan) supposedly flies a stolen jet through the skies of Afghanistan, the producers of the film relied on a painted canvas backdrop on rollers ("we had a distant snow-covered mountain background painted on the canvas"), with the addition of "lighting effects . . . shooting outside and combining zooms and dollies with some plane movement" to create the illusion of flight (Rogers 1997b:19).

Coupled with the fabricated "Otherness" of Hong Kong action star Michelle Yeoh as Wai Lin, the latest in a long series of "Bond girls," Brosnan's game but mechanical performance serves as the anchor for a film that is a triumph of style over substance, spectacle over narrative structure, design and special effects before content. Other contemporary films echo this current strategy of mimicking the past of the Dominant cinema with a surface patina of computer-generated special effects to compensate for the absence of even partial originality. *Tomorrow Never Dies* establishes the villainy of Elliot Carver (Jonathan Pryce) with an opening sequence in which a mechanical underwater drilling device sends the crew of an unsuspecting British naval ship to the bottom of the ocean. The few survivors of the wreck, seeking rescue by the crew members of Carver's pirate vessel, are ritualistically machine-gunned to death in the water, while one of Carver's minions videotapes the entire episode for playback on Carver's global satellite television network.

As head of the Carver Media Group, Elliot Carver's ultimate goal in all of this is as one-dimensional as it is impersonal; he seeks, through an elaborate plot, to be granted an exclusive 100-year lease for global satellite television transmissions in the territory of mainland China. Thus the brutal carnage he has just engineered makes Carver a perfectly appropriate candidate for Bond's unstoppable juggernaut of vengeance. At the film's climax, Carver himself is ground to bits by the same underwater drill he used to destroy the British battleship; as Bond reminds Carver moments before he is blasted into oblivion by his own engine of destruction, one must "always give the public what it wants." Thus, Bond's quest for Carver's death becomes our desired objective, as well. Parenthetically, it is also worth noting that despite the film's ostensible PG-13 rating, the film is a catalogue of carefully choreographed violence, destruction, sadism, and threats of torture, eagerly consumed by the target audience of preteens who comprise most of the film's audience.

Propelled by a series of seemingly endless chase scenes, fist-fights, martial arts combat sequences, explosions, car crashes, beatings, execution-style shootings, and the requisite amount of luxury and splendor one expects from a colonialist artifact, James Bond is the nearly perfect series franchise, adapting from the Cold War to the new international climate with some difficulty, but managing to remain both profitable and contemporaneous nonetheless. For although the expensive sets (built to be destroyed) and the various accouterments of Bond's fantasy lifestyle (yet another fully customized, rocket-launching, remote-controlled BMW automobile) are part of the overall package we are being sold, the key element here is violence—violence both physical and visual, as the film rushes furiously from sequence to sequence, hoping to exhaust us through sheer excess and pacing, and blind us to the film's lack of anything more than the most rudimentary elements of a narrative structure.

Begun without a finished script, stitched together through the intercutting device of a video-screen-filled, hypersurveillant control room presided over by M (Judi Dench), Tomorrow Never Dies is in every way the perfect Bond film for the end of the millennium. Everywhere Bond travels, we follow him through the medium of surveillance cameras. M's assistants track Bond's every move with a variety of robot-controlled remote cameras, experiencing his exploits vicariously along with the members of the audience. Elliot Carver is, in turn, the perfect end-of-the-century criminal mastermind; he seeks not all the gold in Fort Knox (as did Goldfinger) or even a few stray nuclear warheads.

Carver seeks complete domination of the televisual culture that has become our most pervasive and invasive cultural force in the late 1990s. He controls the news globally in every country except mainland China; through his criminal enterprises, he seeks to obtain the "exclusive satellite broadcast rights to China for the next hundred years." Carver seeks to be the sole arbiter of what we see, and do not see, in our homes, on a global scale. Significantly, Carver is supremely disinterested in the mechanisms of the cinematograph, or in the production of feature films—fictive nonnarratives—for an audience that must be constantly wooed on a film-by-film basis to pay to view the spectacles he might create. Carver recognizes that the "news" itself is fiction, manufactured, shaped, edited, and segmented, "news" which (in his case) he creates, but which, no matter its origin, is a series of ready-made images lacking only a means of dissemination (which his satellite network provides) and a corporate sponsor. Though Carver's dream of imagistic monopolization is, through predictable genre requirements, finally destroyed, the message he conveys is (as he admits) one that is only an extension of the philosophy espoused by William Randolph Hearst and immortalized in Orson Welles's *Citizen Kane* (1941): "You provide the pictures, and I'll provide the war." Or as Carver himself notes at one point, "There's no news like bad news."

Predictably, *Tomorrow Never Dies* was launched with a series of expensive and pervasive media tie-ins, plugging everything from BMW cars to Gibson's gin in radio, television, web, and print advertisements. But nowhere was this aggressive commodification of the Bond persona more evident than in a special issue of *Parade* magazine published just a few weeks before the film's release. Comprised of a group of short puff pieces extolling the virtues of limitless gadgetry, the issue represents one of the most ambitious efforts toward commercial cross-plugging in recent media history.

Walter Mossberg and Faith Pennick's article "Seven Products That Will Change the Way We Live: What's *Next?*" uses Pierce Brosnan's "Bonded" image to extol the transfigurative powers of the Ricoh RDC-2 digital camera ("takes up to 38 pictures with sound"); the SkyTel 2-way pager ("it alerts you to Voicemail recordings, and if your friend has the same pager, you can send text messages directly"); web TV Plus, which "enhances television itself by merging regular TV and the web"; along with "laptops that weigh as little as 3 pounds but can do real office work . . . handheld devices—as small as credit cards—that organize information electronically . . . [and] wireless Internet services that deliver information from preselected web sites" (4–5). Much is made of the "revolutionary" nature of these new products, which are displayed by performers Brosnan, Yeoh, and Desmond Llewelyn (in his persona as the gadget-obsessed Q) in a splashy layout that not only promotes the products themselves (all with brand names prominently displayed) but also *Tomorrow Never Dies* with insistent, fetishistic intensity.

What emerges is thus an ad-within-an-ad, dual-advertising masquerading as editorial magazine content, a blitz of images designed to lull us into a fantasy world of perpetual consumption (through the agency of the colonialist exoticism of the aging Bond franchise) and then deliver, crisply and concisely, an array of generally transient and certainly designed-for-obsolescence products, all with prices, model numbers, and availability dates tied to glamorized product shots supposedly demonstrating the inherent essentiality of the products in question.

In Tom Seligson's article, entitled "Should Your Next Camera Be *Digital?*" the author concludes his brief piece with this rhetorical question and response: "Should you buy? Yes, *but don't throw away that 35mm camera. You'll need it to take high quality prints* [emphasis mine]" (8). This last caveat neatly sums up the ephemerality of the product in question which, the author admits two-thirds of the way through the article, can't produce satisfactory paper prints of the images they create: "Digital cameras produce prints with color inkjet printers or specially designed photo printers, but the quality of the prints is poor" (8). But never mind; you can play back the still pictures that you take of your vacation, wedding, or bar mitzvah through your television set, and thus, after a fashion, join the realm of overnight celebrities: "Imagine photographing friends at a party, then instantly turning them into TV stars . . . most digital cameras connect to your set with a simple cable." Never mind the fact that unless you're willing to spend "more than $1,000" for a digital camera with more than one million pixels of resolution ("compare that to a 35mm print of 20 million pixels or a Polaroid shot of 2 million," the author advises), you'll be stuck with a device viewable solely through such televisual apparatus as TV monitors, web pages, or tacked on to e-mail as "gifs" or "jpegs" (computer-compressed imagery) (8).

Similarly, the answer to the question posed by Al Griffin's article entitled "Will I Have to Replace My Music Collection *Again?*" is also "yes . . . but not for a while" (16). As with Seligson's piece, Griffin posits the perpetual consumer of the new and trendy as his ideal target audience. "You've discarded your old turntable and replaced your scratchy vinyl records and hissy tapes with shimmering new compact discs" (16), clearly the right thing to do. Now, are you willing to trade in your CDs for DVS (Digital Versatile Disks), which provide "more than 25 times more data-storage capacity than a CD or a CD-ROM" (16)? Griffin ticks off the numerous other advantages of DVDs:

> The image quality of DVDs is significantly more advanced than that of any other format available. Video resolution is twice that of VHS tapes and even exceeds that of laserdiscs or Digital Satellite Systems. The audio is just as impressive. Most disks feature two different soundtracks: a Dolby Surround-encoded stereo version, playable through *any* audio system (from surround sound to your TV), and a six-channel Dolby Digital version, which requires a Dolby Digital audio-video receiver. The latter approaches the sound quality in a good movie theater. (Griffin, 16)

However, there *are* drawbacks.

> DVD-Video is being challenged by news of a new video-disk format called Divx (Digital Video Express). Whereas DVD was designed for collectors (as are audio CDs), Divx will be pay-per-view. You'll pay about $5 for a movie on Divx, which you must view within 48 hours from the time you drop the disk in your player. You can throw away the disk or keep it for future viewings, to be billed to a preestablished account. Significantly, Divx players will be able to accommodate DVD software, but DVD players won't be compatible with Divx disks. (Griffin, 18)

Thus, the new disk format is already embroiled in what Griffin forthrightly describes as a "format war" (as with Beta versus VHS tapes), and both formats severely restrict the viewer's choice of material, inasmuch as neither of these systems is recordable, and thus only contemporary mainstream cinema or a thin range of certified canonical classics will be available to the consumer. In addition, the pay-per-view aspect of the Divx format makes it truly a "throw away" medium. Nevertheless, the real problem that Griffin sees is getting the goods to the marketplace: "The first hurdles for the new format are the home video and multimedia markets" (16). Creators of films and video games will have to create software compatible with the new format. Until this new format becomes as ubiquitous as a conventional VHS tape, there will be a sales lag.

Yet, as with the previously noted articles by Mossberg and Pennick, and Seligson, the products described are presented in dazzling, enticing photo layouts, with the precise make, model number, and price range information provided for each item. All one has to do is take out one's credit card and purchase the desired item. To be fair, Griffin does note that DVD-RAM,

> a reusable disk format that allows information to be recorded and erased many times, could become not only the next-generation floppy disk for computer-data storage but also the next-generation video recording device. Panasonic has announced it will be shipping DVD-RAM drives, aimed at the PC market, in January 1998. (Griffin, 18)

Significantly, however, no price is given in this case, and given the scarcity of recordable CD machines in the late 1990s, one can imagine that recordable DVDs will be a rather expensive proposition. And so they *should* be, in our consumerist culture, because the purchase of a DVD-RAM announces to the manufacturer that the buyer is inherently not satisfied with programming available in the new format and intends to create her/his own. This threatens the stockpile of existing prerecorded entertainment materials and, as such, is to be discouraged. Wouldn't you rather watch *Dances with Wolves* (1990, dir. Kevin Costner) anyway?

But as all this technological crossbreeding continues to proliferate, creating a myriad of new formats and a plethora of competing cameras, players, recorders, and play-stations, there is an even more all-encompassing technoshift which seeks to alter the televisual landscape we have inhabited since the midcentury mark into an entirely new arena of simulacric desire. As of this writing, digital television transmissions are scheduled to "begin in North America in late 1998." Regular, or analog, television broadcasting "will continue until at least 2006. After that, decoders will let analog sets display digital broadcasts" (Griffin, 18). While digital imaging will dramatically improve the quality of the television image the home viewer receives, once again it will require a considerable outlay in the purchase of a new, digital television set, even as "format wars" continue into the new digital era. Will digital TV necessarily be High Definition TV? Will it have 1,125 lines or 1,140 lines, in contrast to the current 525-line resolution format which has become the VHS standard (bearing in mind that a conventional frame of 35mm still or motion picture film has a theoretical line-resolution of over 2,000 lines)? There is, then, little doubt that the current shift to digital technology will continue to create new equipment, new formats, and new standards to be embraced and ultimately superseded, as today's indispensable item becomes tomorrow's throwaway. Yet even as the hardware changes, inexorably and constantly, the software of images fueling the technological shift will remain an inexhaustible image bank of new and used glyphs, encoding reason and madness, greed and sanctity, brutality and reason for succeeding generations to contemplate.

We may indeed throw out our "scratchy vinyl records and hissy tapes" and embrace the same sounds and images rerecorded in a new medium, but if the current universality of the audio CD proves anything it demonstrates conclusively that, above all, the consumer prizes the memory of the past and will (in the vast majority of cases) seek to purchase anew the same images and sounds that pleased or comforted her/him in their original format. The continuing proliferation of television channels, in some systems running into the many hundreds of individual programming streams, ensures that simply because of the marketplace value for low-cost programming, our collective imagistic past, far from being abandoned as the technology evolves, will be lovingly preserved and reprogrammed, restored and refurbished to provide products for an entirely new generation of viewers and auditors.

Today, echoing the dreams of Elliot Carver's fictive campaign for worldwide control of the televisual and print media, four major entertainment conglomerates control the vast majority of film, television, print, newspaper, cable, and music consumed by the general public: General Electric, Time Warner, Disney/Cap Cities, and Westinghouse. As detailed in an article by Mark Crispin Miller and Janine Jaquet Biden entitled "The National Entertainment State" in *The Nation*, with nearly every magazine we read, every film we watch, every CD we listen to, and every radio station we tune in, we are participating in the activities of one of the arms of this series of all-pervasive four media conglomerates. Time Warner, for example, owns 14.5 percent of Seagrams, 100 percent of Warner Brothers retail stores (selling various character merchandise featuring Bugs Bunny, Daffy Duck, and other Warner commodities), in addition to controlling entirely both live action and animated film production at the Warner Brothers Studio.

As a supplier of prerecorded music CDs and tapes, Time Warner owns 100 percent of Warner/Chappell Publishing, the Atlantic Group (the famous sixties "soul" label featuring Otis Redding, Aretha Franklin, and Wilson Pickett, to name just a few artists in Atlantic's voluminous catalogue), Elektra Entertainment Group, Warner Brothers Records, and Warner Music International; 40 percent of Sub Pop, an "independent" record label; and 50 percent of Columbia House, the lucrative record "club" where members subscribe to a series of monthly offerings. Time Warner also owns all of the Six Flags amusement parks scattered throughout the United States (all of which trade heavily in Warner Brothers cartoon characters as park "mascots"), Cinemax, 50 percent of Comedy Central (Viacom owns the other 50 percent), HBO, CNN/SI, the Sega Channel (a 24-hour video game service available to home cable viewers), as well as all of the various arms of Turner Broadcasting.

Turner, as a subentity of Time Warner, owns the Atlanta Braves and Atlanta Hawks sports franchises, the CNN Interactive web site, Turner New Media (a manufacturer of CD-ROMS and DVDs for home use), Turner Publishing, Hanna-Barbera Cartoons (and thus, the entire back catalogue of HB product, and the ancillary merchandising rights to all HB characters, such as Yogi Bear, Huckleberry Hound, and others), World Championship Wrestling, New Line Cinema, Castle Rock Entertainment, Turner Entertainment (which itself owns more than five hundred MGM, RKO, and pre-1950 Warner Brothers films), as well as the cable networks TBS, TCM (Turner Classic Movies), TNT, the Cartoon Network, CNN Airport Network ("news" designed especially for airport waiting lounges, displayed on remote monitors which operate twenty-four hours a day), Headline News, CNNfn (the Turner financial network), CNN, CNN Radio, and a regional sports network called Sportsouth. Turner Broadcasting also sponsors the Goodwill Games, which are dutifully covered on the various Turner cable networks.

But this is far from the entire picture. As a publisher, Time also owns the magazines *Life, Time, Fortune, Sports Illustrated, Vibe, Money, People, In Style, Sports Illustrated for Kids, Martha Stewart Living, Sunset, Asia Week,* 50 percent of DC Comics (home of Superman and Batman), and 83.25 per cent of *American Lawyer.* Time Warner's book publishing arms include Time-Life Books, Warner Books, Little, Brown and Co., and other firms; in the home video market Time Warner controls Time-Life Video, Warner Home Video, and HBO Home Video. While not a complete picture of Time Warner holdings, this brief overview of the conglomerate's activities should certainly give the reader pause.

Disney/Cap Cities owns a similarly vast array of production companies, book publishers, magazines, and radio and television stations under its corporate umbrella, including 100 percent of Hyperion Books and Chilton Publications; the theatrical motion picture companies Walt Disney Pictures, Touchstone, Hollywood, Miramax, and Buena Vista; the magazines *Institutional Investor* and *L.A. Magazine,* in addition to owning

Fairchild Publications, publishers of the influential fashion journals *W* and *Women's Wear Daily*; ABC radio, which owns twenty-one stations throughout the United States, reaching 24 percent of the entire country's population (indeed, it is the largest radio network in the country and its programming is carried on 3,400 additional radio stations that use *ABC News* and other features as part of their daily programming); ABC's ten television stations; ABC News; and ABC Video. Additionally, Disney/Cap Cities owns eleven newspapers (including the *Fort Worth Star Telegram*, the *Kansas City Star*, the *St. Louis Daily Record*, and other respected dailies; three records labels; two sports teams; and, of course, all the Disneyland theme parks and resorts, including Disneyland, Walt Disney World, 39 percent of EuroDisney, the town of Celebration, Florida, and the Disney Institute (a sprawling "learning center" for adults, featuring backpacking, animation classes, and other life-based programs to lure potentially more adventurous clients), to name just a few of the conglomerate's key properties in this entertainment niche.

By contrast, Westinghouse seems downright modest in its acquisitions, which include CBS (with twenty-one FM stations, eighteen AM stations, fourteen television stations), interests in CMT (Country Music Television), Home Team Sports, and the Nashville Network, as well as the entire CBS Network News operation, which currently generates *60 Minutes*, *Face the Nation*, *48 Hours*, and other news and entertainment features carried by numerous television network affiliates and cable operators throughout the country, as well as "CBS Radio News," which is carried by 450 radio stations in the United States alone. Westinghouse's other interests include Group W Satellite Communications, Thermo King, various telephone networks and wireless communication and security systems. Forty percent of the nuclear power plants in the world use Westinghouse technology. Westinghouse also controls Banker's Trust, Westinghouse Revision Management, Resource Energy Systems, Scientific Ecology Group, Westinghouse Remediation Services, and GESCO (these last four companies specialize in radioactive and hazardous waste disposal). GESCO also services four government-owned nuclear facilities and has installed reactors in the USS *Seawolf*.

Finally, General Electric owns NBC, which as a subentity owns nine television stations, clients of various cable companies (including portions of Court TV, Bravo, AMC [American Movie Classics], A&E, the History Channel, the Independent Film Channel, Prime, Prism, Romance Classics—all these in turn owned in cooperation with other companies such as Time Warner, Rainbow, Microsoft, Cablevision, Hearst, and Disney), as well as NBC Network News (*Today, Meet the Press, Dateline, Nightside,* and other programs). GE further controls a plethora of manufacturing concerns which produce electrical equipment (Electrical Distribution and Control), plastics (GE Plastics), appliances, lighting equipment, aircraft engines, and turbines for nuclear reactors as well as a vast array of holdings in insurance, medical services, and financial investment operations (including the GE Capital Fund). While GE's overall stake in the entertainment industry may not be as pervasive as Time Warner or Disney/Cap Cities, the company itself is ranked first (along with General Motors) in the *Forbes 500* list of U.S. companies (see Miller and Biden 1996:23–26).

This brief overview of the current activities of the four major entertainment conglomerates should convince even the most casual reader that the current tendency is toward increased media consolidation, so that only a very few gigantic, overarching media organizations ultimately fulfill all our entertainment needs. No doubt these corporate entities will undergo additional transformations in the future, but the underlying principle by which they will always operate remains the same. To these enormous conglomerates, we are consumers above any other consideration. That marks us as individual target entities, and Time Warner and Disney/Cap Cities, particularly, seem determined to reach, with their profusion of goods and services, the widest possible demographic, appealing to teenagers and retirees alike. At the core of these four huge companies, then, is an almost childlike demand for continuous consumption, an unending and uninterrupted flow of sounds and images which instruct, entertain, and, most importantly by far, advertise the numbingly numerous iconic and actual wares that the conglomerates have to offer.

Seen from this vantage point, the various "superstar directors" and media personalities, no matter how richly rewarded, remain merely single elements of an overall corporate campaign to enlist us as a virtual and *continual* consumer of goods and services. Within an aggressively organized combination of companies such as these, individual thought is lost. All that remains, then, is to search for some kind of refuge from the machinations of such enormously powerful and profitable entertainment complexes, seeking safety in the domestic sphere, the home which must be entered only by invitation (even by these pervasive entities—at least in this country), a space that we can control, like a children's fort or tree house.

For what is more attractive than the domain of childhood, other than the domain of populist luxury, conferred on the various stars of the cinema by the public's demand for their services? Ismail Merchant shot his film *The Proprietor* (1996) with Jeanne Moreau in the deserted apartment which had once belonged to famed interior decorator Madeleine Castaing, an apartment which had existed in a suspended state since Madeleine Castaing's death in 1994 at the age of ninety-two. "It gave the impression of waiting for something," recalled Jeanne Moreau of the apartment. "At the same time I felt both the presence and absence of the person who lived here" (quoted in Giovanni, 179). When filming of *The Proprietor* was completed, Merchant moved into the apartment, leaving all the draperies, paintings, furniture, and other architectural details intact, just as Castaing had left them. "I felt it would have been a crime to dismantle it without doing something to commit it to memory," observed Ismail Merchant. "It just called out to be used as a movie set" (quoted in Giovanni, 182). Madeleine Castaing's apartment thus passed into the realm of the zone of the cinematograph as a completed construct, a site of faded dreams of empire. As a central location for filming, her plushly appointed, elegantly decorated residence immediately appealed to Merchant precisely because of its meticulous detail and carefully laid-out design; yet, as he worked in the apartment, members of Merchant's film crew noticed that Castaing herself was no stranger to the shortcuts of creating an illusion of grandeur with limited means. "If you moved a chair from its correct position, you exposed a patch of wall that had not been painted. You had the impression she would wake up in the middle of the night to change something, do it in a flurry of improvisation and then climb back into bed. And it stayed that way for years" (quoted in Giovanni, 184). Thus even our living spaces, saturated with the memories of those who have lived there before us, are haptic zones of illusionary artifice, locations of fantasy and self-constructedness.

Jayne Mansfield's "Pink Palace" in Bel Air was decorated with hundreds of magazine covers, posters, and other publicity items the actress had adorned in life. Her garishly ostentatious mansion, complete with a polar bear rug, copper lamé draperies, a study upholstered in red leather, and a gigantic heart-shaped swimming pool in the backyard, in every way epitomized the excessive grandeur of Mansfield's Hollywood ambitions, and, in its isolated and exaggerated splendor, prefigured her desire to live only in the moment, no matter what the eventual cost. Posing on her bed in a negligée, cuddling with her husband Mickey Hargitay next to the swimming pool for the publicity photographers she so assiduously courted, Mansfield's image is at once ephemeral and tragic, the ultimate commodification of the star as a public icon (Champlin, 194–98). Rita Moreno's house in the Pacific Palisades is cool and understated by comparison, yet still the domain of a star, with career artifacts and awards displayed prominently on the mantelpiece above her fireplace (Cheever, 206). As one looks at these images of the stars in their movies, the past and the present become inextricably intertwined into one timeless location of memory, where the gaze of the public meets the returned look of the object to be adored; the star sanctified and enshrined in luxury by the members of the cinema audience.

Bing Crosby eternally sits on the diving board of his swimming pool in 1935, confidently cradling a pipe in his hand, just before the shooting of *Two for Tonight* (1935, dir. Frank Tuttle). He will always be there, radiating health, youth, and luxury, his house immaculately appointed, his relaxed public charm a continual lure for the viewer (Edwards, 215). Producer Gale Anne Hurd relaxes in her Beverly Hills house which dates comfortably from the 1930s (Haldeman, 222), while Colleen Moore still holds court in her Bel Air mansion, posing for photographers in the endlessly mirrored bathroom of her home, next to her yellow onyx bathtub (Tapert, 220). In Coldwater Canyon, Ray Milland and his wife Mal seem comfortable and relaxed in their comparatively modest domain (Harmetz, 190), while Joan Bennett strides boldly across the lawn of her estate in Holmby Hills (Aronson, 173).

Never in all these carefully choreographed, delicately posed publicity shots do we see any hint of future events that will alter these images irrevocably, sometimes canceling them out altogether from the public's memory. When Jayne Mansfield died, her dreams of a glamorous Hollywood life had long since collapsed, and she was reduced to nightclub performances and forgettable B films, but none of that is present here, or is it? How could Joan Bennett, in 1937 divorced with two children and monitoring "the construction of the 14-room French provincial style house that would make her, as she put it, 'one of the landed gentry' " (Aronson, 173), know that her marriage to Walter Wanger, after a streak of hits in the 1940s, would lead to a tragic shooting in the parking lot of MCA, as Wanger shot Jennings Lang (who by then had become romantically involved with Bennett) two times at close range with a .38 pistol. Bennett was convinced that the incident ruined her career.

In 1970, Joan Bennett wrote that "I was excommunicated, and the evidence lies in the fact that before December 13, 1951 [the date of the shooting], I'd made sixty-five films in twenty-three years, while in the decade that followed I made five" (cited in Aronson, 300). Ray Milland's son

Daniel would become a heroin addict and shoot himself fatally in 1981 (Harmetz, 294). Of what benefit were these images now, in a time of irrecoverable loss? To whom do they now appeal? Who *are* the attractive men and women who inhabit these fading images, whether taken in the 1940s or the 1990s, who so proudly pose within their transient domains?

Errol Flynn relaxes in his house in the Hollywood Hills in 1945, lighting a cigarette while sitting "atop a chintz-covered sofa in the living room before a painting by Paul Gauguin"; as his career collapsed in the 1950s, in a haze of cocaine and morphine addiction, Flynn wrote that "no matter where you seek and hide, the world will soon seek you out. And, when you come to think of it, someone who professes to be an actor cannot very well withdraw from life" (Lambert, 213, 215). His carefully designed domain, which he named Mulholland House (where John Barrymore had stayed for three weeks in 1942), was eventually sold to satisfy divorce proceedings against his ex-wife Lili Damita.

Seeking escape, Flynn repaired to his yacht, the *Zaca* (which he lovingly documented in a short travelogue he directed for Warner Brothers, *The Cruise of the Zaca*, 1952), and eventually wound up in Cuba, where he ingratiated himself with Fidel Castro. There Flynn scripted and produced his last film, *Cuban Rebel Girls* (aka *Assault of the Rebel Girls* and *Attack of the Rebel Girls*, 1959), in which Flynn cast himself in his final swashbuckling role as one of Castro's guerrillas. After his death, Mulholland House was sold to the ill-fated actor-singer Rick Nelson, who subsequently died in the crash of his private plane at age forty-five.

At length, the house itself was torn down by a real estate developer, who sold the now-vacant land at a huge profit (Lambert, 285). What remains of Flynn's domain in the wake of his ignominious death? The house is gone, but the still photographs and films survive (including even the disastrous scenes from his self-financed production of *William Tell*, which collapsed in an avalanche of bad debts and was never completed); yet Flynn's image at his peak, in the 1930s to late 1940s, is reused again and again to merchandise repeated televisual screenings of *The Adventures of Robin Hood* (1938, dirs. Michael Curtiz and William Keighley), *The Sea Hawk* (1940, dir. Michael Curtiz), *Objective, Burma!* (1945, dir. Raoul Walsh), and other key films of Flynn's career. Flynn's self-choreographed decaying image in *Cuban Rebel Girls* is almost never revived; the public's hold on the memory of Flynn as a robust man of derring-do is too strong, for all intents erasing the spectacle of his decline.

These luxurious mansions of the past, joined today by the palatial home of Steven Spielberg in Pacific Palisades or Martin Scorsese's memorabilia-jammed New York townhouse, the latter decorated with posters from Jean Renoir's *Grand Illusion* (1937) and *The Golden Coach* (1952), Marcel Carné's *Children of Paradise* (1945), and Jean Cocteau's *Beauty and the Beast* (1946), are repositories of our communal dreams as members of the filmgoing public, but also refuges, or aide-mémoire, for their inhabitants. All this will pass away, leaving only the images to document their existence. For aren't these luxurious homes and apartments, in the last account, only sets and backdrops for the lives of their various inhabitants? As with Madeleine Castaing, who was a professional interior decorator by trade, the various producers, directors, and stars of both classical and contemporary Hollywood seek, in their choice of residences, to create the fantasy of a security that necessarily eludes them.

Within their elegantly appointed halls, behind a screen of unlisted telephone numbers, surveillance systems, security systems, and phalanxes of assistants, contemporary practitioners of the moving image seek to establish the same dominion over their lives as they do in their films, while realizing that such a performative act is an inherent impossibility. In making films, as in designing homes, these artists seek to achieve a measure of comfort and safety, divorced from the concerns of their precarious profession. But plaster peels, wiring goes bad, taxes must be paid. No domain is permanent.

Thus, through all these audience-structuring strategies of the late 1990s, we are given by Hollywood the cinema of spectacle as the domain of sacred violence, the phantom zone of the taboo in actualization; the ontology of the colonialist structures inherent in the supposed "transalterity" of the Dominant Hollywood cinema, in a spectacle that creates a neo-canonical order of sign/system exchanges within world visual culture. This hagiographic address typifies the contemporary biographical cinema; human existence is seen as a series of barely realized diegetic moments. We are left with disaster created solely for consumption, the celebrity of violence and death, the anonymity of the dead without voices. Queer cinema responds to the Dominant cinema by creating a zone of freedom and transgenderal address within a cinema of the margins, which favors the abandonment of the taxonomy of conventional narrative. For the Dominant film spectacle, however, semantic description has become the basic visual strategy of the late 1990s, foregrounded by postnarrative, excessive spectacularity, both visually and aurally.

As an oppositional force to this, in addition to the alternatives afforded by Queer cinema and the truly independent cinema (both created outside the zone of the conglomerates), a few maverick directors—unconcerned with patterns of distribution, advertising, and audience testing, and seeking only to express their own unique vision within the realm of the cinematograph—continue to ply their trade of making personal films with low budgets. For the most part, these filmmakers are content with modest box office returns, and their budgets are correspondingly small. But they remain decisively outside the realm of the blockbuster cinema, creating works of individual passion to please themselves alone. In some cases, the directors do not even seek widespread release of their films, preferring to have them shown at festivals or in various museums and archives throughout the world, rather than submit to the exigencies of the commercial marketplace.

One such filmmaker is Jean-Luc Godard, who began his career as a director in 1959 after a long career as a critic. When originally released (with the exception of his most conventional and accessible narrative film, *Breathless* [aka *A Bout de Souffle*, 1959]), Godard's early films were generally dismissed by most mainstream critics not only as being too didactic, too formalist, and too self-indulgent but also as lacking in cohesion or self-discipline. *Contempt* (*Le Mépris*), Godard's 1963 meditation on the lure and the pitfalls of conventional studio filmmaking, has been restored by Martin Scorsese to its original Franscope (the French equivalent of CinemaScope) splendor in several gorgeous 35mm Technicolor prints. When originally released, the $1 million production received indifferent notices and barely recouped its production costs. Now, with its superb cast of Jack Palance, Brigitte Bardot, Fritz Lang, and Michel Piccoli, as well as Georges Delerue's melancholic yet captivating score, *Contempt* is almost universally hailed as a masterpiece.

Similarly, Godard's other films of the 1960s, notably *My Life to Live* (*Vivre sa Vie*, 1962), *Band of Outsiders* (*Bande à Part*, 1964), *A Married Woman* (*Une Femme Mariée*, 1964), *Alphaville* (1965), *Masculine/Feminine* (1966), and *Weekend* (1967), are now routinely considered as canonical classics of the cinema; yet when first released, all of these films except for *Weekend* barely survived one-week runs in theaters, were subjected (for the most part) to indifferent and/or hostile reviews, and then were dumped by their respective distributors into the limbo of 16mm nontheatrical release. Only with the passage of three decades of increasingly frenetic, big-budget cinema practice can the economy and audacity of Godard's accomplishment with these early films be accurately appraised. One of Godard's most recent films is *For Ever Mozart* (1996). At a relatively brief running time of eighty-five minutes, *For Ever Mozart* is a densely structured *mixage* of sound and image; delicately layered in multichannel stereo and shot almost entirely with natural lighting, it is as assuredly undramatic as *Contempt* is tragically relentless in its narrative structure. As with many of his later films, such as *Hail Mary* (*Je vous salue, Marie*, 1985), *King Lear* (1987), *Germany Year 90 Nine Zero* (*Allemagne Année 90 Neuf Zéro*, 1991), and *Woe Is Me* (*Hélas pour moi*, 1993), Godard is more interested in pushing the limits of what the cinematic sound/image construct can possibly contain than he is entertaining (in a conventional sense) his audience. Once again, Godard is considerably ahead of his time, and in the present theatrical-release climate his newer films find themselves even less assured of receiving the distribution and screenings they so manifestly deserve. As one example, Godard's 1990 film *Nouvelle Vague* (*New Wave*) has never been accorded a theatrical release in the United States (aside from a few desultory museums and festival bookings), despite the fact that an international poll of critics in the June-August 1997 issue of *Film Comment* overwhelmingly voted *Nouvelle Vague* as their number one choice among films deserving release in a list of thirty unreleased foreign films—thirty films which have never received a theatrical release in the United States.

With this sort of near-universal critical approbation, one would assume that *Nouvelle Vague*, *For Ever Mozart*, and other more contemporaneous Godard films (to say nothing of his ongoing series of videos, *Histoire(s) du cinéma*) would surely be aggressively distributed on the art house circuit, at least, but this is not the case. Godard's newer works remain too complex, too fragmented, too rich in imagery and sound for many viewers, and the director himself is too uncompromising in his methods of production for most distributors. Godard's films remain resolutely unspectacular. More and more, the key filming locations of Godard's newer works are hotel rooms, driveways, stretches of barren fields—elegiac zones of contemplation in which people read, engage in inconclusive conversations, stare out windows in the bleak afternoon light, and ponder the transience of their shared mortality.

Godard's visual style has also changed from his earlier works. Gone are the ferociously bright compositions of flat, primary colors, and the flat, direct lighting that lends a near-newsreel aspect to such films as *Masculine/Feminine* and *Weekend*. After experimenting with a variety of lighting strategies from the early 1980s to the early 1990s (the deep saturation of color and "painterly" lighting of *Passion* [1982], the quotidian utilitarianism of his setups in *King Lear*, the sumptuous tracking shots of *Nouvelle Vague*), Godard seems to have found his definitive late cinematographic style with such films as *Germany Year 90 Nine Zero*, *Woe Is Me*, *JLG/JLG*—

Self-Portrait in December (*JLG/JLG—Autoportrait de décembre*, 1994), and *For Ever Mozart*.

In sharp contrast to the near "pop" intensity of such early classics as *Weekend*, Godard now prefers a palette of muted earth-tone colors—greens and browns, with light spilling over into the scene from table lamps, overcast skies, and strategically located windows. Godard's editorial style has also changed; gone are the bold blocks of shots edited together alternatively into long, single-take sequences or rapidly repeated montages, these elements now replaced by a more traditional evaluation of each shot as an individual visual unit, coupled with an editorial rhythm which is at once assured and yet deeply felt. This is true only for Godard's *film* work; his videos are a different affair—a jumble of images rather than a stately procession of tableaux.

Godard, born in 1930, has grown up before our eyes in the cinema, from his first feature film at the age of twenty-nine to the current torrential output of his late sixties. The exuberance of youth has been replaced by the contemplation of old age; Godard seems haunted not only by his own past but also by the lives of Mozart, Woolf, Kafka, Nietzche, Beethoven, Bach, Dvořák, Chopin, Liszt, Caravaggio, and Rembrandt as well as by (and above all) the artists of the cinema—Ford, Eisenstein, Rossellini, Lang, Leontine Sagan, Cocteau, Hawks, and others. As he reveals in *JLG/JLG*, Godard's life is now one of continual self-examination, as lived through books, films, and CDs. In his later works, Godard seems almost obsessed—even overwhelmed—by the history of art and politics, which has become an inexhaustible area of scrutiny for the filmmaker in the penultimate period of his career.

Indeed, *Histoire(s) du cinéma*, Godard's series of videos begun in 1989, comprise an avalanche of images and scraps of sound—blended together into a tapestry of overwhelming, aggressively wearying beauty—in which Godard (in direct contrast to his film works) utilizes the distorting and transformational aspect of video to maximum effect, manipulating clips from old movies, stills, bits of dialogue, strands of music, and hastily written intertitles to create a ferociously personal and daunting overview of our shared cinematic past. The density and unrelenting drive of the videos in this still ongoing series suggests strongly that Godard himself seems tempest-tossed in the inexorable sweep of moving image history, to the extent that he is driven to question and analyze every frame, every sound-bite, every moving image construct from the dawn of cinema to the present, to embrace and yet deeply question a medium that he himself has declared many times to be dead. Starting in the late 1960s, with

Weekend, Godard has been heralding the "end of cinema" with the fervor of a committed revolutionary; now, in his newer works, Godard seems convinced that the cinema will collapse under the sheer weight of the super spectacles that currently crowd the multiplexes of the world, leaving no room for the smaller, more personal visions of Godard and his fellow cinéastes.

In *For Ever Mozart*, Godard once again creates a deliberately fragmented narrative, a deeply self-reflexive film that challenges and confronts its audience. As Godard himself notes in the pressbook he designed for the film, *For Ever Mozart* is composed of "four films which don't necessarily make one. Like the four walls alone of a house." Threading through each of the four segments, or elements, of the film is the figure of the Director, named Vicky Vitalis, an aging and irascible artist who seems permanently dissatisfied with his work. As *For Ever Mozart* begins, the Director is trying to get a film (entitled *The Fatal Bolero*) into production, but soon a multiplicity of logistical problems seem to derail the project. One of the Director's nephews insists that the Director assist a theatrical troupe (of which the nephew is a member) in staging a play by Musset in Sarajevo, *The Game of Love and Chance*. But this enterprise, too, is fraught with difficulties and, typically, the Director abandons both the actors and the play when the war in Sarajevo encroaches on the project. The Director then attempts to complete his abandoned film, but almost gives up when he is unable to direct the actors to his satisfaction. When his film is finally completed, the audience rejects it in favor of the latest ultraviolent spectacle down the street. At length, the Director, exhausted, finds his way into a semideserted concert hall, where a young man (perhaps Mozart himself) plays the piano and conducts an orchestra in a spirited rendition of a Mozart concerto.

As an intertitle early on in the film informs us, *For Ever Mozart* might well be entitled "36 Characters in Search of History." Godard opens *For Ever Mozart* with a humiliating "cattle call" casting session, in which a gallery of actors are commanded to recite a sequence of dialogue but are thrown out, one after the other, after speaking only a few words. As a character in the film notes, "It's the little people who hope. Not the modern world." The dreams of these ordinary performers auditioning for a role in *The Fatal Bolero* are intertwined with their desire for phantasmal immortality, to be represented on the screen by an image of their existence long after their demise. Death, in the cinema as in real life, is an abstraction for Godard: as one character notes, "There is no death, there is only me, me (who is going to die)." Godard is equally skeptical (as always) of the entire enterprise of constructing theatrical and/or cinematic narratives in the face of a reality that is far crueler and more capricious ("One mustn't play at love in Sarajevo").

And yet, in the battle between authentic artistic expression and work for hire, Godard still seems convinced that artistic integrity is of paramount importance in a world that continually forces us to compromise. "As long as there are hacks who scribble away, there will be scoundrels who look to murder," one of Godard's protagonists notes, quoting Victor Hugo. The young actors who travel to Sarajevo are seen by Godard as an impossibly idealistic and impractical troupe of semiprofessionals; when they are caught up in the crossfire of battle (in a series of sequences surprisingly lavish for a late Godard film, involving numerous explosions and the use of actual tanks and mortars as props), their intellectual fervor avails them little as they are literally forced to dig their own graves.

As with all Godard's films, lyricism and brutality go hand in hand, and the desperation with which Godard's characters cling to classicism (books by or on the works of Victor Hugo, George Sand, Goya, Rembrandt, and other artists and writers are brandished about and debated in nearly every sequence in the film) is but one measure of their desire to generate meaning and context out of the chaos of actual existence. Movies and plays are a game, but a serious one; or as Godard states it, "Knowledge of the possibility of representation consoles us for being enslaved to life. Knowledge of life consoles us for the fact that representation is but shadow," an echo of the opening quotation by André Bazin which Godard uses in *Contempt*.

Further, again as with all Godard's films, constituted "authority" is seen as both useless and counterfeit. In *For Ever Mozart*, agents of the International Red Cross debate while civilians are slaughtered; governments attempt to intervene on behalf of the members of the stranded theatrical troupe but can do little more than quibble about technical details, affording no real measure of safety or protection. Rape, torture, and mass executions proceed in an atmosphere of deliberately drab, rundown buildings and muddy fields, as dictators and their stooges argue over trivialities, and screams of agony and gunfire echo in the distance. In the bleak, wintry landscape of Godard's Sarajevo, the thuggery of mass commerce and the violence of military brutality have long ago triumphed over the aspirations of individual artists, although the artists persist, despite all obstacles, in pursuing their goals.

Godard's compositions in *For Ever Mozart* are resolutely utilitarian; no attempt is made to design the shots to satisfy conventional standards of cinematic representation. The sun never seems to shine, the lighting indoors is always funereal and unflattering. The actors in *For Ever Mozart*, as in many late Godard films, deliver their lines in a flat, disinterested monotone, as if directly acknowledging the inherent fraudulence of staged narrative. And yet, despite the atmosphere of a series of disjointed political agit-prop skits, what emerges takes on the feel and appearance of an early Rossellini film: stars, sets, costumes, and conventional narrative tropes are abandoned in favor of a style that at once acknowledges the fictive nature of Godard's world in *For Ever Mozart* but also renders that world poignantly real and concrete.

The drab visuals of *For Ever Mozart* provide, in fact, the perfect vehicle for rendering a world of unceasing exploitation and compromise, for as Godard notes in the pressbook for the film, "War—the theatre of operations—follows theatre. And cinema follows war. In both instances, actors are gotten cheap and will have to pay for it." The world of social upheaval and disjunction limned in *For Ever Mozart* is at once a construct as well as a documentary of real (though staged) events. Godard demands of his protagonists that they sacrifice the safety and closure of conventional narrative for a territory far more tenuous and unexplored—the landscape of perpetual uncertainty, in which there is no solid ground, no "key light." As a visual, aural, and narrative construct, *For Ever Mozart* is a film reduced to a minimum of means in order to convey a maximum of subtextual referents.

In the final segment of *For Ever Mozart*, far from Sarajevo and the actors he has abandoned, the harried and exploited Director tries to get *The Fatal Bolero* back into production. His producers are concerned only with money ("We learned that from the Hakim Brothers," one of them comments) and superficial production values; as for the script, one of the producers vehemently tells the director that at the end of the film, "The girl should die in a twister!" The filming itself is a series of disasters. Asked by the producers to complete a lengthy battle sequence, the Director simply tears the corresponding pages out of his script ("There . . . it's done!"), crediting the strategy to John Ford. An entire morning of filming is spent trying to get a young woman to deliver a single word of dialogue ("Oui") without success. Somehow, the film is finished. But postproduction problems persist.

Without warning, the executive producers of *The Fatal Bolero* abscond with the production money, leaving cast and crew adrift in a sea of bounced checks. But the wily line-producer of *Bolero* has foreseen such a contingency and has held on to the film's negative. In a desperate attempt to avoid bankruptcy, he decides to "open it fast" to make some money. This last-ditch "saturation booking" plan, however, is to no avail; the public hates the finished film. "It's in black and white!" one would-be patron complains. "If it's poetry, I'll walk out!" another declares. "Sorry, kid! there are no tits!" the producer reluctantly informs another audience member. Disgusted by the lack of sex and violence in the film, the audience deserts en masse to see *Terminator 4*, playing down the street. "Come back, my friends!" the producer implores. "We'll change the movie!" But *The Fatal Bolero* is doomed from the start.

As the crowd departs, the theater owner is seen hastily putting up a poster for a different (and no doubt, more commercial) film. The Director wanders alone down the street, deserting the scene of his latest "commercial failure." As *For Ever Mozart* concludes, we see the Director slumped in the hallway of a concert hall, lighting a cigarette as he leans against the banister and the opening notes of a Mozart concerto are heard on the sound track. The film ends with a series of radiant close-ups of the young pianist-conductor leading the ensemble—the only time in the entire film that sunlight has been allowed to penetrate the atmosphere of pessimistic fatalism which has been its predominant theme. *The Fatal Bolero* may be finished and a failure, but the music of Mozart lives on, unencumbered by commerce and compromise. At the end of this "film of intranquility" (Godard's own phrase), one is left with "the music. And for that, you have to know how to turn the pages of the score—life. And to give the tempo."

At eighty-five minutes, *For Ever Mozart* is at once compact and epigrammatic, lucid and complex, yet it is one of Godard's most accessible and beautiful films. His films in the 1990s have been modestly budgeted, yet their aim and scope (with the notable exception of the introspective *JLG/JLG*) seem to be widening to consider the evolving social landscape of the planet rather than merely turning inward. *For Ever Mozart* is indebted to past masters of literature, the cinema, and the visual arts as well as to music, but it is still very much involved in investigating the central concern of Godard's career as a filmmaker: in a medium that inextricably intertwines both art and commerce, how can one responsibly effect political, social, and/or moral change through the cinema?

Disinterested in the politics of distribution, and eschewing the false values of spectacle for the resonance of meditative elegies, Godard has been fashioning films solely according to the dictates of his conscience since 1959; today, he continues as before, creating works that are both disturbing and enlightening. *For Ever Mozart* contains themes Godard has been concerned with since the 1960s, with *Le Petit Soldat* (1960) and *Les Carabiniers* (1963), but it is also a further signpost to a new direction, begun with *King Lear*, *Nouvelle Vague*, and *Germany Year 90 Nine Zero*. In these later films, sound and image have become ever more complex and yet ever more sculpturally pared down, as Godard invites his audience to participate almost as coconspirators in his new epistemological research.

Not so with the creators of the Dominant cinema; as Godard's film clearly demonstrates, they must constantly strive to appeal to the largest spectrum of the public as possible, over and above all other possible considerations. Serving the most widely accepted expectations of the public is thus the contemporary commercial cinema's most urgent and pressing concern. Along with the stars of the Dominant cinema, certain public figures whose lives—in politics, sports, advertising, or commerce—for one reason or another have become inextricably intertwined with pop celebrity and on-demand commercial glamour must also sell themselves aggressively to their constituents. And when one group of constituents falls away, the progressive public politician in the late 1990s must immediately find another.

When the Soviet Union collapsed in the early 1990s, Mikhail Gorbachev was forced to deal with the reality of the political situation and to find other work to keep himself occupied. For a while, his appropriated image was used in a series of billboards for Pabst beer; he has since been seen as the consenting (and compensated) star of a series of commercials for Pizza Hut. When the Third Reich was collapsing under the weight of the combined Allied assault in 1943, both Hitler and his propaganda minister, Joseph Goebbels, tried a different strategy—they simply pretended that it wasn't happening. Victory was assured on all fronts, they thought, if only the Nazis would fight on relentlessly. Accordingly, Goebbels held a huge rally in the Sportspalast in Berlin on February 18, 1943, with the theme of making an all-out effort to conclude the war in Germany's favor. Speaking under an enormous banner emblazoned with the slogan "Totaler Krieg—Kürzesterkrieg" ("Total War—Faster War"), Goebbels whipped his audience into a frenzy of mass participation, asking a series of rhetorical questions designed to secure the German public's wholehearted support for the ongoing conflict, as recorded by Nazi "newsreel" cinematographers covering the event.

GOEBBELS: The English claim that the German people are resisting
   Government measures for total war.

CROWD: Lies! Lies!

GOEBBELS: It doesn't want total war, say the English, but capitulation.

CROWD: Sieg Heil! Sieg Heil!

GOEBBELS: Do you want total war?

CROWD: Yea! [*Enthusiastic applause*]

GOEBBELS: Do you want it more total, more radical, than we could ever have imagined?

CROWD: Yes! Yes! [*Loud applause*]

GOEBBELS: Are you ready to stand with the Führer as the phalanx of the homeland behind the fighting Wehrmacht? Are you ready to continue the struggle unshaken and with savage determination, through all the vicissitudes of fate until victory is in our hands?

CROWD: Yes!

GOEBBELS: I ask you: Are you determined to follow the Führer through thick and thin in the struggle for victory and to accept even the harshest personal sacrifices?

CROWD: Yes! Sieg Heil! [*A chant of "The Führer commands, we follow"*]

GOEBBELS: You have shown our enemies what they need to know, so that they will no longer indulge in illusions. The mightiest ally in the world—the people themselves—have shown that they stand behind us in our determined fight for victory, regardless of the costs.

CROWD: Yes! Yes! [*Loud applause*]

GOEBBELS: Therefore let the slogan be from now on: "People arise, and storm break loose!" [*Extended applause*]

CROWD: Deutschland, Deutschland über alles in der Welt . . . (cited in Welch, 86–87)

It was, all in all, a spectacular performance, one that managed to avoid the reality that the Reich was already coming apart at the seams. Later issues of the *Deutsch Wochenschauen* (the Nazi Party's omnipresent "newsreel") pasted together footage of earlier successful engagements with the enemy, to perpetuate the illusion that victory was still within Germany's grasp. Goebbels, meanwhile, was busily overseeing the production of the last Nazi superspectacle, *Kolberg* (1945, dir. Veit Harlan), an enormous production for which Goebbels actually removed soldiers essential to the war effort from the battle fronts and placed them at Harlan's disposal for the film's costly, and unceasing, battle sequences.

In the meantime, succeeding issues of *Deutsche Wochenschauen* became ever more fantastic in their avoidance of the imminent Nazi collapse. The final edition of the "Newsreel," completed in March 1945, concentrated on images of industrial strikes in the United States, American prisoners of war in German military prison camps, and German soldiers fighting to recapture various towns from which they had been forcibly evicted (Welch, 94–95). The resultant "Newsreel," a pastiche of found, staged, and/or manipulated visual materials, presented not only the "unreality of Goebbels' mental picture of the war" (Welch, 95) but also demonstrated the propaganda minister's skill in presenting strictly those images that he wished the public to see, in precisely the syntactical order required to successfully inflame and reassure an increasingly skeptical and demoralized German public.

Goebbels's view of the war was a construct, and he knew it. In putting together the final edition of *Deutsche Wochenschauen*, Goebbels noted in his diaries that there were specific scenes of defeat which were impossible to incorporate into the finished product: "In the evening the new *Wochenschauen* is submitted to me. It includes some really shattering pictures from the West which we cannot possibly publish. Demolition of the Rhine bridges in Köln, for instance, makes one heavy at heart" (quoted in Welch, 99). But despite the overwhelming evidence of impending defeat, Goebbels kept up a public front that the war was still proceeding in Germany's favor. Indeed, in the final days of the war Goebbels told astonished members of his staff that someday a spectacular color feature film would be made of these trying days for the Reich, and that every one of his staff should therefore conduct him/herself in a manner that would insure history's most favorable posthumous verdict on their actions in time of crisis (Hull, 265).

Goebbels sought to erase from the public's mind any real images of the conflict, just as the United States government succeeded in doing in its "coverage" of the Gulf War, which was so adroitly stage managed and precensored that Jean Baudrillard has correctly likened television reportage of the event to a TV miniseries in which an entire spectacle of conflict is created for viewers out of phantom images whose veracity is never called into question. The Gulf War was above all other considerations a television event, abruptly entered into and hastily concluded, with a scripted "victory" achieved in a matter of days. As Baudrillard notes, "Since this war was won in advance, we will never know what it would have been like had it existed. We will never know what an Iraqi taking part with a chance of fighting would have been like. We will never know what an American taking part with a chance of being beaten would have been like. . . . In this forum of war which is the Gulf, everything is hidden: the planes are hidden, the tanks are buried, Israel plays dead, the images are censored and all information is blockaded in the desert: only TV functions as a medium without a message, giving at last the image of pure television" (1995:61–63).

All is illusion. Just as the animated characters in the cartoons of Tex Avery exist just to be ritualistically maimed, mauled, stuffed into cannons, and thrown off cliffs, fracturing into a million splinters only to be immediately revivified in cartoon after cartoon, so Kenneth Williams, Sidney James, Hattie Jacques, and the other members of the *Carry On* comedy series cheerfully violate history in such films as *Carry On, Cleo* (1964) and *Carry On, Henry VIII* (1971), both directed by Gerald Thomas. Using Antony and Cleopatra's tempestuous relationship and Henry the VIII's numerous marriages as the basis for an endless procession of vigorously tasteless sight gags, these films rewrite both historical fact and convention as a medium for working-class satire.

Coleen Gray, seeking the memory and physical actuality of her lost youth, is sure to be "Forever young! Forever deadly!" as "she live[s] off the life blood of male victims" (according to the film's tag line) in Edward Dein's *The Leech Woman* (1960). When the viewer finishes watching Dein's film, she/he is left with an overpowering sense of loss, of what has not been captured, of the essence that perpetually evades us in our efforts to revivify the dead, to recapture the memory of our former selves. As all lives must end, often unsatisfactorily, we increasingly seek compensatory closure in our escapist films and videos, whether for good or ill. We can control our existence when it is reduced to a series of dyes and stenciled images on an unspooling ribbon of film, or in a series of strategically rearranged magnetic particles on a cassette of videotape, but we cannot live our own lives according to a script. Both order and destiny elude us.

In Edmond T. Greville's *Wild for Kicks* (aka *Beat Girl*, 1960), teenage gang leader Gillian Hills runs with a crowd that includes then-teenagers Oliver Reed, Adam Faith, Peter McEnery, and other disaffected British teens. Seeking to recapture the memory of her dead mother, Hills rejects her new stepmother (Noëlle Adam) and finds escape in stripping at a sleazy Soho nightclub run by a Machiavellian Christopher Lee, playing chicken on the railroad tracks by holding her head on the rails until just before a train passes by, and going to wild, late-night hot-rod races. Only the threat of near rape by club-owner Lee brings her to her senses, and she readily acquiesces to the demands of her father and stepmother, forsaking momentary escape for an engagement in her future as a member of the British Empire.

In Barry Shear's *Wild in the Streets* (1968), Max Frost (Christopher Jones), a wildly popular rock star, succeeds in becoming president of the United States after the voting age is lowered to fourteen, while his appalled mother (Shelley Winters) and a duped congressman (Hal Holbrook) watch helplessly as he confines all those over thirty to concentration camps, where they are force-fed massive doses of LSD. To lend the proper note of verisimilitude to the proceedings, such luminaries as Dick Clark, Walter Winchell, and Melvin Belli appear as themselves; Richard Pryor makes an early appearance as Stanley X, the drummer in Max Frost's band, who also serves as his political hatchet-man. Trapped in the concentration camps for adults engineered by Frost after this social disaster, Shelley Winters is unable to escape the memory of Max as a child, and his betrayal of her. As a last, hopeless gesture, she hangs herself on a barbed-wire fence, unable to deal with the reality she has been forced by film's narrative to inhabit.

Richard Lester's *The Bed-Sitting Room* (1969) is a post-apocalyptic comedy that takes place in a decimated London, shortly after the Third World War. With a cast including Rita Tushingham, Ralph Richardson, Peter Cook, Dudley Moore, Spike Milligan, Michael Hordern, and Mona Washbourne, Lester stages a series of nearly stillborn tableaux in which his motley, Lewis Carroll-ish characters strive to keep the traditions of British colonialism alive in a universe of crumbling monuments and a nonexistent social structure. In Toshio Masuda's bizarre and surreal 1974 film *The Last Days of Planet Earth* (*Nosutoradamusu no daiyogen*), the world is depicted as a horrific kaleidoscope of cataclysmic events heralding the end of human civilization. Val Lewton and Mark Robson's inexpressibly grim *The Seventh Victim* (1943) portrays a bleak world of Satanism in Greenwich Village in which a young girl (Kim Hunter) searches for her sister who has inexplicably disappeared, only to find her involved in a group of devil worshippers.

Sidney Miller's *Get Yourself a College Girl* (1964) spins the tale of a group of young college students who conspire to reelect an aging senator (Willard Waterman) after he espouses the concerns of "the young." In the dream ski resort where the film's action takes place, life is seen as an endless rite of courtship or maritally sanctioned nonstop sex, set to the beat of the Dave Clark Five, the Animals, the Standells, the Jimmy Smith

Trio, and Stan Getz and Astrud Gilberto. Quite predictably, no one ever wants to leave this endless party zone, and the film ends with the bacchanal still in full swing.

Joseph Newman's *The George Raft Story* (1961) stars future horror-film director Ray Danton as Raft in a carefully manicured version of the rise and fall of the 1940s Warner Brothers film star. Al Capone (Neville Brand) and Bugsy Siegel (Brad Dexter) appear as obstacles in Raft's rise to the top, while Jayne Mansfield, Barrie Chase, and Julie London vie for his affections. Here the zone of memory extends into the then-present, as Raft was still alive and working (in Billy Wilder's *Some Like It Hot* [1959] and Leslie Martinson's *For Those Who Think Young* [1964]) when the film was shot. In William Seiter's *The Moon's Our Home* (1936), Henry Fonda and Margaret Sullavan drift carelessly through a breezy comedy about a romance between a movie star (Sullavan) and a novelist (Fonda): in real life, Sullavan and Fonda had been married and divorced before the film was made, thus putting the two protagonists in the uncomfortable position of reliving a relationship that had ended badly for both of them.

Similarly, William Castle teamed Barbara Stanwyck and Robert Taylor, many years after their divorce, in his 1964 fantasy-horror film *The Night Walker*, forcing them to simulate a passion which had long since died, in the service of generic requirements and box office appeal; the postmarital reteaming of Stanwyck and Taylor was good for national comment in the press. In Edward Bernds's *High School Hellcats* (1958), a young girl (Yvonne Lime) falls in with the members of a hell-raising sorority, with disastrous results for all concerned. "What must a good girl do to belong?" the film's advertisements rhetorically wondered, as an incitement to viewers distracted by too many competing films.

Alfred E. Green's *Invasion U.S.A.* (1952) centers around the aptly named Mr. Ohman (Dan O'Herlihy), who hypnotizes a group of patrons in a midtown Manhattan bar into believing that they have been attacked by the Soviet Union, setting off World War III. When Ohman ends his spell, the various denizens of the bar momentarily break out of their self-induced alcoholic torpor, resolving to lead more productive and "patriotic" lives. Arthur Dreifuss's *The Love-Ins* (1967) follows the rise of a Timothy Leary clone (Richard Todd) who urges his followers to "see more, feel more, be more," and stages mass rallies in support of legalizing LSD until he is shot dead during a stadium rally by one of his former supporters. Viewing the film today, it is clear what the Dominant media of the era desired. Disturbed by Leary's appeal to his followers, the film's producers were both forecasting, and to a degree advocating, his death.

In *Hercules in the Haunted World* (1961, dir. Mario Bava) and *Hercules, Prisoner of Evil* (1964, dirs. Antonio Margheriti and Ruggero Deodato), Reg Park as Hercules must face the terror of Hell to save the life of a young princess, and then dispatch a witch "who turns men into werewolves" (Weldon, 317). The list goes on infinitely—whether depicting scenes of domestic chaos or intergalactic destruction, all of these genre films, products of our insatiable desire for spectacle and violence, presented side-by-side with artificially constructed images of domestic tranquillity, seek to hold us in thrall with undreamed-of wonders, something superficially new with each successive scene, creating a hermetically sealed fantasy world that we either seek to escape, or wish to inhabit forever.

But it is important above all to remember that these genre films were primarily product, knocked out on an assembly-line basis to make money, much in the same way that Stanley Tong's *Mr. Magoo* (1997) reduces the former director of Jackie Chan's superb action films of the 1980s to nothing more than a workman for hire within the Hollywood machine, his talents sadly misused, as were Peter Jackson's after his superb film *Heavenly Creatures* (1994). Lured to Hollywood after the success of *Heavenly Creatures*, Peter Jackson was put to work directing Michael J. Fox in 1996's *The Frighteners*, which failed at the box office. After the production of *The Frighteners*, Michael J. Fox quite sensibly went back to television in the sitcom *Spin City*, a project far more attuned to his skills as a light comedian. But for Stanley Tong and Peter Jackson, the message is clear: for most directors, Hollywood is little more than a glorified factory in which one turns out acceptable product to assembly-line specifications, which is what television does more than any other medium. TV needs product for instant consumption, and its appetite is voracious. Reruns are not acceptable, although they are constantly employed: the televisual public, as always, demands superficial novelty in their programming. The film business is, indeed, more product-driven and consumer-driven than ever before.

Recently, a new tactic in motion picture financing has emerged. In addition to product tie-ins and endorsements, directors are now being forced by economic considerations to insert actual commercials into the texts of their films in order to obtain the necessary funding. Nancy Savoca, whose directorial credits include two episodes of the TV movie *If These Walls Could Talk* (1996; Savoca directed the "1952" and "1974" segments), as well as the highly acclaimed theatrical features *Household Saints* (1993), *Dogfight* (1991), and *True Love* (1989), was forced by budgetary concerns to include several actual commercials in her film *The 24 Hour Woman* (1998).

As Jennifer Steinhauer noted when she visited Savoca on the set during production of *The 24 Hour Woman*, "part of the financing [for the film] will come from real commercials for products like Duracell batteries, Blimpie and Fab detergent that are cut into the movie's talk-show sequences. 'We have no shame,' Ms. Savoca said. 'Plus it gives us realism. Fake commercials would have been cheesy, and this paid for a lot of the film' " (7). Certainly this is true, but at the same time, it increases the commercial intensity of the project, linking the images in *The 24 Hour Woman* inextricably to the world of consumerism and human objectification.

But as any contemporary commercial director working today will readily tell you, directing genre pictures is a brutal business, and this has always been the case. It's a fight for time, for money, for creative freedom within a cinematic straitjacket. Numerous classical Hollywood action directors, such as Ray Nazarro, George Archainbaud, and Joseph Kane can attest to this, having worked in Hollywood from the 1930s to the late 1960s, directing both feature films and television programs. In an interview shortly before his death, director Joseph Kane described the rigors of shooting a one-hour action television show in the mid-1960s, on a schedule roughly comparable to that of *ER*, *Walker, Texas Ranger*, *Xena: Warrior Princess*, or other contemporary hour-long dramas. As Kane said of his work as a director on *Rawhide*, *Laramie*, *Bonanza*, and *Cheyenne*, all hour-long Western television shows popular in the early 1960s:

> We had five days to do those one-hour shows. You've got to have forty-eight minutes of story. Twelve minutes of advertising, main title . . . junk. Five days! And that didn't mean you could go nights! You had to start at eight in the morning and be through at six.
>
> So you had forty-five hours. A very tight schedule. You had to knock off around twenty-eight setups a day. Figure it out—you've got to do a setup every fifteen minutes. And you *have* to do it, because the following Monday they start the new one on the same set. They've hired the cast the week you're shooting. The director is getting ready. And you have to get the hell off that set by Friday night. Thursday afternoon, the new scripts arrive on the set, and the crew and the cast are reading the new scripts while you're trying to shoot your show! (Flynn and McCarthy, 322–23)

Thus directors working under such intense pressure become little more than traffic cops, ceaselessly moving the production along, adopting the standard program-director motto of "get it, then forget it."

As audiences became more jaded by contemporary spectacle, they needed ever larger doses of violence to keep them satisfied. Samuel Z. Arkoff, who founded American-International Pictures in the early 1950s with Jim Nicholson, instituted a policy of appealing *solely* to the teen market, making a series of violent, sensational films designed to lure teenagers out of the house and into the theaters, just as *Scream 2* does today. Although AIP sold out to Filmways in 1979, Samuel Arkoff retained, even in later years, a careful sense of why certain pictures clicked, and when. In the early 1960s, AIP moved into the *Beach Party* series (directed, for the most part, by William Asher), sensing that what teens of that era required more than anything else were escapist visions of a teenage life without adult supervision, but with plenty of money (and the things it buys) in evidence in every luxuriously appointed sequence. Thus such films as *Beach Party* (1963, dir. William Asher), *Bikini Beach* (1964, dir. William Asher), *How to Stuff A Wild Bikini* (1965, dir. William Asher), *Ski Party* (1965, dir. Alan Rafkin), and *The Ghost in the Invisible Bikini* (1966, dir. Don Weis) catered to a preexisting need for teen escapist fantasy during this era, following trends rather than trying to set them. The audience, in short, is coproducer of the spectacle it witnesses and helps to create. As Arkoff explained to Linda May Strawn,

> We made those pictures because we sensed a trend. We were not trying to create new areas that young people didn't want to go into or had blocks against or weren't ready for. We were trying to fathom how far and how fast the youth changes were occurring. . . .
>
> From the beach pictures, we went to rebellious youth. *The Wild Angels* [1966, dir. Roger Corman], *Wild in the Streets* [1968, dir. Barry Shear]. Open rebellion. Just as the other companies started to get into that, we got out. Kent State was a tip-off. The kids turned off. When they saw students could get killed, they realized it was serious. . . .
>
> The young people had turned off. They want escapism. Not old-fashioned romantic pictures, [which] the young public doesn't want to look at today. (Strawn, 265)

This seems remarkably in line with the findings of the researchers at Teen Research Unlimited; teens then, as now, want escapism without risk, and when it gets too close, they lose interest. Hyperreality is not the issue here; the key is *unreality, unrelenting* and *unremitting.* The movie viewer, ensconced in her/his seat in the darkness, seeks above all to *avoid* reality, to put off for as long as possible the return to normalcy, when they push past the upturned boxes of popcorn and spilled sodas and make their way through the doors into the world outside. But are they ever satisfied? The entire key behind contemporary genre films is to keep the viewer hooked, perpetually wanting more, to be satisfied yet still hungry for a return to the same world, the same characters, the same general plotline, with only minor variations. This explains why every cast member not killed in *Scream* (1996) is back for *Scream 2* (1997); audiences want continuity, and *Scream 3* is already in preproduction. Today's genre films are really serials above all else, in which formulaic thrills and formula entertainment are dispensed in two-hour bursts, with the promise of more to come held out in the final scenes of each new work.

Perhaps this is why the spectacle of the death of Princess Diana so captured the popular imagination; here was one spectacle of disaster and opulence which *could not be repeated*, because the protagonist was truly dead, not fictively deceased, awaiting resurrection in a sequel to her years as a member of the Royal Family. Diana's rise to power and prominence was a real-time, continually unfolding genre entertainment, one whose plot twists were as unpredictable as any suspense film, and whose characters captured the popular imagination through a variety of charitable deals, displays of wealth, and travel to exotic locales, where only the truly wealthy can afford the tariff. And it was a one-time-only spectacle, in which the violent end seemed bizarrely appropriate for a life lived at high speed for the past fifteen years.

Now there will be no "happily ever after"; there will be no "ever after" at all. Diana's death seals up forever the possibility of a sequel, reminds the audience that, in this instance, there is no hope of shooting additional scenes to complete a sequence that was badly directed: the spectacle is over, and only the memory remains. Perhaps this is why, months after Diana's death, "documentaries" of hastily assembled clips of her life still dominate the airwaves, why her every motion, her smiles, her waves to the adoring members of her public have been so carefully catalogued and preserved. Diana's image will be forever young, the mask that age cannot wither because the original owner has passed from our view. Every instant of Diana's life can now be charted, and it seems that the public appetite for it is nearly limitless. Is it the certainty that she will never be able to change her image that satisfies the public? Is it the sameness of her likeness that audiences hunger for, like the sameness of the sequel? Every "new" image of Diana will always replicate an existing glyph. Diana's only future is in her past.

When Maria Falconetti is burned at the stake in Carl Theodor Dreyer's *The Passion of Joan of Arc* (1928), we can marvel at Dreyer's artistry in staging the spectacle of Joan's conflagration, but we know that what we are witnessing is an illusion. When Richard Todd as U.S. Senate Chaplain Peter Marshall in Henry Koster's *A Man Called Peter* (1955) is stricken with a second, and fatal, heart attack within the narrative confines of Koster's film, we know that we are merely witnessing the cinematic "death" of a person who is portraying the historical figure of Peter Marshall, who did indeed die after a heart attack at a relatively young age. The "real" Peter Marshall, whose life was marked by an avoidance of spectacle and who was never the star of a film, will likely never be seen by us again except in old newsreel clips which survive in vaults in the National Archive, clips that perhaps no one will ever view. Yet his copy lives on, cinematically and iconically, ready to repeat the homogenized details of Marshall's career over and over for our communal satisfaction.

We also know that the Dorothy Gale in Walter Murch's *Return to Oz* (1985) is not the one we are familiar with from Victor Fleming's 1939 version; in Murch's revisualization of L. Frank Baum's story, Dorothy escapes from a dank, dark Kansas sanitarium to return to an Oz ruled by the evil Nome King, an Oz bereft of any of the charm or splendor of the earlier version. This is not the Oz we know, and we reject it implicitly. When an anonymous gigolo who has been loitering in Vivien Leigh's courtyard in José Quintero's film of Tennessee Williams's play *The Roman Spring of Mrs. Stone* (1961) is at length admitted by Leigh to her apartment, we know (because it has been foretold by Lotte Lenya) that he will kill her for her jewelry and money, even as the film ends before this final desecration can occur.

Conversely, we know that Lotte Lenya, who rose to prominence in Bertolt Brecht and Kurt Weill's *The Threepenny Opera*, which she performed on stage numerous times before she appeared in the film version directed by G. W. Pabst in 1931, is also convincing as the brutal, sinister Rosa Klebb, James Bond's memorable nemesis in *From Russia with Love* (1963, dir. Terence Young), as she tries to stab Bond to death with a poisoned blade hidden in her sensible but clunky black Soviet shoes. As the passage of time deprived her of the iconic bloom of youth, Lenya realistically assessed the situation and was more than willing to appear as a dowdy or waspish villain, as were Bette Davis and Joan Crawford in the final days of their respective careers.

When the traditional western collapsed, it was necessary to reinvent it, as the Italian cinema did during the 1960s with such ultraviolent "spaghetti westerns" as *Four Dollars for Vengeance* (1965, dir. Alfonso Balcazan), *A Taste for Killing* (1966, dir. Tonino Valerii), *Day of Anger* (aka *Day of Wrath*, 1967, dir. Tonino Valerii), *Hate for Hate* (1967, dir. Domenico Paolella), starring fading American cowboy icon John Ireland, *Hate Thy Neighbor* (1969, dir. Ferdinando Baldi), and *Have a Good Funeral, My Friend . . . Sartana Will Pay* (1971, dir. Anthony Ascott). This list, of course, does not include the most famous "spaghetti westerns," Sergio Leone's *A Fistful of Dollars* (1964), *For a Few Dollars More* (1965), and *The Good, The Bad, and the Ugly* (1966), three "breakout" westerns that resuscitated the career of Clint Eastwood, then only a minor former TV-star with several seasons of *Rawhide* under his belt.

In all these films, dialogue and motivation are minimal; violence is all. The lack of dialogue in Leone's films, particularly, made it easier to dub them into English, French, or German, so that Eastwood's transient fame could be exploited by the Italian-German-Spanish coproducers who underwrote the film's minimal production costs (Weisser, 114). This is what Geoffrey O'Brien referred to as "The Italian System," in which fading Hollywood genres and stars were recycled in the 1960s by the bustling studios of Cinecitta, which tackled everything from sword-and-sandal spectacles to westerns to science fiction to horror films, with only a few costume changes and the barest suggestion of sets to carry off the deception (O'Brien 1993:149–72).

In much the same way, Diana breathed new life into a Royal Family increasingly seen as being out of touch with its constituents, as being devoid of charm or charisma, and arrogant rather than approachable. That her death was both capricious and dramatically violent further enshrined her in the pantheon of pop immortals. In Atom Egoyan's film *The Sweet Hereafter* (1997), a group of fourteen schoolchildren are killed when their school bus falls through the ice of a semifrozen lake; as John Powers recounts, "The movie's most haunting sequence is the fatal crash, which makes a mockery of Hollywood razzle-dazzle. The yellow school bus simply skids off the road, rolls onto a frozen lake, and then plunges through the ice—easy as ABC. The accident is terrifying precisely because it's so quick, so banal. There are accidents, and they can happen to anyone" (Powers, 168).

But Diana's death was not as undramatic as Egoyan's fictive construct; her Mercedes was traveling at a high rate of speed at the point of impact from all accounts, as befits the violent, spectacular death scenes offered to the public by the commercial cinema. Thus, in the manner of her death as in the way she led her life, Diana was the new "chic" embodiment of royalty. Even after her divorce from Charles, she was widely perceived by the British public as having gotten out of a bad situation with grace and style, with fortune, children, and title intact. Yet not everyone agreed with this assessment. Even in Britain, there were many who publicly denounced the wave of self-abasement and lachrymose sentiment that surrounded her death, funeral, and interment.

Ron Press, a retired engineer, sent this letter to the newspapers:

> I find the media coverage of Diana's death intolerable. Only intimate friends and family noted and mourned the death of my wife, and that is how it must be. Have we lost all sense of proportion? (Jack and Marlow, 29)

Maggie Winkworth, a psychologist, noted that "Diana was very good at being a celebrity. But if she'd had a harelip none of this would ever have happened. I don't mean to be cruel, but can you deny the truth?" (Jack and Marlow, 18). Brendan Martin complained that "following acres of newsprint praising Diana's compassion and concern for victims of injustice, *The Guardian* burie[d] news of the drowning of 400 poor black Haitians [in the back of the paper]" (Jack and Marlow, 32). And Elizabeth Stern, a student of piano living in London whose parents had been killed in an automobile wreck in Florida six months before Diana's death, summed up the feelings of many Britons who felt that the observances of Diana's death were becoming unseemly with these words:

> What I feel and what those crowds outside the palaces felt seem completely unrelated. Flowers, cards, teddy bears—you don't send condolence letters to the person who's died, for heaven's sake! People wanted to feel grief so that they could feel part of it all. Fine. But they shouldn't imagine they were grieving. When I was on the Tube and I saw all those women with flowers in their arms on their way to Buckingham Palace, I just wanted to go up and shake them. One of my friends spent fifty pounds on flowers and sent them to the palace. And yet she didn't buy flowers for me when my own parents died. I find it hard to speak to her. My brother, who's a doctor, feels the same as I do, and so do all his colleagues. During the minute's silence one of the doctors at his hospital carried on working—somebody had to—and the nurses there actually shouted at him to stop. It was unbelievable. (Jack and Marlow, 22)

But whether one likes it or not, the death and burial of Diana Spencer became a media event nearly without parallel, a chance for both sponsors and networks (cable, satellite, and broadcast) to cash in on a ready-made spectacle of disaster (the crash) and memory (Diana's life within the confines of the Monarchy). With that in mind, for one last moment, let us watch the video of Diana's funeral together. More than 2.5 billion people watched the live broadcast worldwide; who knows how many have seen it since, captured forever on videotape? Before the funeral, on Friday, September 5, at 6 P.M., Queen Elizabeth spoke to the public at the behest of Prince Charles on the death of Princess Diana, saying in part that

> we have all been trying in our different ways to cope. It is not easy
> to express a sense of loss, since the initial shock is often succeeded
> by a mixture of other feelings: disbelief, incomprehension, anger—
> and concern for those who remain. We have all felt those emotions
> in these last few days. So what I say to you now, as your Queen and
> as a grandmother, I say from my heart. (Author's transcript)

The next day, at 11 A.M. in Westminster Abbey, a one-hour funeral service took place. Against a backdrop of organ music by Dvořák, Bach, Ralph Vaughan Williams, Elgar, and Mendelssohn, the funeral cortége entered the abbey, as the congregation watched. Princes William and Harry laid wreaths near their mother's coffin as a gesture of ceremonial remembrance. After a series of readings by Diana's sisters in memory of her death, Elton John sang a revised version of his song "Candle in the Wind," which would go on in a matter of weeks to becoming the best-selling pop single of all time. In his eulogy, Diana's brother, Earl Spencer, stood and delivered a stinging indictment not only of the press and its alleged role in Diana's death but also of the Royal Family's treatment of her, warning the Queen, in essence, that if the House of Windsor did not adequately protect and nurture Diana's sons William and Harry, then her "blood relatives" would. After more prayers, a blessing, and one minute of silence which was observed (as we have seen) nationwide, Diana's coffin left Westminster Abbey for the trip to Althorp at a few minutes past noon.

Outside Buckingham Palace, various bystanders offered their views on Diana's life and work as the funeral cortége slowly continued its journey to Diana's ancestral home. On CNN one bystander is heard commenting on Elton John's "Candle in the Wind" that although "the song was originally intended for Marilyn Monroe, I didn't really have much of an association with [it]. But I am exactly the same age as Princess Diana, and it just seems so appropriate that that song was rewritten for her, and I think for me that was probably the most moving part of the service today. . . . It's just been fantastic to be here, in a sad ironic way, to participate in this event, which is probably the event of the century."

On the road to Althorp, the funeral procession stops momentarily to clear away some flowers thrown by well-wishers, which are blocking the driver's view. Richard Branson, head of the Virgin Group, is seen smiling and laughing outside Buckingham Palace, where thousands of well-wishers remained to pay their respects. On CNN an announcer reminds the viewer that "in case you missed any part of Diana's funeral, the funeral will be replayed in its entirety in a very short time." Then it's time for a commercial, cushioned with especially designed "bumpers" featuring Diana at her most glamorous, waving to onlookers in ethereal slow motion. After a series of advertisements for computer software, Walt Disney World Cruises, and the American Pharmaceutical Industry, coverage continues.

A British journalist contrasts the style of mourning her generation adopted ("People like myself, who grew up in the 1940s, before Diana was born, were taught that we grieved privately, with dignity . . . and there's been a lot of criticism, particularly among the younger people in England, who felt that the Royal Family didn't express their grief publicly enough . . . it's a generational difference in how to cope with something very, very tragic") with the public outpouring of grief that attended Diana's death, finding that it ultimately satisfied both younger mourners (with Elton John's tribute) and older (with the singing of "I Vow to Thee My Country," one of Diana's favorite hymns). "We will never have the like again, of such color, such glamour, such life," the journalist concludes, as the procession continues down the M1 to Diana's final resting place.

After many more commercials, and a great deal more "color" commentary, the group of automobiles arrives in Harlestone Village, where cameras have been staring at the empty road at the edge of the village for many minutes, feeding a live transmission of the vacant strip of asphalt to millions of viewers around the globe. As the image splits into two screens in one, we watch as Diana's hearse exits off the M1 toward the village. As the onlookers wait, another advertisement for Walt Disney World Cruises, a preview trailer of the British independent film *The Full Monty* (1997, dir. Peter Calfaneo), and an ad for Crunch and Munch popcorn interrupt our visual surveillance of the funeral cortége's progress. All along the route, remote cameras, situated on overpasses, bridges, and other key vantage points, offer us a second-by-second account of the cortége's painstaking trip to the place of Diana's interment.

As the procession finally passes directly in front of our view at the edge of Harlestone Village, with Diana's coffin in plain view inside the glass-walled hearse, the crowd bursts into spontaneous applause. Like the footage of the Kennedy motorcade in Dallas, directly before JFK's assassination, as John F. Kennedy smiles and waves to the spectators moments before he is fatally shot, this footage will be "looped" and rerun again and again on local, national, and international television broadcasts over the next several days. This is the shot that the media have been waiting for, the "money shot," the close-up of the coffin that contains Diana's remains, just as the wreck of the Mercedes in Paris contained her dying body almost a week before. The video footage of Diana's wrecked automobile in Paris, fetishized and strobe-lit to abstract perfection by the news media, became a video loop ceaselessly played and replayed by the broadcast and cable television networks, even as Diana fought for her life in a Paris hospital not far away. Now, even in death, Diana is still the unceasing object of the news media's inquisitive and penetrating gaze.

At length, the hearse finally approaches the gates of Diana's ancestral estate, as the crowd continues to press in on all sides, throwing flowers, cheering, applauding. "There she is!" one child shouts, as the hearse passes him by. But these, however, are the last moments in which Diana's mortal remains will remain on display. Within seconds, the hearse passes mercifully out of the gaze of the public and the news cameras, into the gates of Diana's family estate; and as the crowd continues to cheer and applaud, the gates swing shut for a private burial the media—and by extension the world, both real and televisual—will not be allowed to attend.

All that is left now for CNN, CSPAN, MSNBC, NBC, CBS, ABC, E! Entertainment, and all the other news and entertainment channels is to replay, again and again, over and over, the footage of the funeral, clips of Diana's life, interviews and speeches, colorful or banal commentary from members of the press who have dedicated their lives to surveilling the Royal Family—and this they will do for the next several days. Montages of Diana's marriage to Charles, the birth of her two sons, footage of Diana visiting the poor and the infirm are all blended together in a "music video" scored to the rewritten "Candle in the Wind." One villager in Althorp tells an inquiring member of the press that she thinks having Diana buried here "will change the life of this village forever," as it probably will. Within minutes of the final shot of the hearse disappearing behind the gates of Diana's family estate, all the networks are running the funeral again, directly from the beginning, complete with a repeat of the progress of the funeral procession toward Althorp.

In death as in life, Diana's image—or even the memory of it, or of the coffin which has now come to symbolize her iconic presence in these last moments of public display—is recyclable, repeatable, endlessly renewable so long as videotape can be rewound and video footage pulled from various news archives. The trade in Princess Diana memorabilia is brisk. Tea towels, mugs, banners, T-shirts, CDs, videos—anything that can be imprinted with an image of Princess Diana is being sold and eagerly consumed by the public. On the Internet, this message was posted on a web discussion group: "I really would like to know the value of my Princess Diana Bride Doll by the Danbury Mint. If anyone has a clue I would really appreciate a response."

Wouldn't we all? As the months pass by, and the near hysteria surrounding the death of Diana recedes in the public memory to some degree, who knows the value of *any* of the many images taken from life on both film and video, and graven as likenesses on dolls, dinner plates, and other memorabilia of Diana Spencer, Princess of Wales? That her death was a disaster there can be no doubt; that she constructed her life as a carefully choreographed media dance also seems fairly certain. She could have chosen seclusion, as many celebrities, royal or otherwise, do; but instead Diana actively courted the world press, using it to shape public perceptions of herself and her children, enlisting sympathizers in her divorce proceedings with Prince Charles, and finally securing for herself a comfortable niche in civilian life that promised both power and prestige. But all that is ended now, and those of us who felt left outside this international spectacle of mourning are left to speculate on the reasons behind Diana's celebrity appeal. Diana was attractive, knew how to deliver a speech with confidence and poise, and was a consummate master of the photo op. But so are many other figures who catch the public's fancy. Perhaps Diana engaged so much public sympathy and interest because, in contrast to the other members of Britain's Royal Family, she seemed both modern and immediate, a pop celebrity in her own right. She knew where to stand, how to dress, and how to hit her "mark" precisely on target, so that she would be shown in precisely the right key light on formal public occasions.

In her off-duty public moments, when she took her sons to amusement parks or on skiing holidays, Diana still retained a degree of control over the press that would be the envy of many a Hollywood star. When scandal came, she weathered it with the insouciance of a Robert Mitchum, who refused to apologize to his public for a late 1940s marijuana bust that might easily have ended his career. Rather than knuckling under, Diana continually crested on the wave of publicity, reinventing herself visually and textually throughout her sixteen years in public life with style and grace, and an instinctive understanding of what would appeal to her public. And now, in death, she has become, along with James Dean, Marilyn Monroe, and a select few others, a legendary pop culture icon. We are right to be suspect of the maudlin outpouring of grief that attended Diana's death, even if it was genuine. For in her violent death, Diana ultimately sacrificed herself on the altar of celebrity martyrdom, thus fulfilling the public's darkest need to witness both the fairy tale beginning, and the tragic conclusion, of a very short and very public life.

SELECTED BIBLIOGRAPHY

Aronson, Steven M. L. 1996. "Joan Bennett: Star of *Woman in the Window* and *Father of the Bride* in Holmby Hills." *Architectural Digest* (April): 172–77, 300.

Atkinson, Michael. 1995. "The Eternal Return." *Village Voice* (Film Special Section), November 21, pp. 4–5.

August, Marilyn. 1997. "Grace, Diana Had Much in Common," *Lincoln (Neb.) Journal Star*, September 2, p. 5A.

Bart, Peter. 1995. "The *Other* Arnold." *GQ* (October): 89, 90, 94.

Bashe, Philip. 1992. *Teenage Idol, Travelin' Man: The Complete Biography of Rick Nelson*. New York: Hyperion.

Baudrillard, Jean. 1995. "*Crash.*" In *Simulacra and Simulation*, 111–19. Translated by Sheila Faria Glaser. Ann Arbor: University of Michigan Press, 1994.

——. *The Gulf War Did Not Take Place*. Translated by Paul Patton. Bloomington: Indiana University Press.

——. 1994. *The Illusion of the End*. Translated by Chris Turner. Stanford, Calif.: Stanford Univeristy Press.

——. *Seduction*. 1990. Translated by Brian Singer. New York: St. Martin's.

Berger, Meyer. 1937. "500 Pupils and Teachers Are Killed in Explosion of Gas in Texas School; 100 Injured Taken from the Debris." *New York Times*, March 19, p. 1.

Bhabha, Homi K. 1994. *The Location of Culture*. New York: Routledge.

Biel, Steven. 1996. *Down with the Old Canoe: A Cultural History of the Titanic Disaster*. New York: Norton.

Blanchot, Maurice. 1995. *The Writing of the Disaster*. Translated by Ann Smock. Lincoln: University of Nebraska Press.

Blevisky, Marshall. 1992. *American Mythologies*. New York: Oxford University Press.

Bogdanovich, Peter. 1971. *Allan Dwan: The Last Pioneer*. New York: Praeger.

Bordwell, David. 1989. *Making Meaning: Inference and Rhetoric in the Interpretation of the Cinema*. Cambridge: Harvard University Press.

Bourdon, David. 1989. *Warhol*. New York: Abrams.

Bragg, Rick. 1997. "Drop of Virus from a Monkey Kills Researcher in Six Weeks." *New York Times*, December 14, p. 16.

Brennan, Timothy. 1997. *At Home in the World: Cosmopolitanism Now*. Cambridge: Harvard University Press.

Butler, Judith. 1997. *The Psychic Life of Power*. Stanford, Calif.: Stanford University Press.

Carr, C. 1997. "Magnificent Obsessions: The Art and Artifacts of the World According to Jack Smith." *Village Voice*, December 2, pp. 39–40.

Caute, David. 1994. *Joseph Losey: A Revenge on Life*. New York: Oxford University Press.

Champlin, Charles. 1996. "The Actress's Pink Palace on Sunset Boulevard." *Architectural Digest* (April): 194–98, 292.

Chang, Suna. 1997. "The Royal Line." *Entertainment Weekly*, November 21, pp. 37–38.

Cheever, Susan. 1996. "Rita Moreno: The Dynamic Star of *West Side Story* in the Pacific Palisades." *Architectural Digest* (April): 204–209.

Clark, Candace. 1997. *Misery and Company: Sympathy in Everyday Life*. Chicago: University of Chicago Press.

Conley, Tom. 1991. *Film Hieroglyphs: Raptures in Classical Cinema*. Minneapolis: University of Minnesota Press.

Corliss, Richard. 1986. "Calling Their Own Shots: Women Directors Are Starting to Make It in Hollywood." *Time* 24 (March 1986): 82–83.

Corso, Gregory. 1989. *Mindfields*. New York: Thunder's Mouth.

Crowther, Bosley. 1951. "*Hard, Fast, and Beautiful*" (review). *New York Times*, July 2, p. 16.

D'Emilio, Frances. 1997. "Co-Stars in This Nativity: Princess Diana, Versace." *Lincoln (Neb.) Journal Star*, December 7, p. C1.

Davis, Douglas. 1993. *The Five Myths of Television Power; Or, Why the Medium Is Not the Message*. New York: Simon and Schuster.

Deivert, Bert. 1995. "Shots in Cyberspace: Film Research on the Internet." *Cinema Journal* 35, no. 1 (fall): 103–24.

Dempsey, John. 1997. "Cable Ops Caught in Nets." *Variety*, February 17–23, pp. 1, 84.

Dillard, Annie. 1998. "The Wreck of Time." *Harper's* (January): 51–56.

Diprose, Rosalyn. 1994. *The Bodies of Women: Ethics, Embodiment, and Sexual Difference*. London: Routledge.

"Di Would Have Been Next Body to Guard." 1997. *Lincoln (Neb.) Journal Star*, November 19, p. 4A.

Dixon, Wheeler Winston. Forthcoming. "When I'm 63: An Interview with Jonathan Miller." *Popular Culture Review*.

——. 1998. *The Transparency of Spectacle: Meditations on the Moving Image.* Albany: State University of New York Press.

——. 1997. *The Exploding Eye: A Revisionary History of 1960s American Experimental Cinema.* Albany: State University of New York Press.

——. 1997. *The Films of Jean-Luc Godard.* Albany: State University of New York Press.

——. 1995–96. "The Digital Domain: Some Preliminary Notes on Image Mesh and Manipulation in Hyperreal Cinema/Video." *Film Criticism* 20, nos. 1–2 (fall–winter): 55–66.

——. 1995. *It Looks at You: The Returned Gaze of Cinema.* Albany: State University of New York Press.

Donati, William. 1996. *Ida Lupino: A Biography.* Lexington: University Press of Kentucky.

Downing, David B. and Susan Bazargan. 1991. *Image and Ideology in Modern/Postmodern Discourse.* Albany: State University of New York Press.

Doyle, Jennifer, Jonathan Flatley, and José Estaban Muñoz. 1996. *Pop Out: Queer Warhol.* Durham, N.C.: Duke University Press.

Edwards, Anne. 1996. "Bing Crosby: The *Going My Way* Star in Rancho Santa Fe." *Architectural Digest* (April): 210–15, 289.

"1,800 Drown as Excursion Steamer Capsizes, Loaded to Capacity, in the Chicago River; Top-heavy, She Was Started While Moored." 1915. *New York Times*, July 25, p. 1.

Elias, Justine. 1997. "The Taskmaster Who Made *Titanic*." *New York Times*, December 14, sec. 2, pp. 17, 26.

Elley, Derek. 1984. *The Epic Film.* London: Routledge.

Ellis, Robert. 1950. "Ida Lupino Brings New Hope to Hollywood." *Negro Digest* (August): 47–49.

Farnsworth, Clyde H. 1970. "Youth Hostel Takes Main Force of Fatal Avalanche in the French Alps; 39 Die in France Under Snowslide." *New York Times*, February 11, pp. 1, 14.

Fleming, Dan. 1996. *Powerplay: Toys in Popular Culture.* Manchester: Manchester University Press.

"Flood Costs 3,000 Lives in Two States; $100,000,000 Worth of Property Wiped Out; Fires Add to Horror in Stricken Dayton." 1913. *New York Times*, March 27, p. 1.

Flynn, Charles and Todd McCarthy. 1975. "Interview with Joseph Kane, September 2, 1973." In Todd McCarthy and Charles Flynn, eds., *Kings of the Bs: Working Within the Hollywood System*, 313–24. New York: Dutton.

Foster, Gwendolyn Audrey 1995. *Women Film Directors: An International Bio-Critical Dictionary.* Westport, Conn.: Greenwood.

Foster, Hal. 1996. *The Return of the Real: The Avant-Garde at the End of the Century.* Cambridge and London: MIT Press.

"400 Caught in Mine, All Believed Dead." 1909. *New York Times*, November 14, p. 1.

"1,400 Dead in Ecuador Earthquake; New Shocks Cause Panic in Ambato." 1949. *New York Times*, August 7, pp. 1, 24.

Frankel, Max. 1997. "No Pix, No Di." *New York Times Magazine*, September 21, p. 53.

Frow, John. 1995. *Cultural Studies and Cultural Value.* Oxford: Clarendon Press.

Fuller, Graham. 1991. "Ida Lupino." *Interview* (April): 118–21.

Gabler, Neal. 1997. "The End of the Middle." *New York Times Magazine*, November 16, pp. 76–78.

Giovanni, Joseph. 1996. "Ismail Merchant: The Producer-Director Takes on Madeleine Castaing's Paris Apartment." *Architectural Digest* (April): 178–85, 302.

Giroux, Henry A. 1994. *Disturbing Pleasures: Learning Popular Culture.* New York: Routledge.

Gleick, James. 1997. "Addicted to Speed." *New York Times Magazine*, September 28, pp. 54–61.

Goldfarb, Jeffrey C. 1991. *The Cynical Society: The Culture of Politics and the Politics of Culture in American Life.* Chicago: University of Chicago Press.

Griffin, Al. 1997. "Will I Have to Replace My Music Collection *Again?*" *Parade*, November 30, pp. 16, 18.

Halberstam, Judith and Ira Livingston, eds. 1995. *Posthuman Bodies.* Bloomington: Indiana University Press.

Haldeman, Peter. 1996. "A 1930s Beverly Hills House for the Producer of *The Terminator.*" *Architectural Digest* (April): 222–29, 299.

Harmetz, Aljean. 1996. "Ray Milland: In Coldwater Canyon with *The Lost Weekend*'s Star." *Architectural Digest* (April): 190–93, 294.

Hartung, Philip. 1949. "*Not Wanted*" (review). *Commonweal*, August 12, p. 438.

Hearty, Kitty Bowe. 1997. "From Trooper to Trouper." *Interview* (December): 73.

Heller, Scott. 1995. "Scholars Contemplate the Future of Film Studies in a World of Fast-Changing Technology." *Chronicle of Higher Education*, October 27, p. A17.

Hewitt, Andrew. 1993. *Fascist Modernism: Aesthetics, Politics, and the Avant-Garde.* Stanford, Calif.: Stanford University Press.

Hill, John. 1986. *Sex, Class, and Realism: British Cinema, 1956–1963*. London: BFI Publishing.

Hill, John and Martin McLoone, eds. 1995. *Big Picture, Small Screen: The Relations Between Film and Television*. Luton, Bedfordshire: John Libbey.

Hirschberg, Lynn. 1997a. "Lawrence Gordon and Christine Vachon." *New York Times Magazine*, November 16, pp. 104–106.

———. 1997b. "Lili Taylor, Sharon Stone: A Dialogue." *New York Times Magazine*, November 16, pp. 79–81.

Hirschhorn, Clive. 1983. *The Universal Story: The Complete History of the Studio and Its 2,641 Films*. New York: Crown.

Hitchens, Christopher. 1997. "Throne and Altar." *The Nation*, September 29, p. 7.

Hope, Ted. 1995. "Indie Film Is Dead." *Filmmaker* (fall): 18, 54–58.

Huhtamo, Erkki. 1995. "Seeking Deeper Contact: Interactive Art as Meta-commentary." *Convergence* 1, no. 2 (Autumn): 81–104.

Hull, David Stewart. 1969. *Film in the Third Reich: A Study of the German Cinema, 1933–1945*. Berkeley: University of California Press.

"I Have Lost 20 lbs. of Fat." 1934. Front-page text advertisement in *Reynold's Illustrated News*, September 23.

"Invisible Man Series: Program Titles." (No date.) Unpaginated manuscript in the collection of the British Film Institute, London.

Jack, Ian and Peter Marlow. 1997. "Those Who Felt Differently." *Granta* 60: 9–35.

Jarman, Derek. 1991. *Queer Edward II*. London: BFI Publishing.

———. 1986. *Caravaggio: The Complete Film Script and Commentaries*. London: Thames and Hudson.

Jarvis, Everett Grant. 1996. *Final Curtain: Deaths of Noted Movie and TV Personalities*. 8th ed. Secaucus, N.J.: Citadel/Carol.

Jones, Michael Wynn. 1976. *Deadline Disaster: A Newspaper History*. London: David and Charles/Newton Abbot.

Kakutani, Michiko. 1996. "Designer Nihilism." *New York Times Magazine*, March 24, pp. 30, 32.

Keylin, Arleen and Gene Brown. 1976. *Disasters from the Pages of the New York Times*. New York: Arno Press.

Kirn, Walter. 1997. "Robert Redford Has This Problem." *New York Times Magazine*, November 16, pp. 82–85.

Koch, Stephen. 1973. *Stargazer: Andy Warhol's World and His Films*. New York: Praeger.

Koestenbaum, Wayne. 1997. "Femme Noire." *Vogue* (December): 182.

Koning, Dirk. 1995. "No Sex, Please: Congress and the Courts Threaten

Censorship of Cable Access, Internet." *The Independent* 18, no. 10 (December: 6, 7.

Koszarski, Richard. 1976. *Hollywood Directors, 1914–1940.* New York: Oxford University Press.

Kristeva, Julia. 1995. *New Maladies of the Soul.* New York: Columbia University Press.

Kroker, Arthur and Marilouise. 1996. *Hacking the Future: Stories for the Flesh-Eating '90s.* New York: St. Martin's.

Kuhn, Annette. 1995. "Introduction: Intestinal Fortitude." In Kuhn, ed., *Queen of the "B's": Ida Lupino Behind the Camera,* 1–12. Westport, Conn.: Praeger.

Lambert, Gann. 1994. "Errol Flynn: A Swashbuckling Life at Mulholland House." *Architectural Digest* (April): 212–15, 285.

Leonard, John. 1997. "The New Puritanism: Who's Afraid of *Lolita*? (We Are)." *The Nation,* November 24, pp. 11–12, 14–15.

——. 1997. *Smoke and Mirrors: Violence, Television, and Other American Cultures.* New York: New Press.

Levin, Eric, ed. 1997. *The Diana Years: Commemorative Edition of People Weekly.* New York: Time Inc.

Lidz, Franz. 1997. "Never Say 'No More' About Bond." *New York Times,* December 14, sec. 2, p. 17.

"Liner Sinks in 14 Minutes with 954 Lives; 'Empress of Ireland' Lost in St. Lawrence; Wireless Brings Prompt Aid; 433 Are Saved." 1914. *New York Times,* May 30, p. 1.

Lourie, Eugene. 1985. *My Work in Films.* New York: Harcourt Brace Jovanovich.

Lupino, Ida. 1967. "Me, Mother Directress." *Action* 2, no. 3 (May-June): 14–15.

——. 1953. "Ida Lupino Retains Her Femininity as Director." Feature article in pressbook of *The Hitch-Hiker,* p. 4.

Lyotard, Jean-François. 1984. *The Postmodern Condition: A Report on Knowledge.* Translated by Geoff Bennington and Brian Massumi. Minneapolis: University of Minnesota Press.

MacCabe, Colin. 1985. *Tracking the Signifier. Theoretical Essays: Film, Linguistics, Literature.* Minneapolis: University of Minnesota Press.

Manovich, Lev. 1997. "What Is Digital Cinema?" *Blimp* 37: 29–38.

McDonald, Myra. 1992. *Representing Women: Myths of Femininity in the Popular Media.* London: Edward Arnold.

McKinley, James C., Jr. 1997. "Searching in Vain for Rwanda's Moral High Ground." *New York Times,* December 21, sec. 4, p. 3.

Michaels, Lloyd. 1998. *The Phantom of the Cinema: Character in Modern Film*. Albany: State University of New York Press.

Miller, Jane. 1991. *Seductions: Studies in Reading and Culture*. Cambridge: Harvard University Press.

Miller, Mark Crispin and Janine Jaquet Biden. 1996. "The National Entertainment State." *The Nation*, June 3, pp. 23–26.

Morton, Andrew. 1992. *Diana: Her True Story*. New York: Simon and Schuster.

Mossberg, Walter S. and Faith Pennick. 1997. "Seven Products That Will Change the Way We Live: What's *Next?*" *Parade*, November 30, pp. 4–6.

"Munition Ship Blows in Halifax Harbor, May Be 2,000 Dead; Collision with Belgian Relief Vessel Causes the Disaster; Two Square Miles of City Wrecked; Many Buried in Ruins." 1917. *New York Times*, December 7, p. 1.

Nichols, Bill. 1994. *Blurred Boundaries: Questions of Meaning in Contemporary Culture*. Bloomington: Indiana University Press.

O'Brien, Geoffrey. 1997. "What Does the Audience Want?" *New York Times Magazine*, November 16, pp. 110–11.

——. 1993. *The Phantom Empire*. New York: Norton.

Orvell, Miles. 1995. *After the Machine: Visual Arts and the Erasing of Cultural Boundaries*. Jackson: University Press of Mississippi.

Owen, Frank. 1997. "Death and the Media Maiden." *Village Voice*, September 16, p. 51.

"Pakistan Estimates Quake Killed 4,700 in 9 Towns." 1974. *New York Times*, December 31, pp. 1, 2.

Parla, Paul Anthony. 1986. "Remembering *The Thing That Couldn't Die*: That Forgotten Second Feature." *Midnight Marquee* 35 (fall): 21–25.

Parish, James Robert. 1993. *The Hollywood Celebrity Death Book*. Las Vegas: Pioneer.

Parish, James Robert and Lennard De Carl. 1976. *Hollywood Players: The Forties*. New Rochelle, N.Y.: Arlington House.

Parker, Francine. 1967. "Discovering Ida Lupino." *Action* 2, no. 3 (May–June): 19.

Philips, Caryl. 1997. "Another Course Change Toward Seriousness." *New York Times*, September 7, sec. 2, pp. 6, 42.

Pinedo, Isabel Cristina. 1997. *Recreational Terror: Women and the Pleasures of Horror Film Viewing*. Albany: State University of New York Press.

Pizzello, Stephen. 1997. "Driver's Side: Director David Cronenberg Pulls Over to Answer *American Cinematographer*'s Questions About *Crash*." *American Cinematographer* (April): 43–47.

Pollan, Michael. 1997. "Town Building Is No Mickey Mouse Operation." *New York Times Magazine*, December 14, pp. 56–63, 76, 78, 80–81, 88.

Powers, John. 1997. "Movies: *The Sweet Hereafter*" (review). *Vogue* (December): 168, 170.

Pressbook for *Love and Kisses*. 1965. Universal City: Universal City Studios.

"Quake Hits Iran; Toll Estimated at 2,000 to 4,000." 1972. *New York Times*, April 11, pp. 1, 7.

Redhead, Steve. 1995. *Unpopular Cultures: The Birth of Law and Popular Culture*. Manchester: Manchester University Press.

Reid, Mark A. 1997. *PostNegritude Visual and Literary Culture*. Albany: State University of New York Press.

"Rescuers Perish in Blazing Pit." 1934. *Reynold's Illustrated News*, September 23, p. 1.

Rickey, Carrie. 1980. "Lupino Noir." *Village Voice*, October 29–November 4, p. 43.

"*Riptide*: Biography of Producer Ralph Smart." (No date.) Unpaginated manuscript in the collection of the British Film Institute, London.

Rogers, Pauline. 1997a. "Making Goo: Dean Cundey, ASC, Brings *Flubber* to Life." *International Photographer* (December): 38–43, 55.

——. 1997b. "Shooting a New Tomorrow: *Tomorrow Never Dies*." *International Photographer* (December): 17–21, 45.

Roper, Jonathan. 1995. "The Heart of Multimedia: Interactivity or Experience?" *Convergence* 1, no. 2 (Autumn): 23–28.

Ross, Robert. 1996. *The Carry On Companion*. London: Batsford.

Rushdie, Salman. 1997. "Crash." *The New Yorker*, September 15, pp. 68–69.

"Salvador Quake Kills 1,000 in One City; Other Towns Hit." 1951. *New York Times*, May 8, pp. 1, 12.

Safire, William. 1997. "The Full Monty." *New York Times Magazine*, November 16, pp. 62, 64.

Sayre, Nora. 1982. *Running Time: Films of the Cold War*. New York: Dial.

Scharres, Barbara. (No date.) "Ida Lupino." *Film Center Gazette* 16, no. 2: 4.

Scheib, Ronnie. 1980. "Ida Lupino: Auteuress." *Film Comment* 16 (January): 54–64.

Schelde, Per. 1993. *Androids, Humanoids, and Other Science Fiction Monsters: Science and Soul in Science Fiction Films*. New York: New York University Press.

Schrag, Calvin O. 1997. *The Self After Postmodernity*. New Haven: Yale University Press.

Seiter, Ellen. 1993. *Sold Separately: Children and Parents in Consumer Culture*. New Brunswick, N.J.: Rutgers University Press.

Seligson, Tom. 1997. "Should Your Next Camera Be *Digital?*" *Parade*, November 30, p. 8.

Seltzer, Mark. 1992. *Bodies and Machines*. New York: Routledge.

Selvin, Joel. 1990. *Ricky Nelson: Idol for a Generation*. Chicago: Contemporary Books.

Sharkey, Jacqueline. 1997. "The Diana Aftermath." *American Journalism Review* (November): 19–25.

Shaviro, Stephen. 1993. *The Cinematic Body*. Minneapolis: University of Minnesota Press.

Sontag, Susan. 1996. "The Decay of Cinema." *New York Times Magazine*, February 25, pp. 60–61.

Spoto, Donald. 1997. *Diana: The Last Year*. New York: Harmony.

Stacey, Jackie. 1995. "The Lost Audience: Methodology, Cinema History, and Feminist Film Criticism." In Beverly Skeggs, ed., *Feminist Culture Theory: Process and Production*, 97–118. Manchester: Manchester University Press.

Steinhauer, Jennifer. 1997. "A Director Who Films What She Knows Best." *New York Times*, December 28, sec. 2, p. 7.

Stevenson, Jack. 1997. "A Secret History of Cult Movies: A Biblical Tale of the Holy Unlikely." *Blimp* 37: 66–75.

Strawn, Linda May. 1975. "Interview with Samuel Z. Arkoff, February 11, 1974." In Todd McCarthy and Charles Flynn, eds., *Kings of the Bs: Working Within the Hollywood System*, 255–66. New York: Dutton.

Svetkey, Benjamin, with Chris Nashawaty. 1997. "The Reich Stuff." *Entertainment Weekly*, November 21, pp. 8–9.

Tapert, Annette. 1996. "Colleen Moore: The Original Flapper in Bel Air." *Architectural Digest* (April): 216–21, 294.

Thompson, Kristin and David Bordwell. 1994. *Film History: An Introduction*. New York: McGraw-Hill.

Thurman, Judith. 1994. "Martin Scorsese's New York: An 1860s Town House for the *Age of Innocence* Director." *Architectural Digest* (April): 248–55, 290.

Todorov, Tzvetan. 1995. *The Morals of History*. Translated by Alyson Waters. Minneapolis: University of Minnesota Press.

"Turn Your TV into a Christmas Wonderland" (advertisement). 1997. *Parade Magazine*, December 7, p. 15.

"TV Film 'Could Cause Hatred.' " 1959. *The Chronicle*, November 17, n.p.; news clippings collection of the British Film Institute, London.

Vahimagi, Tise. 1994. *British Television: An Illustrated Guide*. Oxford University Press.

Viladas, Pilar. 1994. "Steven Spielberg: The Director Expands His Horizons in Pacific Palisades." *Architectural Digest* (April): 242–47.

Virilio, Paul. 1995. *The Art of the Motor*. Translated by Julie Rose. Minneapolis: University of Minnesota Press.

Vogt, Hannah. 1981. *The Burden of Guilt: A Short History of Germany, 1914–1945*. New York: Oxford University Press.

Warhol, Andy and Pat Hackett. 1980. *Popism: The Warhol 60s*. New York: Harcourt Brace Jovanovich.

Watson, Lyall. 1995. *Dark Nature: A Natural History of Evil*. New York: HarperCollins.

Weaver, Tom. 1988. *Interview with B Science Fiction and Horror Movie Makers: Writers, Producers, Directors, Actors, Moguls, and Makeup*. Jefferson, N.C.: McFarland.

Weeks, Janet. 1997. "Hollywood Is Seeing Teen: Younger Set Favors Movies Above All." *USA Today*, December 22, pp. D1, D2.

Weiner, Debra. 1977. "Interview with Ida Lupino." In Karyn Kay and Gerald Peary, eds., *Women and the Cinema*, 169–78. New York: Hutton.

Weinraub, Bernard. 1997. "Making a Trailer Pull a Movie." *New York Times*, December 14, sec. 4, p. 2.

Weisser, Thomas. 1992. *Spaghetti Westerns—The Good, the Bad, and the Violent*. Jefferson, N.C.: McFarland.

Welch, David. 1988. "Goebbels' Götterdämmerung, and the *Deutsche Wochenschauen*." In K. R. M. Short and Stephan Dolezel, eds., *Hitler's Fall: The Newsreel Witness*, 80–99. London: Croon Helm.

Weldon, Michael. 1983. *The Psychotronic Encyclopedia of Film*. New York: Ballantine.

Wertheimer, Alan. 1996. *Exploitation*. Princeton: Princeton University Press.

Whitney, Dwight. 1966. "Follow Mother, Here We Go, Kiddies!" *TV Guide*, October 8, p. 16.

Wiegman, Robyn. 1995. *American Anatomies: Theorizing Race and Gender*. Durham, N.C.: Duke University Press.

Willett, Cynthia. 1995. *Maternal Ethics and Other Slave Moralities*. New York: Routledge.

Yacowar, Maurice. 1995. "The Bug in the Rug: Notes on the Disaster Genre." In Barry Keith Grant, ed., *Film Genre Reader II*, 261–79. Austin: University of Texas Press.

Zakaria, Fareed. 1997. "Peace Is Hell." *New York Times Magazine*, November 16, pp. 131–32.

Zavarzadeh, Mas'ud. 1991. *Seeing Films Politically*. Albany: State University of New York Press.

INDEX